The Netflix Vision of Horror

The Netflix Vision of Horror

A Narrative Structural Analysis of Original Series

SOTIRIS PETRIDIS

McFarland & Company, Inc., Publishers
Jefferson, North Carolina

This book has undergone peer review.

ISBN (print) 978-1-4766-8422-2
ISBN (ebook) 978-1-4766-4312-0

Library of Congress and British Library
cataloguing data are available

Library of Congress Control Number 2021027837

© 2021 Sotiris Petridis. All rights reserved

No part of this book may be reproduced or transmitted in any form or by any means, electronic or mechanical, including photocopying or recording, or by any information storage and retrieval system, without permission in writing from the publisher.

Front cover image © 2021 mrjo/Ethiriel/Shutterstock

Printed in the United States of America

McFarland & Company, Inc., Publishers
Box 611, Jefferson, North Carolina 28640
www.mcfarlandpub.com

This research is co-financed by Greece and the European Union (European Social Fund—ESF) through the Operational Programme (Human Resources Development, Education and Lifelong Learning) in the context of the project "Reinforcement of Postdoctoral Researchers–2nd Cycle" (MIS-5033021), implemented by the State Scholarships Foundation (IKY).

Operational Programme
Human Resources Development,
Education and Lifelong Learning
Co-financed by Greece and the European Union

Acknowledgments

This book is part of my postdoctoral research conducted at Aristotle University of Thessaloniki, Greece, and financed by the Greek State Scholarships Foundation. I am indebted to Christina Adamou, the supervisor of the research, for her valuable help and constant guidance. I would like to express my gratitude to my best friends, Manolis Kapnopoulos and Tania Nanavraki, for their treasured support. Also, I am thankful to Penny Bouska for being by my side during the most challenging times of this research.

I dedicate this book to my friends and family, who are always encouraging me to continue doing what I love. Finally, I would like to thank my peer reviewers for their time and feedback.

Table of Contents

Acknowledgments — vi
Introduction — 1

ONE. Netflix Original Horror Series: Films in Disguise — 7

TWO. The Narrative Structure of the Complex Discovery Plot — 40

THREE. The Narrative Structures of Triple and Double Function Plots — 101

Conclusion — 157

Filmography — 163
Appendix A: Series Corpus — 165
Appendix B: Three-Act Structures — 167
Appendix C: Types of Plot and Horror — 169
Chapter Notes — 171
Bibliography — 177
Index — 185

Introduction

Television is an audiovisual medium that is part of our everyday lives. Until recently, the medium appeared to be "free of charge," easily available to use, and with a plethora of content allowing you to see something of your choice with no extra cost or effort. As Anne Dunn comments, "Television is literally 'part of the furniture' and is consumed in a domestic setting, subject to interruptions, some of which—the commercial breaks—are scheduled."[1] Here lies the big difference from cinema, because television has to work harder to keep the audience committed. The viewer of television has total control of the medium and can change channels and fictional programs in a heartbeat. On the other hand, movie audiences make an effort in order to go to the cinema and see the film of their preference.

As expected, this fundamental difference between the two mediums has considerable influence on the narratives of their fictional works. Television relies on fragmented narratives that are distributed on a periodical basis, while films are concrete audiovisual narratives that are structured in a manner that forces the audience to watch them in one sitting. Moreover, television was built around the term that Raymond Williams famously coined as television "flow"; he argued that watching television actually meant watching television flow, not watching a particular program.[2] It is common for a television audience to change between channels and not pay attention to a specific show. On the other hand, cinema demands from the audience the appropriate level of attention for one specific fictional narrative at a time.

Watching television differs from watching a film in the cinema also in the sense that each TV show is aired at a specific, regular time and the audience must be there in order to watch the new installment of the narrative. Because of this particularity of the medium, in almost every contemporary society, television is linked with narrative forms and genres that have been highly formulaic.[3] The structuring methods of television

Introduction

series are based on potential spots for cliffhangers in order for the network to have slots for commercial breaks.

In order to ensure that viewers will watch the next segment, act, episode, or even season, the structuring norms of television dictate the placement of multiple cliffhangers, leaving the viewers with all sorts of open questions. At the same time, one of the biggest challenges of a TV serial narrative is to maintain viewer comprehension. As Jeremy Butler points out, "Series are based on the assumption that individual episodes may reach a certain amount of closure, but no definitive closure, which would forestall a continuation of the series."[4] In other words, viewers can expect only partial closure, and therefore television aims for the creation of an endless narrative with many possibilities. Jason Mittell stated: "American commercial television differs from much of the world in how it privileges a narrative model in which a successful series never ends, with a final episode typically regarded as a sign of commercial failure and/or creative exhaustion, and often programs end by abrupt cancellation more than planned conclusion."[5]

Conventional television practices have now been overthrown by the technological evolution of the medium, which has drastically changed the landscape of the audiovisual industry. New online platforms based on subscription video-on-demand practices made their appearance and changed the viewing habits of the audience. While the typical practice was to watch an episode of a series on a daily or weekly basis, now the viewers tend to consume enormous portions of a series in a short period of time. In broadcast television, continued viewing meant watching a succession of different segments, including advertisements, while contemporary binge-watching tends to be associated with watching one episode after another of the same series.[6]

Apart from that, the new form of series consumption led to the elimination of the need for cliffhangers within episodes, since ad-free streaming does not have advertisement breaks. This new characteristic makes irrelevant the traditional episodic structure that fits into broadcast television flow. Online platforms now have the freedom and the ability to adjust the structure of their series according to their distribution models and minimize repetitive exposition to better fit the new streaming flow. This streaming flow urges us to view and consume a series as an extended whole and not as a fragmented narrative.

It is widely observed that the lines between television and cinema are blurred, and the audiovisual sector has started to embrace media convergence. Both mediums share the same semiotic rules that are

Introduction

based on the audiovisual language, while their narratives are starting to use similar structuring approaches. Since the technological evolution of the online platforms has introduced a more concrete model of narration, contemporary series have started to behave like long-form filmic texts. Online platforms are creating content that is meant to engage the audience in continuous viewing.

One of the main players in the contemporary streaming wars and the first platform to create original content for online consumption is Netflix. Ted Sarandos, the chief content officer at Netflix, explains, "Our brand is personalization. We didn't want any show to define Netflix."[7] This platform tries to satisfy its subscribers by building their experiences based on their needs, with Timothy Havens stating that the Netflix brand identity is indeed personalization.[8]

In accordance with this brand identity, Netflix started to create original content under the label "Netflix Originals." This content does not need to fit into a broadcast schedule and consequently it does not need to have stable episode or season lengths. Moreover, these streaming series do not obey the conventional rules of the television medium regarding their structuring methods. The narratives of these online shows are organized in a manner similar to how cinema builds its concrete narratives. We no longer have a fragmented narration, but rather a continuous audiovisual narrative that has not been created in order to fit into a slot of a television flow.

In other words, Netflix Original series use an episodic format in order to narrate their stories, but the series are structured according to filmic rules of classical narration. Proceeding from this observation, this book will examine the structuring methods of a specific audiovisual genre from a specific online platform, the Netflix Original horror series.

The selection of this particular genre was made according to qualitative and quantitative data. One of the first genres that Netflix produced in 2013, the starting year of Netflix Originals, was indeed horror, with *Hemlock Grove* (Netflix, 2013–2015) being one of the three series by the platform that year. Then, from 2013 to 2019, the starting point of this research, Netflix produced and distributed a number of horror series that show a substantial deviation from the standardized TV narrative structures. Also, the selection of Netflix as the only source of the audiovisual works that will be part of this study is not accidental. Even if there are plenty of subscription video-on-demand platforms, a lot of them are keeping conventional distribution patterns that do not require alternative structuring methods. For example, Apple TV+ distributes

Introduction

The Morning Show (Apple TV+, 2019–present) on a weekly basis, while Disney+ uses the same distribution pattern for *The Mandalorian* (Disney+, 2019–present).

A systematic and thorough research of the episodic genre on this platform will show the great influence of the new ways of distribution and consumption on the structuring methods of the narratives under study. This book will shed light on the evolution and the impact of the changing face of series based on the new narrative norms that online platforms have brought to the medium. I will argue that these narratives are organized and designed as unified audiovisual works that have more in common with films than with television shows.

This research will be done systematically and methodically and will be based on an audiovisual corpus consisted of thirteen Netflix Original horror series. Based on specific criteria, the corpus covers all the original content produced by Netflix that belong to the horror genre. More specifically, the final series corpus of this study, created by fictional narrations of Netflix Original horror series on the U.S. version of the platform that premiered through the end of 2019, were created by Netflix and are widely acknowledged as part of the horror genre.

In the first chapter, I formulate the theoretical framework on which this research will be based. Based on screenwriting theories about filmic classical narration and three-act structure models, I examine the narratives of each series of the corpus, and according to the collected data, I articulate an outline of the new forms of television narration. Horror plots have four essential functions (onset, discovery, confirmation, and confrontation), according to which different plot categories can developed. By comparing the narrational methods of series that obey the three act-structure to the essential functions of their plots, we can sort the series into different categories: the complex discovery plot, which works as the prototype model of narration and features all of the four functions, and other sub-categories, like triple and double function plots, which select three or two of the essential functions to incorporate into their plots. Depending on which plot category series belong to, their narratives are organized differently, and the three-act model of narration is adjusted in order to satisfy their needs.

The next two chapters of the book will be devoted to the methodical study of each plot category and the norms of the overarching story's three-act structure. More specifically, the second chapter will analyze the complex discovery plot, a type of narration that has a more balanced distribution of the action, since the proportionate lengths of each act are

Introduction

very similar to those of the initial three-act structure. The series that will be analyzed in this chapter are *Chilling Adventures of Sabrina* (Netflix, 2018–present), *Diablero* (Netflix, 2018–present), *Ghoul* (Netflix, 2018), *Hemlock Grove* (Netflix, 2013–2015), *Marianne* (Netflix, 2019), *Stranger Things* (Netflix, 2016–present), *Typewriter* (Netflix, 2019–present), and *V Wars* (Netflix, 2019–present).

Finally, the third chapter will analyze the triple- and double-function plot categories that are in the series corpus and how these narratives differentiate their structuring forms from the prototype complex discovery plot category and from the standardized three-act structure. Particularly, the categories are the discovery plot that *Chambers* (Netflix, 2019) and *The Haunting of Hill House* (Netflix, 2018) follow, the discovery/confirmation/confrontation plot that *Santa Clarita Diet* (Netflix, 2017–2019) and *The Order* (Netflix, 2019–present) follow, and the discovery/confrontation plot, the only double function category, which *Black Summer* (Netflix, 2019–present) follows.

The theoretical framework introduced in this book has innovative elements that highlight issues which have not been analyzed before, as its goal is to fill the gap in the academic literature with regards to narrative studies concerning structuring methods and models about television series. The results of Netflix Original horror series will be a timely and needed addition to the academic analysis of both episodic horror and television studies in general.

Chapter One

Netflix Original Horror Series
Films in Disguise

SVOD Platforms, Netflix and the Case of Binge-Watching

The last decade has been marked by the technological evolution and growth of new media that have led to the fruition of audiovisual fictional programs on different platforms. Nowadays, audiovisual works can be found in many different media that surpass the conventional ways of content consumption. Today, knowledge and information are accessible by everyone with Internet access (around 40 percent of the world population, and 88.5 percent of the U.S. population),[1] and users have become more active than ever. This activeness of the spectator and the increase of Internet accessibility with higher speeds has helped the creation of a variation on the television medium, the subscription video on demand (SVOD) platforms.

SVOD platforms are similar to traditional TV packages that allow users to consume as much content as they desire at a flat fee per month. Unlike conventional broadcast networks whose economic model is primarily dependent on revenue provided by advertisers in exchange for a network's inclusion of ads within their broadcasts, the subscription model is based on a direct economic relationship between the institution and its subscribers, who pay a fee in exchange for access to programming.[2] Currently, a lot of production companies, like Disney and WarnerMedia, have created SVOD platforms to host their content, recognizing the future of audiovisual consumption. A characteristic projection of the future of the medium is seen in a study indicating that by 2025, Disney+, the SVOD platform of Disney, will amass 101 million subscriptions, and when combined with Netflix, Amazon Prime Video, Apple TV+ and HBO Max, the platforms will have 529 million subscriptions.[3] According to Maíra Bianchini and Maria Carmem Jacob

The Netflix Vision of Horror

de Souza, these platforms deal with at least three associated features: "1. international market expansion; 2. the creation of a system to regionally and globally identify, attract, assess, retain, and expand subscribers; and 3. the combination of a set of products that live up to the diversity and wishes both of its wider and its niche audiences."[4]

Apart from giving new life to older audiovisual works by making them accessible to the wide public through an alternative way of consumption, SVOD platforms create audiovisual works that premiere online and are accessible for viewing exclusively on these platforms. This phenomenon is what Amanda Lotz describes as "internet-distributed television"—professionally produced content circulated and consumed through websites, online services, platforms, and apps, rather than through broadcast, cable, or satellite systems.[5] Netflix is a pioneer on this field, since it was the first SVOD platform that created original content, and according to its co-founder and CEO, Reed Hastings, the platform has employed familiar industry strategies, with HBO's strategic planning as main reference.[6]

Netflix is presently the major global, subscription video-on-demand service, but it is not, however, the first such service with global aspirations, since various transnational channels, including CNN, MTV, Al Jazeera, and CGTN, came before it, along with digital platforms such as YouTube.[7] Netflix launched in 1997 and its initial task was to rent and sell DVDs, a progressive decision at the time, since the company decided to exclude the older VHS technology.[8] This innovation continued, and in the next decades Netflix became a multinational SVOD service that spans national borders and operates simultaneously in a large number of countries.

Nowadays, Netflix produces original content that belongs to a wide range of audiovisual genres: from drama and sitcoms to science fiction and crime shows. Its content has expanded to include a wide combination of Netflix Original productions and older or contemporary audiovisual works that are available to be re-seen in this different manner. Of course, when an audiovisual work, and more specifically an episodic show, is created to be exclusively consumed in this relatively new medium, it acquires different norms and conventions that are more suitable for these platforms. Conventional television demands different things from the audience, and therefore its narratives are structured around these needs. Netflix, however, and all the other SVOD platforms, abandoned some archaic television practices and gave space to the possibilities of the new medium.

These observations will be the foundation of the research of this

1. Netflix Original Horror Series

book. Based on thorough analysis of the narratives of Netflix Original series that belong to the horror genre, I will study the structure of their conventions and norms, and I will demonstrate that these works function more like extensive and long-form filmic texts rather than television series. Conditions for fictional storytelling have considerably altered in recent years, since the production, distribution, and consumption of narratives across a range of media have become increasingly digitalized and linked to the Internet.[9] Since the medium has evolved in a new direction and created a new relationship with the audience, the narratives offered for consumption have to change. The audience is more active, selective, and ready to consume bigger portions of the product, so the audiovisual work must be structured accordingly.

Continuing its innovations, Netflix was the first online and SVOD platform that decided to create original content for its subscribers. In 2013, the platform introduced the audience to the new digital age of online series by producing *House of Cards* (Netflix, 2013–2018), *Hemlock Grove* (Netflix, 2013–2015) and *Orange Is the New Black* (Netflix, 2013–2019), the first original audiovisual works to be created for an online service. One of the first series, *Hemlock Grove*, belongs to the horror genre and started a tradition for the platform, with many other horror series to follow. After the success of Netflix Original series, the platform also produced original films, but this research will solely focus on episodic programs and the consumption of these works. TV series are usually fragmented audiovisual pieces that are distributed in different manners, so the scope of the present research does not include films, since they are unified audiovisual works of a specific duration.

Apart from the differentiation between episodic shows and filmic texts, we have to make another distinction among the series that are labeled Netflix Originals. As Netflix is a worldwide SVOD platform, one of its policies is to acquire exclusive international licensing rights to foreign audiovisual works and present them to the rest of the world as Netflix Originals.[10] For example, in Greece Netflix presented the two first seasons of *Scream* (MTV, 2015–2016)—which are centered around the story of Emma Duval (Willa Fitzgerald), a teenage girl set in the fictional town of Lakewood, who is linked to the horrific events of the town's past—as part of Netflix Originals, but the series was first presented in the USA at MTV with a conventional screening on a weekly basis. However, since this show has never appeared in Greece, and Netflix has its exclusive rights for the territory, it can present it as part of Netflix Originals, even though it was not an in-house production.

9

The Netflix Vision of Horror

This is a common marketing tactic of Netflix that goes back to the starting point of Netflix Originals. The first show that was branded with this label in late 2012 was *Lilyhammer* (NRK, 2012–2014), a Norwegian show to which Netflix acquired exclusive international licensing rights. Even if *Lilyhammer* was presented almost one year earlier than the other original shows, everybody recognizes as the first original Netflix series the above-mentioned audiovisual works, since they were *produced* by Netflix.

The thing that makes Netflix Original series stand out and create a new path that is uniquely based on the norms of the new medium is that they renounce the conventions of traditional serial distribution by making the entire season available at once.[11] Netflix considered the new viewing habits of the audience that already had started with DVD releases or Internet streaming of older series and create an innovative way of presenting its new shows to its subscribers.[12] The platform incorporated these characteristics into the production and distribution processes of its original content by building a model of individualized viewing practices and self-scheduling of shows that are more suited to the active spectator of the new medium.[13] The audience wanted to immediately consume these products, and the daily or weekly appointment with their favorite show was no longer an option for Netflix.

The new feature that became synonymous with Netflix is binge-watching, a term that describes the practice of watching a show's episodes in a row within a short timespan.[14] The purpose of this new distribution pattern is to make available to the audience the option to consume a whole "season" of a show in just a few days, or even hours. In a strategic move, in 2012 the platform set up the "post-play" default system to automatically keep playing one episode after another in order to increase the audience's desire for binge-watching.[15] In an interview posted the day before Netflix released the first season of *House of Cards* in 2013, showrunner Beau Willimon stated, "Our goal is to shut down a portion of America for a whole day."[16] The intention of the creators of these shows is to lure the audience to see the whole audiovisual work instantly and not regularly over a long period of time. The weekly appointment in front of a television to see the new adventures of our favorite characters is now almost obsolete in the content that is originally produced and distributed by Netflix.

As of this writing, Netflix has produced a wide variety of original series content using this distribution pattern of releasing whole seasons at once. As expected, this model of distribution influenced the

1. Netflix Original Horror Series

structuring methods of these series and shifted the discourse from television storytelling techniques to more innovative narrative models. Since these audiovisual works are not created in order to be seen weekly or daily, the episodes must maintain a model of narration that does not assume empty time between the consumption of each episode. In other words, this type of structuring demanded some changes in order for the audience to want to see more episodes, or even the whole season, at once.

One of the first to examine the new narrative structures of series created by Netflix was Mario Klarer. In his article "Putting Television 'Aside': Novel Narration in *House of Cards*," Klarer examined the narrative of the first season of *House of Cards* and compared it to a novel's narrative, stating, "*House of Cards* sets this new online serial format aside from the older television series by combining two major narrative conventions, the traditional filmic mode of storytelling with that of the traditional novel, thereby producing a hybrid or composite format with great narrative potential.[17]"

The combination of the audiovisual language with conventions from the novel form is done via the first-person narrator, since the main character of *House of Cards*, Frank Underwood (Kevin Spacey), is speaking directly to the camera—and therefore the audience. This breaking of the "fourth wall" is an innovative (for the medium) technique that introduces the first-person narrator into the audiovisual language. Of course, this is an exception to Netflix's other original content, so it is not used as a general approach. This series indeed uses a convention from novels by incorporating first-person narration into the show, but it is the only Netflix Original series that extensively uses this practice. *House of Cards* is one isolated example of the new kinds of SVOD narrative; however, the answer to the narrative problem of these episodic shows lies in the structuring methods not of novels, but of filmic texts.

These series are based on the conventions of audiovisual language, while they tell a story within a specific duration, so the new form of distribution and consumption treats these works as unified films. Since films tell a story usually with a closed ending and within an average duration of two hours, their structure can be used as a model of examination for series created for SVOD platforms. The question that arises is whether the structures of these series obey classical filmic narrative conventions.

The big difference between a conventional TV series and a film lies in the progression of their narratives. While a film usually obeys

The Netflix Vision of Horror

the rules of classical narration and has a complete story with an ending, a TV series is an ever-evolving narrative for both the story and the characters, which leads to a number of formal characteristics, such as a lack of definitive closure, the occurrence of cliffhangers, and a tendency towards minimal exposition.[18] According to Sean O'Sullivan, a TV series is a continuing narrative distributed in installments over time, and its narratives can be divided into six basic elements. The first three—iteration, multiplicity, and momentum—primarily address patterns within installments, or explicit discursive connections between installments, while the other three—world-building, personnel, and design—primarily address the varieties of scope that serials can create as their installments accumulate and the audience's understanding of the serial's narrative self-consciousness builds.[19] Most television narratives do not use the classical modes of narration that cinema has established; we expect that television narrative will give us multiple story threads and temporary or partial resolutions.[20]

Since the overarching story of a conventional series can last for several seasons and consequently years, episodes are the key unit of communication with the audience. So, when we are talking about the narrative structure of a TV series, usually the discourse is around the structure of each episode.[21] From the four-act and five-act structures of TV drama to the two-act structure of sitcoms, TV fiction has been versatile and adaptive to the needs of each narrative and each network. As Jeremy Butler observes, the series is a repeatable form with a particular plot pattern that is distributed on a daily or weekly basis.[22] In practical terms, the more acts an episode has, the more act breaks that serve as places for potential commercial breaks and therefore big cliffhangers that will manage to bring the audience back because they want to see what happens.[23]

While arguing against binge-watching of older TV series, Jim Pagels made two valuable points about the structure of their narratives: first, episodes have their own integrity, which is blurred by watching them in a row; and second, cliffhangers and suspense between episodes need time to breathe.[24] These points are in complete harmony with the aforementioned structuring method and reinforce the argument. But what happens when a series is created exclusively for binge-watch consumption in an online platform like Netflix that does not have commercial breaks? Veronica Innocenti and Guglielmo Pescatore note, "The single episode is now little more than a departure point for the engagement of the user, who is increasingly asked to interact with the serial product in a participatory way."²⁵ In these cases, online series have been created to be viewed all at once, hence the focus of this discourse has to change. As Kathryn VanArendonk argues, "In shows like this, the episode has become, if not a completely invisible force, then something with much less power than it used to have."²⁶

Based on these observations, it is easily understood that Netflix Original series are not perceived as conventional television shows, but rather share more similarities with films that obey a classical model of narrative structure. But what exactly is a classical filmic narrative?

Classical Narration and the Three-Act Structure

One of the most dominant models of narration in Hollywood and in popular cinema in general is the classical narrative style. David Bordwell defines it as "a particular configuration of normalized options for representing the fabula and for manipulating the possibilities of syuzhet and style."²⁷ Bordwell's analysis is based on Russian formalism and the concepts of "fabula" (the *chronological* order of the events contained in the story), and "syuzhet" (the *narrative* order of the events contained in the story).²⁸ However, Bordwell's approach does not focus solely on the story and the structure of the narrative, but incorporates other elements into the analysis, such as shots, framing, editing, and the mise-en-scène.

In the present study, the theoretical tools that will be used focus on the structuring of the story in order to better analyze the influence of the new medium on the overarching stories of these shows. The best tools for this task come from screenwriting studies. Based on screenwriting methods, the majority of filmic texts are part of the classical narrative model and obey some fundamental rules, following a three-act structure, because they have a beginning (a first act), a middle (a second act), and an end (a third act).²⁹ Common opinion has it that the three-part structure has its roots back in 335 BC in Aristotle's *Poetics*,³⁰ but the three-act structure as we know it today was introduced in 1978 by Constance Nash and Virginia Oakey³¹ and became famous with Syd Field's *Screenplay: The Foundations of Screenwriting* in 1979.³²

As Matthias Brütsch points out, the dominance of this model is so strong that many of the seemingly alternative approaches of other academics and screenwriting experts using a higher number of smaller units confirm its validity by stating how the units that are proposed in their models can be fitted into the three acts³³ (for example, Christopher

The Netflix Vision of Horror

Vogler's twelve stages of the hero's journey of 1998,[34] Paul Joseph Gulino's eight-sequence structure of 2004,[35] and Blake Snyder's fifteen beats of 2005[36]).

The three-act structure is usually a powerful tool for arranging or analyzing a feature film, but a lot of screenwriting studies have been using this tool to analyze the structures of short films.[37] The success of this tactic proves that the duration of the audiovisual work is an irrelevant element regarding structuring, and therefore on a theoretical level it could be applied to lengthier audiovisual works, like series.

Regarding the fundamentals of this narrative model, the basic characteristic of the three-act structure is that the story is centered around a main conflict, and each act has its own purpose regarding the progression of the narrative towards the resolution of this conflict. More specifically, the function of the first act is to present all the necessary information about the fictional world and the main characters as well as the main conflict of the plot; the second act develops the story and complicates the actions around the main conflict with more antagonistic forces and obstacles; and the third act is used to solve the main conflict. Moreover, the classical approach dictates that the three acts cover stable and approximately symmetrical portions of narrative time: 25 percent for the first and third acts and 50 percent for the second act.[38]

As we can see in fig. 1, the proportioned arrangement of the acts is enriched by some structural points that are important to the story. More specifically, at the beginning of the narrative we can spot the inciting incident, an event that aims to attract the attention of the audience while it creates the central dramatic question, the answer to which the audience will seek out at the end of the narrative.[39] In other words, in that specific structural point, the main conflict is introduced to the audience. They will have to see the whole narrative in order to find out if and how the conflict will be resolved. Before the inciting incident, there is the introduction to the fictional world of the audiovisual work

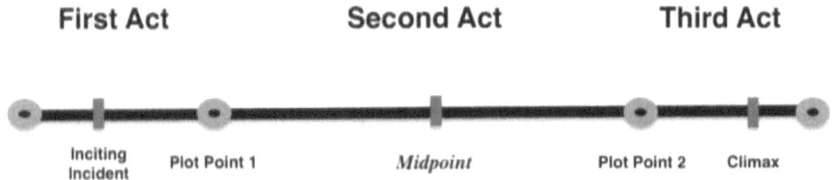

Figure 1: The Three-Act Structure

and to our main characters, who will be called to face the main conflict. After the inciting incident, there is further act-one development with the introduction to the backstory of the character and/or the antagonist, the introduction of more rival forces that will be the subject of possible minor or major conflicts, and further development of the main conflict.

Dividing the three acts, there are two plot points that carry the narrative from one act to the next one. Both plot points have the same features, since they change the narrative's course to a new direction, reinforce the main conflict, and therefore repeat the dramatic question that has been established in the inciting incident.[40] Since these structural points are important and alter the facts of the story by forcing the characters into new territories, it is logical that the main question arises again; because there are new facts around the main conflict, the audience wonders if the resolution of the conflict is still manageable.

At the middle of the narrative and consequently the middle of the second act, there is another structural point, the midpoint. There, the narrative introduces some new facts and the action starts to get tougher for the main characters. Just before the end, there is the climax, in which the audience feels that the story has ended, as they get all the answers they needed—or in other words, the main conflict is resolved.[41]

Since there are a plethora of variations of the three-act structure, the aforesaid breakdown is just a general outline of this narrative model. As it was mentioned before, there are plenty of approaches that break down the three-act structure into smaller pieces in order to better understand the functioning of each act and each structural point. The greater the number of structural units, the better the functioning of the theoretical tool, since there will be no room for generalizations.

In order to deepen the examination of the three-act structure and create a concrete theoretical tool of analysis, we have to consider Blake Snyder's beats approach. In this method, Snyder breaks down the three-act structure and creates a sheet with fifteen manageable sections called beats, each with a specific goal for the overall story.[42] Snyder builds his theory around a prototype filmic narrative of an estimated time of 110 minutes, and based on that he calculates the time of each beat. Like the general outline of the three-act structure, this approach does not solely concern feature films, but with a simple mathematical equation we can adjust it to the duration of any audiovisual work. The fifteen beats and their estimated lengths are as follows:

The Netflix Vision of Horror

1. ***Opening Image*** (1 min.): The first beat is self-explanatory, since it's the first scene of the audiovisual work that the audience sees. This beat sets up the tone, type, and initial impression of the work, and therefore it is the introduction to the fictional world of the narrative.

2. ***Theme Stated*** (5 min.): Around the beginning of the audiovisual work, there is a scene or a piece of dialogue that betrays the theme of the narrative to the audience. This beat is the heart of the narrative, or, in other words, what our story is about.

3. ***Setup*** (1 min.–10 min.): The first part of the narrative is always an introduction to the fictional world and the main characters of the story. The audience has to be introduced to the fictional world while at peace, and then the narrative can move on to the possible obstacles. As we can observe, the setup beat incorporates the other two beats into its duration.

4. ***Catalyst*** (12 min.): After the presentation of the fictional world at peace, the narrative has to introduce the main conflict. This beat has the same functionality as the inciting incident, meaning that there is an action that attracts the viewer's attention and creates the central dramatic question. After that, the audience waits for some answers, and this is why the spectator watches the whole audiovisual work, in order to know if the conflict will be resolved.

5. ***Debate*** (12 min.–25 min.): Afterwards, there is the further act-one development, in which more information is given to the audience. In this beat, the main characters doubt the journey they must take after the events of the catalyst, and the audience is uncertain about the characters' upcoming decisions.

6. ***Break Into Two*** (25 min.): Then the narrative enters the second act. This beat has exactly the same function as the first plot point in the generalized outline of the three-act structure. With the new facts that are introduced to the story, this beat is considered the point of no return for the main characters, since they have been committed and obliged to follow the journey they are called to take.

7. ***B Story*** (30 min.): Usually, in the second act, the narrative introduces a secondary story in order to fill the biggest act of the structure. This subplot is usually in line with the theme of the audiovisual text and works as a unified narrative with the main plot.

8. ***Fun and Games*** (30 min.–55 min.): The first part of the second act is also known as "the promise of the premise." In this beat, the difficulties that our main characters face are perceived as fun and games, since the stakes start to get higher from the midpoint onwards.

1. Netflix Original Horror Series

    9. ***Midpoint*** (55 min.): At exactly the middle of the second act and consequently of the whole narrative, there is the midpoint. In this beat, the stakes start to get higher and the situation begins to look more difficult for the characters.

    10. ***Bad Guys Close In*** (55 min.–75 min.): After the midpoint, everything seems more difficult than before. Both internally (the characters' problems) and externally (when the "bad guys" seem to win), this beat is the point of the narrative where the pressure is greater than ever.

    11. ***All Is Lost*** (75 min.): After the higher stakes and the difficult situation, the next beat concerns the part of the narrative when everything seems lost for the characters. At this point, defeat looks inevitable for the main characters.

    12. ***Dark Night of the Soul*** (75 min.–85 min.): The title of the last beat of the second act is self-explanatory, since it is the point of the narrative when the characters have lost all hope and all the obstacles seem difficult to overcome. Something that seemed manageable and achievable now looks harder than ever before.

    13. ***Break Into Three*** (85 min.): The narrative enters its third and final act. The 13th beat has exactly the same function as the second plot point of the three-act structure. This beat is the part of the narrative when the characters are at their lowest point but decide to fight back again.

    14. ***Finale*** (85 min.–110 min.): This beat is the longest part of the third act. In it, the audience gets all the answers they wanted. At this point, the main conflict is resolved (either in a good or in a bad way for the characters), the audience gets all the answers needed, and the narrative comes to an end. The Finale beat incorporates into its duration the previous and the next beat; it is technically the entire third act of the narrative.

    15. ***Final Image*** (110 min.): The 15th and final beat of Snyder's approach is the final scene of the narrative. This is the final step and the contrasting image to that of the first beat (opening image), which works as a proof that change has taken place through the progression of the narrative in both the fictional world and the main characters of the story.

    Snyder's approach keeps the three-act structure intact. As a matter of fact, the first five beats are the first act, the next seven beats are the second act, and the rest of the three beats are the third act. The

The Netflix Vision of Horror

only ostensible difference in this three-act model is that at first glance, it seems that the second act is slightly longer, while the other two acts are marginally shorter (instead of 25 percent–50 percent–25 percent, the timetable of Snyder's approach looks like 23 percent–54 percent–23 percent). Of course, Snyder's beats are describing big parts of the narrative, which cannot last just one minute. For example, the 6th beat, the break into the second act, starts at the 25th minute of the narrative, but it is almost impossible for a plot point to last only a few seconds. The structural points can take anywhere from one scene to a whole sequence. So, if we study in depth Snyder's approach, we will see that ultimately it obeys the 25 percent–50percent–25 percent rule.

Combining the generalized three-act structure that has at its center the 25 percent–50 percent–25 percent rule with the minutes of each of the fifteen beats, Snyder's approach could be easily reformed as following: the Opening Image is at 1 percent, the Theme Stated is at 5 percent, the Setup is from the beginning until 9 percent, the Catalyst is at 11 percent, the Debate is from 11 percent to 25 percent, Break Into Two is at 25 percent, the B Story starts at 27 percent, Fun and Games is from 27 percent to 50 percent, the Midpoint is at 50 percent, Bad Guys Close In is from 50 percent to 68 percent, All Is Lost is at 68 percent, the Dark Night of the Soul is from 68 percent to 75 percent, Break Into Three is at 75 percent, the Finale is from 75 percent to 100 percent, and the Final Image is at 100 percent of the total narrative.

It is clear that this approach keeps the general outline of the three-act structure and adds more details in order to create a more comprehensive model. As Brütsch points out, the general three-act structure approach is sometimes a matter of interpretation of the analyst and can be a field for possible mistakes in the examination of an audiovisual work.[43] For this reason, this work chooses Snyder's approach of the fifteen beats as a more detailed theoretical tool which offers a thorough analysis of an audiovisual narrative.

The three-act model of narration is a powerful tool for analyzing filmic texts, but it has not been systematically used for the overarching stories of conventional TV series. Netflix has blurred the line between television and filmic works; as Adam Hart states, there is a convergence of film and television on streaming services.[44] These series are not fragmented into pieces that broadcast each week but are concrete structures that operate as steps in a larger narrative.

Since Netflix is based on binge-watching practices, the three-act structure can be used as a theoretical basis for analyzing the narratives of Netflix Original series. Moreover, some creators even admit that they have used this structure when they outlined the overarching story of a season, like the writers from *Bloodline* (Netflix, 2015–2017). More specifically, Todd Kessler, one of the creators of the series, stated in an interview that the new aspects of the medium in the SVOD era

> allowed us to say, we're going to approach the first three episodes as the first act of our story, Episodes 4, 5, 6 and 7 is the second act of our story, and then 8 through 13 is the third act. So, we're feeling more like, we're taking advantage of this storytelling medium, meaning you can watch multiple episodes, you can watch the whole first act at once, which is very different than a network or a cable show, unless you watch it after it's already aired. And so, for us, that desire is, we can go deeper, and hopefully create a stronger bond between the audience and the characters.[45]

From the above statement, we can clearly see that even the creators of these shows admit that their work is subject to the new norms of series consumption. Hence, the focus of the present study will be to prove that these shows are actually long-form films that are distributed as series and adapt the classical norms to their needs. Of course, the scope of this book is limited to a specific genre, so before I go any further, I will define its characteristics and outline the audiovisual texts of this analysis.

The Horror Genre and the Series Corpus Creation

As Netflix has an abundance of original content, this study will focus on an individual genre. Audiovisual genres are usually treated as dynamic texts that are constantly developing and adapting the genre's conventions to the circumstances, because they are better understood when viewed as evolutionary processes.[46] Focusing on one popular audiovisual genre like horror can give us more concrete results. Literary historian J.A. Cuddon defined horror as a piece of fiction of variable length which shocks, frightens, or even induces a feeling of repulsion or loathing.[47] As Rick Worland observes, horror is universal and has appeared in a variety of forms and media in almost every human culture.[48] Although this audiovisual genre has existed since the birth of cinema, its systematic theoretical study began in the mid–1970s, about the same time that film studies were introduced to universities.

The definitions of the genre of horror differ. Many authors have tried to create a description that would be able to completely distinguish

The Netflix Vision of Horror

and separate horror from other similar and close genres, like science fiction and thriller, but they have always encountered difficulties.[49] Dominic Strinati characterizes horror "as a genre that represents the need for suppression if the horror shown is interpreted as expressing uncomfortable and disturbing desires which need to be contained."[50] The horror genre covers an abundance of subgenres and cycles with audiovisual texts from a wide range of narratives, from raw realism to purely paranormal narrations. What makes these particular audiovisual texts a concrete genre is the fact that they are meant to scare the audience. In particular, the fear of death is an essential part of audiovisual horror texts, in the senses both of a natural process of the human body and the eternal punishment of the immortal soul.[51] As Brigid Cherry argues, being scared can itself become the main pleasure of watching horror works, and not the particular works themselves.[52]

Horror was always present in the television medium. TV scholars tend to categorize television production history into three broad periods referred as TVI, TVII, and TVIII. Roberta Pearson points out that the division of television history into certain periods is helpful as it provides broad guideposts in a complex discursive formation of what we understand as television. She summarizes the periods of U.S. television as follows:

> In the United States, TVI, dating from the mid–1950s to the early 1980s, is the era of channel scarcity, the mass audience, and three-network hegemony. TVII, dating from roughly the early 1980s to the late 1990s, is the era of channel/network expansion, quality television, and network branding strategies. TVIII, dating from the late 1990s to the present, is the era of proliferating digital distribution platforms, further audience fragmentation, and, as Reeves et al. (2002) suggest, a shift from second-order to first-order commodity relations.[53]

Television has a long history regarding fictional horror programs. In their book *TV Horror: Investigating the Darker Side of the Small Screen*, Lorna Jowett and Stacey Abbott conduct an in-depth study of the relationship between television and horror, and they show that the genre has been prominent on TV in the USA in all three of these periods.[54] Of course, the horror genre is frequently considered to be an outcast because is excessively violent and graphic; this is one reason there is little consideration of TV horror, since TV is a mainstream medium that cannot easily host the vivid nature of the genre. As Matt Hills notes, horror on TV is often "generically nominated in ways that render horror relatively invisible," such as in *Twin Peaks* (ABC, 1990–1991) being referred as a postmodern drama.[55] Even one of the masters of horror, Stephen King himself, argued in his *Danse Macabre* that television horror lacks the capacity "to put on the gruesome mask and go 'ooga booga'!"[56]

So, when we hear audiovisual horror, most of the time our minds turn to films rather than television series, since TV horror has been widely criticized. Yet, despite the criticism, there are many TV shows that belong to the genre, such as the following examples: *Twilight Zone* (CBS, 1959–1964), *Thriller* (NBC, 1960–1962), *Alfred Hitchcock Presents* (CBS, 1955–1965), *Dark Shadows* (ABC, 1966–1971), *Kolchak: The Night Stalker* (ABC, 1974–1975), *The X-Files* (FOX, 1993–2002), *Buffy the Vampire Slayer* (WB-UPN, 1997–2003), *Supernatural* (WB-CW, 2005–present), *The Vampire Diaries* (CW, 2009–2017), and *The Walking Dead* (AMC, 2010–present). Through its technological nature, television connected the public with the private life, and therefore it was always suitable for hosting horror narratives. As Drew Beard observes, "With the growth of cable television and home video, the television set over the past 30 years has become an ever-widening portal, connecting the public sphere to the private sphere and occupying a space of wonder and dread that would in turn become occupied by the Internet."[57]

Regardless of the negative criticism about the limitations on portraying certain ideas and narrative themes on television, the medium has changed significantly in the last decades, after entering what is often called the post-network era.[58] Cable television and contemporary SVOD platforms released the genre from the burden of its previous difficulty in representing gore and violent stories. Of course, as Abbott argues, "One cannot base a serial horror drama upon a string of shock effects and graphic displays of gore, which would, in fact, serve to diffuse the horror through repetition."[59] So, apart from the problems of the medium that were overcome, another issue regarding television horror is seriality itself. Netflix, on the other hand, eliminated this problem too, since its series are distributed all at once and the episodes are intended to be consumed in a short period of time.

Having all that in mind, the next step in this academic research is to identify and outline the analyzed material. But when we talk about audiovisual genres, things get complicated. When we refer to two or more audiovisual texts and place them in the same genre, we automatically accept that these works share some common elements. These elements may be part of the narrative or aesthetic norms and conventions. The problem, however, is the equivalent of the "chicken or the egg"

The Netflix Vision of Horror

causality dilemma: first select the audiovisual works that belong to a genre and then analyze their characteristics, or identify the characteristics of a genre and then choose the works that can be part of it? Andrew Tudor has called it the "empiricist dilemma": audiovisual works are first required to be isolated, for which a criterion is needed, but this criterion will emerge from the empirically common features of the works.[60]

Of course, because we are talking exclusively about Netflix, this dilemma does not exist, since the SVOD platform and its algorithm places its audiovisual works into genres and categories. In order to avoid a possible confusion regarding the rhetorical question "What is horror?" and consequently "Which texts belong to the horror genre?," this book will start from the assumption that every series that is labeled by Netflix as horror is in fact part of the genre.

As Christine Gledhill observes, genres are first and foremost a boundary phenomenon,[61] so in order to better strengthen my study, I began the present research by creating a corpus of online series that will be the foundation of this analysis of narrative structure, enhancing it with tangible quantitative results. Since the research is about particular series of a commercial genre produced by a specific SVOD platform, the audiovisual corpus is mostly based on Netflix categorization. The audiovisual texts that were included in this initial creation of the corpus had to be listed as a horror series and as part of Netflix Originals. Also, since we are talking about dozens of hours of audiovisual narratives and because every series has a repetitive formula from season to season, the research will only cover the first season of each series. Based on the above, the original corpus created included the first seasons of twenty-four horror series listed as Netflix Originals on the U.S. version of the platform through the end of 2019, the year that this research started. Then, in order for the research to be more specific, some more criteria had to be implemented.

As was mentioned, the fact that an audiovisual text is labeled as Netflix Originals does not necessarily mean that this work was produced by Netflix. Not all of the twenty-four series were written and produced exclusively by Netflix, and some of them had their initial premieres as conventional TV shows, usually on a weekly basis. Thus, their narratives were not structured for a binge-watching experience. Of the initial twenty-four series, five of them were produced and screened in another country, and Netflix acquired them afterwards as an exclusive international distributor: *Glitch* (ABC, Netflix, 2015–2019), from Australia; the first season of *Slasher* (Super Channel, Chiller, Netflix, 2016–present),

1. Netflix Original Horror Series

from Canada; *Immortals* (BluTV, 2018), from Turkey; *Crazyhead* (E4, Netflix, 2016), from U.K.; and *Kabaneri of the Iron Fortress: The Battle of Unato* (Araki, 2019), a film that premiered in theaters in Japan on May 10, 2019, and which Netflix acquired and made available in three episodes.

Another criterion for the present research is that the series must have a fictional narration. Two of the initial twenty-four series, *Prank Encounters* (2019–present) and *Haunted* (2018–present), are reality shows, something that excludes them from this study. Also, some of the remaining seventeen Netflix Original series were not perceived by the public as part of the horror genre, and Netflix used this term for publicity reasons. Thus, the fourth criterion is to be listed as a horror in either IMDb or Rotten Tomatoes, two of the most popular websites regarding audiovisual works. Based on this criterion, four of the initial series had to be excluded from the final corpus: *Daybreak* (Netflix, 2019), which is listed as Action and Adventure; and *Castlevania* (Netflix 2017–2018), *Devilman: Crybaby* (Netflix, 2018), and *Love Death + Robots* (Netflix, 2019–present), which are listed as Animation/Anime.

So, the final series corpus of this study is composed of the first seasons of Netflix Original horror series on the U.S. version of the platform that premiered through the end of 2019, were produced or ordered by Netflix, have fictional narration, and are acknowledged as part of the horror genre by either IMDb or Rotten Tomatoes. The final corpus consists of thirteen series that were created by Netflix and distributed for a binge-watching consumption. The thirteen series are as follows:

Table 1. Netflix Horror Series in the Corpus

Series	Number of Episodes	Total Duration (minutes)	Country	Year (1st Season)
Black Summer	8	257	USA	2019
Chambers	10	412	USA	2019
Chilling Adventures of Sabrina	10	560	USA	2018
Diablero	8	302	Mexico	2018
Ghoul	3	127	India	2018

The Netflix Vision of Horror

Series	Number of Episodes	Total Duration (minutes)	Country	Year (1st Season)
The Haunting of Hill House	10	555	USA	2018
Hemlock Grove	13	656	USA	2013
Marianne	8	350	France	2019
The Order	10	445	USA	2019
Santa Clarita Diet	10	262	USA	2017
Stranger Things	8	383	USA	2016
Typewriter	5	234	India	2019
V Wars	10	395	USA	2019

One initial observation is that not all of the series come from the United States. Four of them are from different countries: two from India, one from Mexico, and one from France. Nevertheless, all of them are produced by Netflix, so all of the series will be addressed equally and there will not be an analysis regarding the country of origin. Netflix is a worldwide, online platform and this study will treat its content as a global phenomenon. Moreover, the foreign audiovisual sample is relatively small and from different continents; consequently there are not sufficient data to study these specific works regarding their country of origin.

A second observation is that some of the series of the corpus are not a pure expression of the horror genre but could be characterized as hybrid narratives. For example, *Santa Clarita Diet* is a comedy horror series, while five series can be categorized as fantasy horror narratives (*Chambers, Chilling Adventures of Sabrina, Hemlock Grove, Stranger Things,* and *The Order*). Industries of the medium rely on genres in producing their programs, while at the same time most of the texts have some generic identity, fitting into well-entrenched generic categories or incorporating genre mixing.[62] According to Mittell, genre mixing "is a cultural process, enacted by industrial personnel, often in response to audience viewing practices."[63] Hybrid narratives are not a new phenomenon on television, since the emergence of quality TV pushed the medium into creating a style of television programming that is of higher quality due to its subject matter, style, or content and not based on genre tactics.[64] So, regardless of the hybrid nature of some of the series, this study will treat them as horror narratives, since this is how they are promoted by Netflix and perceived by the public (see the fourth criterion of the creation of the series corpus).

Finally, in order to calculate the total duration of a series, I had to deal with each season as a unique and concrete audiovisual narrative, so I did not include the end credits of each episode. Even Netflix itself treats end credits as something out of the narrative and unnecessary by automatically transferring the viewer to the next episode.[65] The platform cuts the end credit sequence short so that you can keep watching, a technique that strengthens the binge-watching experience.[66] As we can see, there is a wide range of total durations—from the minimum 127 minutes of *Ghoul* to the maximum 656 minutes of *Hemlock Grove*. Also, the number of the total episodes of each season is diverse, ranging from three to thirteen episodes.

Horror Plot Categories

As we are talking about the narrative structuring of audiovisual texts, and therefore their plots, we have to take into account the conventions of this specific genre regarding this matter. One of the most important and thorough studies of the genre is Noel Carroll's *The Philosophy of Horror, or Paradoxes of the Heart*. In this book, Carroll systematically explores some different plot categories of the genre and deconstructs them into vital functions. The study of Carroll concerns different types of horror, from short written stories to TV shows. This approach tries to find the essence of the genre regarding its plots and regardless of the medium. Carroll identifies four essential functions that can be found in the narratives of the horror genre: onset, discovery, confirmation, and confrontation.[67]

More specifically, according to Carroll, during the onset function the monster's presence is established for the audience, while in the discovery, the monster arrives and an individual or a group learns of its existence. The discovery of the monster may come as a surprise to the characters, or it may be part of an investigation.[68] The confirmation function involves the discoverers convincing some other group of the existence of the monster and of the proportions of the mortal danger at hand, while in the confrontation humanity marches out to meet the

The Netflix Vision of Horror

monster and the confrontation generally takes the form of a debacle. Often, there is more than one confrontation. Furthermore, the confrontation movement may also adopt a problem-and-solution format.[69]

The main problem with this approach is the fact that Carroll is narrowing down the genre by having the presence of a monster as a prerequisite. Horror is an umbrella term that incorporates many audiovisual texts that do not have a monster as the evil force. The evil force is usually a defining element of the horror genre, and there are several categorizations of particular audiovisual texts according to the monster. One of these categorizations is by Charles Derry, who spoke about three major categories of audiovisual horror based on the evil force: the Horror of Personality, the Horror of Armageddon and the Horror of the Demonic.[70] In the Horror of Personality, the evil force is represented as a human being, the Horror of Armageddon deals with aspects of nature that are acquiring abnormal features, while the Horror of the Demonic represents the evil force as a metaphysical being with demonic elements.

Therefore, it is a fact that monsters can take various forms in these narratives—metaphysical (vampire, werewolf, etc.), human (insane scientists, murderer, etc.) or practices related to nature (animals, extreme weather, etc.). Of course, in our everyday lives, the term "monster" usually has a metaphysical and/or paranormal nature and does not include the above-mentioned forms. Hence, to avoid confusion, only the term "Other"[71] (with a capital first letter) will be used in this book, which is a term that can cover all aspects of evil and, based on Kevin Thomas, refers to different groups that are undoubtedly excluded from something or someone else.[72] The terminology is not accidental, as this term was formulated by important scholars, scientists and philosophers, including Georg Wilhelm Friedrich Hegel and Johann Gottlieb Fichte,[73] Jean-Paul Sartre,[74] Simone de Beauvoir,[75] Emmanuel Levinas,[76] Julia Kristeva,[77] and Jacques Lacan.[78]

Appropriately, the theories of the term Other in the present study are the ones best applied to the genre of horror and to Carroll's approach about the different categories of horror plots. The Other in not unfamiliar to television scholars, with Vivian Sobchack pointing out, "In the age of television the drawbridge is always down; the world intrudes. It is no longer possible to avoid the invasive presence of Others."[79]

Lacan was a pioneer in this academic discourse and coined one of the most well-known and complex uses of this term. He made a distinction between the "little other," symbolizing him with a (from the French term *autre*), and the "big Other," symbolizing him with A (from the

1. Netflix Original Horror Series

French term *Autre*).[80] The little other is the one who is not really other, but a reflection and projection of the Ego and is thus entirely inscribed in the imaginary order. On the other hand, the big Other describes radical alterity, an illusory otherness of the imaginary, something that it cannot be assimilated through identification.[81] In simple terms, Lacan spoke of two categories of Other, where in the first one there is a view of the self, while in the second the diversity prevails. According to Patrick Jemmer, the general process of perceiving the Other is concretized through the creation of binary distinctions, such as identity/difference, us/them, subject/object, in/out, certain/uncertain, true/false, male/female, Self/Other.[82]

Based on Lacan's approach, Slavoj Žižek speaks of an Other who operates on a symbolic level and is the unwritten constitution of the society, a force that is present, conducting and controlling the actions of community members. As Žižek himself says, "When I violate a certain rule of decency, I never simply do something that the majority of others do not do—I do what 'one' doesn't do."[83] On the same note, Kristeva's approach speaks about the abject, a term that refers to the human reaction to an imminent collapse in the light of the loss of distinction between subject and object, or between the self and the Other.[84]

Having that in mind, we can better understand an approach that was created exclusively for the horror genre by Robin Wood. Wood, while using psychoanalytic theories, defines society and its forms of oppression in the collective unconscious, but then a crucial question arises: what about those who do not keep up with the social constraints? Wood talks about the concept of the Other, which puts at risk the normality of Western society.[85] The Other, who can take various forms—from class and national to political and ideological—does not keep up with the rules of the bourgeoisie, so, society either tries to reject him or make him conform to its own terms. Based on Wood, every audiovisual horror text has an Other that disturbs normality, and therefore the main characters must confront him because, as Cary Morrison states, these evil forces "reflect the deepest fears of a culture, mirroring those issues that confront us on primal levels."[86] In the same manner, Stephen Asma observes that terror and monsters have always been politically useful,[87] since from archaic times through the present, monsters have been impregnated with political demonization and dangerous propaganda.[88]

Returning to Carroll's approach, all of the four functions that he distinguishes are about the Other of the narrative and its interaction with normality. In the first function the audience learns about the existence

The Netflix Vision of Horror

of the Other, in the second function the fictional characters discover the Other, in the third function the now-knowing characters try to convince the rest of the group that the Other exists, while in the fourth and final function, the fictional characters confront the Other. Not all of the narratives of the horror genre incorporate all four functions, but Carroll identifies different plot categories based on their selection of these four essential functions.

The first category that works as a prototype model of narration of the genre is the complex discovery plot, in which all of the four functions are part of the narrative. The plots of these audiovisual texts are arranged so that first the audience learns about the threat, then some of the characters realize the danger, then they convince the rest of the protagonists about the possible threat, and then they confront the danger.

After defining the complex discovery plot, Carroll describes other categories of horror plot that may omit one or more of the above four essential functions. Thus, Carroll describes the possible triple-function plots: the discovery plot (onset, discovery, and confrontation),[89] the confirmation plot (onset, discovery, and confirmation),[90] the onset/confirmation/confrontation plot, and the discovery/confirmation/confrontation plot, whose names are self-explanatory.[91] In the discovery plot there is no need for some characters to convince the rest about the existence of the Other, since they discover its presence all together. In the confirmation plot there is no confrontation of the Other, usually leaving the narrative with an open ending. The onset/confirmation/confrontation plot lacks a discovery component and therefore it is usually found in narrative contexts where the monster is already known to exist, usually for sequels, franchise plots, etc. In the discovery/confirmation/confrontation plot there is no available evidence of the onset of the Other until the moment of discovery, which means that audience and characters learn at the same time about the threat.

Then, after distinguishing the prototype and the triple-function plot categories, Carroll shows that a horror story can also be a double- or a single-function plot. He identifies the following formats: the double-function categories are the onset/discovery plot, the onset/confirmation plot, the onset/confrontation plot, the discovery/confirmation plot, the discovery/confrontation plot, and the confirmation/confrontation plot, while the single-function categories are the onset plot, the discovery plot, the confirmation plot, and the confrontation plot.[92] In conclusion, based on the four functions and the selection each narrative makes, Carroll identifies fourteen different categories of horror plots.

1. Netflix Original Horror Series

According to these four functions, Carroll tries to study in depth the mechanisms of horror plots regardless of the medium. Even if this academic approach does not provide much information about the structuring of horror narratives, nevertheless it delivers a thorough presentation of the possibilities a horror plot can have. Consequently, if we combine the structuring methods from screenwriting studies analyzed above with Carroll's approach, it can be vital for the analysis of the series corpus and of audiovisual horror in general.

Netflix Original Horror Series

Having reviewed the two most important theoretical tools of this study, the three-act structure and the categories of horror plots, the analysis of every series of the corpus will unveil to us the structuring methods of the binge-watch digital era. Of the thirteen chosen series, the following eight follow the complex discovery plot by incorporating all of the four functions in their narratives: *Chilling Adventures of Sabrina* (Netflix, 2018–present), *Diablero* (Netflix, 2018–present), *Ghoul* (Netflix, 2018), *Hemlock Grove* (Netflix, 2013–2015), *Marianne* (Netflix, 2019), *Stranger Things* (Netflix, 2016–present), *Typewriter* (Netflix, 2019–present), and *V Wars* (Netflix, 2019–present). The rest of the series are divided into triple- and double-function plot categories. More specifically, two series—*Chambers* (Netflix, 2019) and *The Haunting of Hill House* (Netflix, 2018)—follow the discovery plot, two series—*Santa Clarita Diet* (Netflix, 2017–2019) and *The Order* (Netflix, 2019–present)—follow the discovery/confirmation/confrontation plot, while only one series, *Black Summer* (Netflix, 2019–present), follows a double-function category, the discovery/confrontation plot.

From fig. 2, we can clearly see that there is a preference in the complex discovery plot category, since more than 61 percent of the audiovisual texts in the corpus favor the use of all of the four essential functions. The rest of the series are divided into three other categories, but there is a tendency towards triple-function plots and only one example with a double-function plot. Carroll's analysis is about every category of horror plot, from a short story to a long series. As the corpus of the present study consists of long-form narratives, it is logical that the plot categories that are being used incorporate as many functions as they can. Double- and single-function plots are relatively short and are rarely observed to be part of a long narrative form, since they

The Netflix Vision of Horror

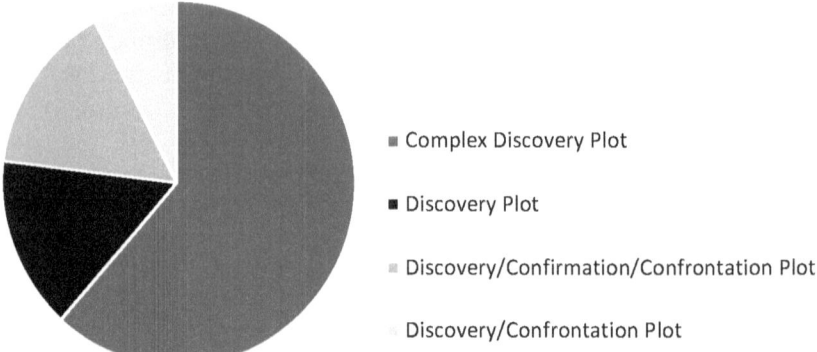

Figure 2: The Plots of the Series Corpus

are usually intended for short horror stories. Therefore, *Black Summer* and its double-function plot category is an exception to the general rule.

Apart from the plot categories, the second fundamental issue is regarding the structuring of the narratives. Even if most of the series have more than one protagonist and in some episodes break the linearity of time—basic characteristics of a classical narrative—they are still following the three-act structure as a construction tool of their overarching story. In order to strengthen the argument, a brief overview of the generalized three-act structure of each series follows:

Black Summer is a series of 8 episodes with a total of 257 minutes, and it is the only one that follows the discovery/confrontation plot. The series centers around the early days of a zombie apocalypse, when complete strangers come together to find the strength they need to survive and get back to their loved ones. The inciting incident occurs at the 18th minute, when the two main characters meet and one promises the other to help her find her daughter. The first plot point happens at the 41st minute, when all the people attack the soldiers and cross the gates. The midpoint is at the 110th minute, when one of the main characters dies and becomes a zombie, while the second plot point occurs at the 186th minute, when the seven basic characters come together to confront several zombies. The season ends with the climax, in which the remaining characters find the missing daughter and the main conflict is resolved.

Chambers is a ten-episode series of a total of 412 minutes, which

1. Netflix Original Horror Series

follows the discovery plot. The story is about Sasha (Sivan Alyra Rose), a woman who survives a heart transplant and then begins to develop the personality traits of the deceased girl who was the donor. The inciting incident is placed in the 46th minute, in which Sasha first sees the deceased girl in her own reflection on the mirror. The first plot point occurs at the 132nd minute, when Sasha starts to be violent by killing a friendly mouse. The midpoint is at the 215th minute, when Sasha's skin becomes white around the wound in her hand, while the second plot point is at the 305th minute of the narrative, when with the help of the deceased girl's brother, Sasha takes a drug in order to connect with the girl. The season ends with Sasha killing some members of the cult who were responsible for this metaphysical experience with the great powers she has obtained.

Chilling Adventures of Sabrina is a complex discovery plot comprising ten episodes with a total duration of 560 minutes. Regarding this series, a clarification has to be made regarding an eleventh episode, which was arguably part of the first season. A couple of months after the initial release of the first season, a new episode appeared that was a Christmas special, but because it was not part of the binge-watching experience, I am not incorporating it into the first season and therefore into the present analysis. The series is about Sabrina (Kiernan Shipka), a half-witch, half-mortal girl, who must choose at her 16th birthday between the witch world of her family and the human world of her friends. The inciting incident is at the 58th minute, when Sabrina has a bad vision regarding her upcoming dark baptism. The first plot point is at the 118th minute, when the dark lord—through the school principal—tells Sabrina that she will be his no matter her denial of the baptism. The midpoint is at the 287th minute, when Sabrina confronts her teacher about her identity and she lies to her. The second plot point occurs in the 427th minute, when Sabrina kills one of the witch sisters in order to complete a sacrifice and bring back from the dead her boyfriend's brother. Finally, the season concludes with Sabrina being visibly changed at the academy with the other witches, something that works as the answer to the main conflict of the overarching story.

Diablero is a Mexican 8-episode narration with a total of 302 minutes. The story is about a priest, a legendary demon hunter, and a modern-day, possessed superhero who join forces to battle evil. The inciting incident happens at the 38th minute, when the three main characters go to the place where the little girl was kidnapped in order to find clues. The first plot point occurs at the 75th minute, when a woman finds and saves the little girl. In the midpoint, at the 148th minute of the narrative, the woman that protects the children is revealed to be evil. The second plot point is at the 230th minute, when the main characters go to the place the evil woman lives but find she has left with all four of the kidnaped children. The season concludes with the main conflict having been resolved and the characters being together and happy, after having defeated the evil forces.

Ghoul is the shortest narrative of the corpus, since its 127-minute duration could be easily compared with an average feature film. The story is set in a totalitarian, near-future India, when a mysterious prisoner is sent to a remote military interrogation center where he turns the tables on his captors by exposing their most shameful secrets and unleashing a demon from Arabic folklore. The inciting incident occurs at the 17th minute, when the main protagonist, Nida (Radhika Apte), betrays her father and gives information to the regime, something that leads to his imprisonment. The first plot point is at the 32nd minute, when Nida arrives at the remote military interrogation, but the major does not trust her because of her past. The midpoint is at the 60th minute, when the ghoul makes one soldier kill the other. The second plot point happens at the 96th minute, when the major orders the arrest of Nida and the colonel. The season ends with Nida at her cell starting the ritual of inviting the ghoul, the Arabic demon, just like the first scene of the series, in which her father invited it.

Hemlock Grove is one of the first Netflix Originals and the first horror series. Its total duration is 656 minutes. The series follows the peculiar events in Hemlock Grove, a fictional town in Pennsylvania, where Roman Godfrey (Bill Skarsgård), heir to the town's wealthy Godfrey family and a vampire, befriends the town's newcomer, Peter Rumancek (Landon Liboiron), a young werewolf. The two work together to shed light on the brutal murders that are happening in the town, while also hiding their own dark identities. The inciting incident is at the 94th minute, when Roman for the first time sees Peter turn into a wolf. The first plot point is at the 145th minute, when Peter agrees to team up with Roman in order to find the killer of the mysterious murders. The midpoint is at the 319th minute, when the two main characters fight, while the second plot point is at the 493rd minute, when the vargulf kills the twin daughters of the sheriff. The season ends with the killing of the vargulf—the main conflict of the season—and the introduction of a new status for both the protagonists.

1. Netflix Original Horror Series

Marianne is a French 8-episode series of 350 minutes centering on Emma (Victoire Du Bois), a famous and successful horror writer, who is forced to return to her hometown after the woman who haunted her dreams fifteen years ago begins to reappear. The inciting incident occurs at the 51st minute, when for the first time, in her nightmare, Marianne demands that Emma write about her again. The first plot point is at the 97th minute of the narrative, when Emma starts to write again about Marianne and then, the next morning, Emma's mother returns from the woods. The midpoint is at the 190th minute, when the infant child of a main character disappears. The second plot point is at the 263rd minute, when the main characters are gathered in the school. The inspector says that Marianne has possessed him, and then he commits suicide. The season ends with Emma winning over the spirit of Marianne with the help of her local friends, while she learns from a vision of Marianne that she is pregnant.

Santa Clarita Diet is a comedy horror series with a total duration of 262 minutes. The story is about Sheila (Drew Barrymore) and Joel (Timothy Olyphant), a married couple who are real estate agents in Santa Clarita, California. When Sheila dies, their lives take a dark turn since she turns into a zombie that wants to eat human flesh. The inciting incident occurs at the 27th minute, when Sheila eats her first victim alive. The first plot point is at the 54th minute, when Joel promises Sheila to stay together as a family and help her kill people in order to eat them. The midpoint is at the 130th minute, when one of Sheila's victims becomes a zombie. The second plot point is at the 183rd minute, when Sheila loses her little toe, something that means she is starting to decompose. The season ends with the family being apart: Joel is locked up at a psychiatric clinic and Sheila is locked up in their house's basement, while their daughter tries to find a cure.

Stranger Things, one of the most popular Netflix Original series, is part of the horror genre. The first season has an 8-episode structure and a total duration of 383 minutes. The story is set in the fictional town of Hawkins, Indiana, in 1983, and focuses on the investigation of the disappearance of Will (Noah Schnapp), while supernatural events are occurring around the town, including the appearance of a girl with psychokinetic abilities, Eleven (Millie Bobby Brown), who helps the missing boy's friends in their search. The inciting incident occurs at the 46th minute, when the three boys find Eleven in the woods. The first plot point is at the 100th minute, when the "monster" kills Barb (Shannon Purser). The midpoint is at the 196th minute, when the sheriff finds out

The Netflix Vision of Horror

that the dead body of Will is fake. At the 291st minute there is the second plot point, when someone follows Mike (Finn Wolfhard), Dustin (Gaten Matarazzo), and Eleven, while Lucas (Caleb McLaughlin) sees the following person and informs them. The narrative concludes with the group of the boys being reunited, while Will has some paranormal experiences but does not share them with anyone.

The Haunting of Hill House is a mini-series consisting of ten episodes of a total duration of 555 minutes. The story is about the Crain family, who confront haunting memories of their old house and the terrifying events that happened there. The plot is structured around two timelines, one following the five adult Crain siblings, whose paranormal experiences at Hill House continue to haunt them in the present day, and the other using flashbacks depicting events leading up to the eventful night in 1992 when the family escaped from the house. Even if the series looks like it occurs in non-linear time, the narrative is structured in a linear manner, with the story demanding that both past and present coexist (this issue will be thoroughly analyzed in the third chapter of the book). So, the narrative is in fact following the three-act structure and has all the structural narrative points of the classical model. More specifically, the inciting incident is the suicide of Nell (Victoria Pedretti) in the 58th minute; the first plot point is the statement of Luke (Oliver Jackson-Cohen) that Nell's death was not a suicide, at the 209th minute; the midpoint is at the 277th minute, when the audience learns that bent-neck lady was Nell all along; and the second plot point is at the 430th minute, when Luke goes to burn down the house. The series concludes with the death of their father and the survival of the rest of the Crain siblings.

The Order is a fantasy horror series; its first season has a total duration of 445 minutes. The series centers on Jack (Jake Manley), a college student, who pledges to a secret order to avenge his mother's death and lands in a war between werewolves and practitioners of dark magic. The inciting incident is at the 48th minute, when Jack fights with Kyle (Jedidiah Goodacre), who tried to set him up, but then a werewolf attacks them. The first plot point is at the 96th minute, when Jack meets with the werewolves of the Knights of Saint Christopher. They invite him to be a member too, but he refuses. The midpoint is at the 222nd minute, when Jack and Alyssa (Sarah Grey) are sleeping together, while the sickness returns to the witch. The second plot point happens at the 320th minute, when Jack brings Alyssa to help the werewolves and all together try to find Randall (Adam DiMarco). Finally, the climax of the

1. Netflix Original Horror Series

first season is at the end, when the order puts a spell on Jack to forget everything.

Typewriter is a 5-episode, Indian series with a total of 234 minutes. The story is about three young friends in Goa who plan to search an old villa for ghosts. When a new family moves in, the home's hidden past resurfaces. The inciting incident is at the 27th minute, when a mysterious man (later on the math teacher of the kids and ultimately Fakeer's son) kills the man who did not succeed in bringing him the typewriter from the villa. The first plot point is at the 48th minute, when the typewriter writes on its own the phrase "ghosts do exist" and then a figure identical to Jenny (Palomi Ghosh) appears next to the bed while she is asleep. The midpoint is at the 100th minute, when Sam sees the evil Jenny killing a man and then finds the real Jenny at the church. The second plot point occurs at the 178th minute, when Sam (Aarnaa Sharma) tells her friends everything that she learned about Fakeer and that his soul is trapped inside the typewriter. Finally, the climax of the season is when the friends manage to destroy the typewriter, leading ultimately to the victory of the main characters.

V Wars is the most recent produced series incorporated into the corpus of this study and has a total duration of 395 minutes. The series centers on Dr. Luther Swann (Ian Somerhalder), who tries to find a cure for a virus that has been released from ice melting due to climate change and turns humans into vampires. The inciting incident of the first season occurs at the 53rd minute of the narrative, when Luther kills his wife, who was turned into a vampire. The first plot point is at the 90th minute, in which Luther says that the people infected by the virus are in fact victims, but Calix (Peter Outerbridge) seems to disagree and be plotting something behind Luther's back. This leads to Department of National Security's statement declaring Michael (Adrian Holmes), the first vampire, to be a public threat. The midpoint is at the 207th minute, when Luther finds out that his son is infected. The second plot point is at the 290th minute, when the FBI saves Luther and his kid from a camp. The season ends with the uprising of the Bloods under the leadership of Calix and their taking Luther's son as a hostage.

Having analyzed the thirteen Netflix Original horror series according to the generalized three-act structure, we can identify the acts of each narrative and extract some initial data from which, if we combine it with the horror plot categories of each series, we can draw some first conclusions. Based on all the aforementioned plot points, here is a table with the three-act structure of each series:

The Netflix Vision of Horror

Table 2. Three-Act Structures of the Series

Series	First Act	Second Act	Third Act	Plot Category
Black Summer	16%	56%	28%	Discovery/Confrontation Plot
Chambers	32%	42%	26%	Discovery Plot
Chilling Adventures of Sabrina	21%	55%	24%	Complex Discovery Plot
Diablero	25%	51%	24%	Complex Discovery Plot
Ghoul	25%	50%	25%	Complex Discovery Plot
The Haunting of Hill House	37%	40%	23%	Discovery Plot
Hemlock Grove	22%	53%	25%	Complex Discovery Plot
Marianne	28%	47%	25%	Complex Discovery Plot
The Order	22%	50%	28%	Discovery/Confirmation/Confrontation Plot
Santa Clarita Diet	20%	50%	30%	Discovery/Confirmation/Confrontation Plot
Stranger Things	26%	50%	24%	Complex Discovery Plot
Typewriter	21%	55%	24%	Complex Discovery Plot
V Wars	23%	51%	26%	Complex Discovery Plot

1. Netflix Original Horror Series

From the above table, we can make two essential observations that can work as the foundation of the rest of this research: all of the thirteen series follow the generalized three-act structure and their narratives can be studied as an extensive filmic text, while the plot category significantly affects the percentage of each act. All the above Netflix Original horror series work as unified narratives that are meant to be watched continuously and not on a periodical frequency. The significance of the structuring is being transferred from the unit/episode to the entity/season. But as was expected, each narrative adapts the conventions and norms of the three-act structure to its needs.

More specifically, the series with the complex discovery plot feature all of the four functions and have a more balanced distribution of the action into their acts, since the percentages of each act are very similar to the standard three-act structure. More specifically, their first acts range from 21 percent to 28 percent (with an average of 24 percent), their second acts from 47 percent to 55 percent (with an average of 51 percent), and their third acts from 24 percent to 26 percent (with an average of 25 percent). These narratives follow faithfully the generalized outline of the three-act structure with their first and third acts having almost identical lengths, while the second act is as long the two others combined.

The series with the discovery plots that incorporate the onset, discovery, and confrontation functions redefine the percentages of each act. More specifically, the first acts of these two series are 32 percent and 37 percent, the second acts are 42 percent and 40 percent, while the third acts are 26 percent and 23 percent. On average, the discovery plot three-act structure is 34 percent–41 percent–25 percent, which means that these narratives keep intact the duration of the third act but have a longer first and a shorter second act.

Following the same pattern, the two series that follow the three-part discovery/confirmation/confrontation plot rearrange the percentages, with the first acts being 20 percent and 22 percent, both second acts being 50 percent, and the third acts being 30 percent and 28 percent. On average, this plot category has a three-act structure of 21 percent–50 percent–29 percent, which means that these narratives have a longer third and a shorter first act, but they keep intact the second act. Finally, the only series of the corpus that follows a double-function plot category, the discovery/confrontation plot, has a three-act structure of 16 percent–56 percent–28 percent. This means that this narrative has a much smaller first act and slightly longer second and third acts.

Moving forward this argument and having in mind that the four functions follow a linear time sequence, we can easily link each function with a specific act. When the narrative incorporates all of the four functions, the percentages of each act are balanced and based on the general outline of this classical model. Comparing the series of the corpus, we can see that the discovery and confrontation functions are integral parts of all of the narratives, and there is no show that excludes them from its plot. This is to be expected, since each horror narrative is based on a main conflict between the protagonists and the Other that starts with the discovery of the Other by the characters and ends with their ultimate confrontation. Series that lack the onset function tend to have shorter first acts, since they do not have to introduce the Other's presence and they can move faster to the implications of the second act. In contrast, series that lack the confirmation function tend to have shorter second acts since the narrative can move quickly to the confrontation and possible resolution of the final act. So, even if all the Netflix Original horror series are functioning as long-form films, they adapt the three-act structure by choosing which of the four functions are incorporated into their plots.

The generalized approach of the three-act structure does not offer an in-depth view of the narrative but gives us a simplified interpretation of the structure of the narratives. For a better understanding of the new norms that were created in series horror due to the SVOD conventions, we have to use Snyder's approach of the fifteen beats. It is remarkable that all of the series of the corpus follow the fifteen beats and adjust them based on their narration needs. The next chapters of this book will be dedicated to a comprehensive and detailed analysis of the structure of the series of the corpus in order to establish and thoroughly analyze the unified models of narration of each plot category for horror that has been created for binge-watching experience.

Conclusion

It is widely accepted that the landscape of television has drastically changed since Netflix became a global network in a form of an SVOD platform. Binge-watching has become synonymous with Netflix, and for most of its original content, it releases all episodes at the same time. The distribution and consumption of fictional programs have been radically altered, and as is reasonable, these new methods have affected the narrative structures of these shows, because they change the way they are supposed to be viewed.

One of the audiovisual genres that is flourishing on Netflix is horror, and based on strict criteria, a series corpus was created in order to form the basis of this study. There were two main theoretical tools of this analysis: the three-act structure, a well-known and timeless instrument that helps filmmakers build their classical narratives, and Carroll's categorization of horror plots based on four essential functions. Based on these theories, I analyzed the case studies and concluded that each of the series follows the three-act structure but adapts it to its own needs. These results prove the main hypothesis of this book: that these audiovisual works are functioning as extensive and unified audiovisual narratives—like long-form films, rather than like TV series, which are based on episodic narration that will be aired and therefore consumed weekly.

Based on these results, the next chapters of this book will be based on an in-depth analysis of the narrative of each of the thirteen series of the corpus, using Snyder's approach. More specifically, the second chapter will address the complex discovery plot and the structuring norms of the eight series that belong to this category, while the third chapter will focus on the triple- and double-function plot categories that can be found in the corpus.

Chapter Two

The Narrative Structure of the Complex Discovery Plot

Complex Discovery Plot: The Prototype Model of Narration

As was established in the first chapter, the complexity of the structuring methods of the long-form narratives that belong to the corpus is highly influenced by the category of the horror plot each series follows. Depending on the number of plot functions each series incorporates into its overarching story, the percentages of each of the three acts are highly influenced. Many of the series incorporate into their narratives all of the four functions and follow the complex discovery plot. More specifically, eight out of the thirteen narratives have the onset, discovery, confirmation, and confrontation functions. This chapter will focus on these audiovisual works and study in depth their structuring norms and choices in order to define and outline the conventions of this plot category, which works as the prototype model of narration of the genre.

The linear arrangement of events in these series is established in a methodical way. The Other is introduced to the audience with the onset function; some of the characters then begin to be aware of the danger that is approaching, in the discovery function; however, they first have to convince the rest of the protagonists in the confirmation function before they challenge the Other in the confrontation function. The complex discovery plot has a balanced distribution of action with the percentages of each act being similar to the classical three-act structure. More specifically, the narratives of these series follow the standardized outline with their first and third acts having almost identical lengths, while the second act has double the duration of the others.

This chapter will analyze this horror plot category and thoroughly study the functions of these specific narratives. The series that will be

2. The Narrative Structure of the Complex Discovery Plot

analyzed in this chapter are *Chilling Adventures of Sabrina* (Netflix, 2018–present), *Diablero* (Netflix, 2018–present), *Ghoul* (Netflix, 2018), *Hemlock Grove* (Netflix, 2013–2015), *Marianne* (Netflix, 2019), *Stranger Things* (Netflix, 2016–present), *Typewriter* (Netflix, 2019–present), and *V Wars* (Netflix, 2019–present). First, there will be a structural analysis of each of the aforementioned series in an alphabetical order, and then the chapter will conclude with a methodological approach to the complex discovery plot based on the data collected from each of the eight case studies. The goal of this chapter is to create a unified approach to the complex discovery pot and define the norms that govern it, so that in the next chapter it can be used as the prototype model that can help us better understand how the narratives of the series with fewer essential functions in their plots actually operate.

Chilling Adventures of Sabrina—*A Structural Analysis*

Chilling Adventures of Sabrina is an American fantasy horror series based on the Archie comic book series of the same name and created by Roberto Aguirre-Sacasa. The series is centered on Sabrina Spellman (Kiernan Shipka), who must reconcile her dual nature as a half-witch, half-mortal while fighting the evil forces that threaten her, her family and the humans around her.[1] In September 2017, it was reported that a live-action television series based on the homonymous comic book was being developed for CW, but in December 2017 the project moved to Netflix and two seasons, comprising ten episodes each, were ordered by the streaming service.[2] CW president Mark Pedowitz pointed out that Netflix had the ability to offer a two-season commitment, a fact that tempted Warner Bros. Television to move the series to the SVOD platform.[3]

The series' TV predecessor, *Sabrina, the Teenage Witch* (ABC, WB, 1996–2003), an American sitcom TV series created by Nell Scovell and based on the same comic book series, belongs to a completely different genre, since sitcom conventions demand stereotypical characters and situations in order to create comedic elements. *Chilling Adventures of Sabrina* took a completely different path and was structured as a fantasy horror that, according to Aguirre-Sacasa, was inspired by famous horror films. Aguirre-Sacasa stated, "The idea was to do a dark horror version of Sabrina, something that was more of a slow-burn horror,

The Netflix Vision of Horror

like *The Exorcist* and *Rosemary's Baby* and all those great satanic horror movies from the 1960s and 1970s."[4] The reception for this different approach was mainly positive. Constance Grady states that when the series fully commits to its dark goth horror aesthetic, it is at "its most thrilling,"[5] while Meagan Navarro points out that this dark version of Sabrina's world bears a much closer resemblance to the likes of classic horror films than to *Bewitched* (ABC, 1964–1972).[6]

The first season consists of 10 episodes and a total duration of 560 minutes. It was made available on Netflix on October 26, 2018. The episode's duration is approximately one hour and ranges from 50 to 63 minutes (including the end credits). As it was mentioned in the first chapter, there is an eleventh episode that was released as a Christmas special, but it is not part of the overarching story of the first season.[7] Even the creator of the series admitted that this episode was not planned from the beginning. While working on the first episode of season two they realized that they had done a Halloween and a Thanksgiving episode in season one, so they decided to create a Christmas episode between the two seasons.[8]

The construction of the overarching story follows faithfully the three-act structure, with the episodes working as units of an overall and extensive narrative. The narrative does not only fit into the generalized three-act model; it also follows each of the fifteen beats that Blake Snyder introduced. These fifteen beats of the series are the following:

Opening Image (1 min.): The series starts with Sabrina, her boyfriend Harvey Kinkle (Ross Lynch), and her friends being at the cinema and watching a horror film. Outside the theater, they see Mary Wardwell (Michelle Gomez), Sabrina's favorite teacher and mentor at Baxter High, who was at the film, but leaves to go to her house. Sabrina and her friends talk about the horror film they watched. The opening image of the series is setting the tone of the narrative, in which horror elements are at its core. Even if it is not based on scary components, this image is the appropriate opening for a series that refused the legacy of the former TV version of Sabrina and turned to the horror genre. Moreover, this first beat introduces all the main characters of the story.

Theme Stated (33 min.): Harvey and Sabrina are talking about her upcoming birthday. Sabrina says that she has to go to another school, and Harvey thinks she is hiding something from him. Sabrina decides to show him the truth, and both the characters go to the forest. There, she tells him about the upcoming dark baptism and her true half-witch, half-mortal nature. Harvey does not take it well and tries to leave, but

2. The Narrative Structure of the Complex Discovery Plot

Sabrina puts a spell on him in order to forget everything. Harvey does not remember anything, and both characters leave the forest. This sequence sets the theme of the whole narrative, since the entire series is about the battle between the dual natures of the main character. As the narrative progresses, the clash between the witch world and the human world occurs, something that leads to Sabrina's impending choice of preference. This internal battle of the main character is the theme of the narrative that creates a concrete and comprehensive overarching story.

Setup (1 min.–50 min.): The first part of the series is dedicated to the setup of the main components of the narrative. More specifically, in the first fifty minutes of the whole narrative, the audience is introduced to the fictional world of the series, the main characters and antagonists are presented, and the protagonist's internal conflict begins to develop. We see how the antagonistic force takes the place and the form of Sabrina's best teacher, and how Sabrina is hesitant about the upcoming dark baptism and the fact that she is not her real self in either world: in the human world no one knows that she is half-witch, while in the witch world they bully her because she is not pure blooded. The entire setup of the narrative take the majority of the first episode of the season, while the end of the episode is reserved for the next two beats.

Catalyst (58 min.): Near the end of the first episode, Sabrina goes to the old tree in order to eat an apple and search for the answer to whether she should be baptized. She starts to have a vision, in which the apple is rotten with worms, while some witches are hanged in the tree. A demon comes out of the tree and tries to grab Sabrina. She spits out the apple, and the vision ends at the same time her boyfriend comes to pick her up. This is the moment when the inciting incident occurs and the main conflict is established in its entirety. Even if information has already been given to the audience about the hesitance of the protagonist to be baptized, this beat creates a tangible conflict in which Sabrina has evidence that the dark baptism will lead to unwanted consequences. From this scene on, the narrative has an external conflict that simultaneously works with the theme of the narrative and creates the central dramatic question: whether Sabrina will choose her human or her witch nature.

Debate (58 min.–118 min.): The next sixty minutes of the narrative are dedicated to the debate beat, in which Sabrina doubts her calling to be baptized. She does not know if she has to answer to her internal call and cancel the dark baptism. There is a conflict inside her between the mortal and the witch world that represents the two natures of her true identity. Before she answers her internal call, there is a moment of doubt about the upcoming journey she is going to take. Additionally, this moment of doubt resurfaces the theme of the narrative. This beat develops at the end of the first episode and in the second episode.

Break Into Two (118 min.): After the first five beats, it is time for the narrative to enter the second act. At the end of the second episode and until the start of the third episode, there is the first plot point, in which the narrative's course goes a new direction that reinforces the main conflict. At this beat, Sabrina refuses to proceed with her dark baptism, while her aunt, Zelda (Miranda Otto), says that her actions have embarrassed her and the family. Sabrina tells her aunt about her vision in which her parents tell her to run away from her baptism. Then, at her school, she has another vision in which the dark lord speaks to her through the principal and says that he will force her to sign the baptism and then be his. Sabrina runs away from the principal's office, but she still hears his words until she meets Miss Wardwell. She does not tell Miss Wardwell anything. Based on the actions of the first plot point, Sabrina decides to take the journey of maintaining both her natures, while trying to balance between the mortal and the witch worlds.

B Story (125 min.): The narrative having entered its second act, some secondary plotlines are introduced in order for the longest act to be developed. At this point of the narrative, the main B story starts to unfold, in which we see how the dark lord claims Sabrina through legal actions. This leads Sabrina into the court of witches, which ultimately wins. Sabrina has to go to both her mortal school and the academy for witches. Of course, since we are talking about a long-form audiovisual narrative, there are other secondary storylines that work and develop simultaneously with the main story.

Fun and Games (125 min.–287 min.): The first part of the second act is dedicated to actions whose stakes are not yet high. At this point of the narrative, the audience sees how Sabrina tries to balance her mortal and magical sides. The judicial controversy with the dark lord and Sabrina's victory, her arrival at the witch academy and the bullying towards her, and her victory over a demon in her family's house are just some of the components of the fun and games beat. The main dramatic question is always here and the narrative tries to answer it, but at this point the obstacles are not extremely important and the main character seems carefree.

Midpoint (287 min.): The stakes get higher. In this beat, Sabrina realizes that her best teacher, Miss Wardwell, is not who she really thought. Because of this, she goes to her home and asks to find out who

2. The Narrative Structure of the Complex Discovery Plot

she really is. Miss Wardwell lies to Sabrina and tells her that her (Miss Wardwell's) father put her in this place to protect her from possible threats. The audience knows that she is lying, since in the first episode a demonic force killed Miss Wardwell and took her form. This new direction of the narrative establishes greater potential risks for Sabrina and creates a new tone for the rest of the second act. The midpoint is taking place exactly at the middle of the entire narrative, where it was supposed to be.

Bad Guys Close In (287 min.–384 min.): After the midpoint and the higher stakes, the antagonistic forces seem to be closer to the protagonist than ever. Sabrina starts to trust Miss Wardwell with everything around her witch identity, but Miss Wardwell tries to push her into the wrong choices, like the exorcism of Susie's uncle. After that, the cannibalistic Feast of Feasts occurs, where there is a lottery for Queen of the Feast, who is sacrificed and eaten at the feast. Sabrina spends the week trying to convince Prudence (Tati Gabrielle) to reject her selection, in which she ultimately succeeds. Finally, the three witch sisters are opposed by Harvey, since his family were witch hunters. In this beat, we see that the problems of the main character are greater than before, but they remain centered on the main conflict and based on the theme of the narrative. Sabrina is determined to balance the mortal and the witch worlds, no matter how difficult things get.

All Is Lost (284 min.): The eleventh beat of the narrative raises the stakes even higher, since it seems that the character has lost every chance of accomplishing her goal. In this season, this beat occurs when Prudence's two sisters make voodoo against Harvey and his brother while they are inside the mine, in order to take revenge on their family. At this point, everything seems lost because the two worlds of Sabrina collide and every hope for balancing her two identities is gone.

Dark Night of the Soul (384 min.–427 min.): At this point, Harvey's brother Tommy (Justin Dobies) dies. Sabrina knows that is the witches' fault since they made voodoo against him. This is why she considers using dark magic to resurrect him. Sabrina goes into Wardwell's office and takes the book with this precise spell. Miss Wardwell watches her and tries to push her into her ultimate destruction, something that will start with this spell. As the second act comes to an end, the main protagonist seems more lost than ever. After trying to balance the mortal and the witch worlds around her, Sabrina understands that this is not possible and considers using her powers to interact with the humans around her.

The Netflix Vision of Horror

Break Into Three (427 min.): At the middle of the eighth episode, the second plot point occurs when Sabrina, the three witch sisters, and Nicholas (Gavin Leatherwood) are in the middle of the forest and perform the resurrection spell. Based on this spell, Sabrina has to sacrifice one of the sisters in order to be complete. This is why Sabrina kills one of the witch sisters. With this action, the narrative enders into the third and final act. As this is a plot point, it changes the course of the narrative and reinforces the main conflict. Therefore, this beat repeats the central dramatic question that has been established in the inciting incident, meaning the ultimate fate of the main character regarding her dual identity.

Finale (427 min.–560 min.): This beat is the biggest part of the third act, in which we get all the answers we were searching for from the beginning. Tommy is resurrected but is not his true self. At the same time, Sabrina, with the help of her cousin, resurrects the witch sister who was sacrificed for the spell. The friends of Sabrina learn about her secret and her witch identity, while the attack of the thirteen witches begin. In order to save her friends and the mortal world around her, Sabrina decides to proceed with her dark baptism and signs the book of the dark lord. Then everything gets back to normal, but Sabrina has lost her mortal friends and more importantly her boyfriend, who was forced to kill his brother. The climax of the narrative is incorporated in this beat, based on which the dramatic question gets answered: Sabrina has to choose the witch world in order for the mortal world to be balanced.

Final Image (560 min.): The last beat of the season is the final image of the narrative. The mortal friends and the boyfriend of Sabrina are talking about her. They all agree that Sabrina's character and behavior have substantially changed. We see Sabrina at the witch academy with the three sisters. From her appearance to her attitude, Sabrina seems altered. The last image is the epitome of the change that has occurred due to the progression of the narrative. In the first beat, the opening image of the narrative is Sabrina, an ordinary girl who is just hanging around with her friends. In contrast, the final image is the exact opposite that comes as a result of the main conflict and the way it was resolved. Sabrina is now embracing her witch identity and is not the mortal girl of the opening image anymore.

These fifteen beats prove that the season follows the three-act model. More specifically, the series has a first act of 21 percent, a second act of 55 percent, and a third act of 24 percent. At the same time, the narrative reinforces the statement that episodes are no longer the

2. The Narrative Structure of the Complex Discovery Plot

important element of the structuring in a SVOD series. Even the plot points are not placed at the ends of episodes, where usually have cliffhangers, but at the middle of their individual narratives.

Moreover, this three-act structure has all of the four functions from Noel Carroll's approach. The onset is at the beginning of the narrative in the Setup beat, when Miss Wardwell is murdered and the dark force takes her form. With this action, the audience learns that someone is after Sabrina, while the main characters do not yet know the danger that is approaching. The discovery function is at the Break Into Two beat, when Sabrina realizes that the dark lord is after her. Of course, even if the main character knows the danger, the rest of the characters do not believe her. The confirmation comes at the B-Story beat with the legal actions and her victory in the court. Then, all the members of the family come to believe her about the danger that is after her. Subsequently, every action by Sabrina, and by the rest of the main characters, that is meant to oppose the evil forces that are after them, is part of the confrontation function, which mainly takes place at the Finale beat.

According to the analysis, we can clearly see that *Chilling Adventures of Sabrina* is a fine example of a complex discovery plot that follows the three-act structure and works as a united narrative, not as a fragmented audiovisual text. Even if it is a series, its narrative structuring methods are forcing the audience into more continuous consumption. According to Snyder's approach, each of the fifteen beats are placed in the exact point they should be and each has the same functionality it would have in a unified filmic text.

Diablero—A Structural Analysis

Diablero is a Mexican series, one of the four foreign audiovisual texts of the corpus of this study. The series, which premiered on Netflix on December 21, 2018, is based on Mexican writer Francisco Haghenbeck's book *El Diablo me obligó*.[9] After Netflix greenlighted this Spanish-language horror series, it raised the company's number of original productions in Latin America to 50, a fact that proves its interest in becoming a global network.[10]

The story is centered around Father Ramiro Ventura (Christopher Von Uckermann), a priest who asks for the help of the legendary demon hunter Elvis Infante (Horacio Garcia Rojas) in order to find and save his little daughter. This narrative is a pure example of the Horror of Demonic category. Kristen Lopez observes that even if it is a Spanish-speaking, Mexican production, it draws heavily from its U.S. counterparts,[11] and Mikayla Daniels compares it with *Supernatural* (CW, 2005–present).[12] Of course, the place the events occur has an important role in the narrative. On this matter, Joel Keller states, "While a show like Diablero can work just about anywhere, having it take place in Mexico City, a mainly Catholic city that is one of the most populous cities in the world, takes the narrative to another level."[13]

The first season consists of eight episodes and has a total duration of 302 minutes. The episodes are approximately 40 minutes with a range from 35 to 44 minutes (including end credits). The series faithfully follows the three-act structure, with its constructing choices underlining the unified model of narration. The plot has all of the four functions, which makes it part of the complex discovery category. Furthermore, the narrative progresses according to the fifteen beats of Snyder's approach, which will help us better understand the functioning norms of this series. The fifteen beats are the following:

Opening Image (1 min.): The opening image of the narrative sets the tone for the entire season while introducing the audience to the paranormal world of *Diablero*. The first scene is centered around a mother who lulls her daughter Mariana (Cassandra Iturralde) to sleep. Even though the girl thinks that she saw something, the mother reassures her that there is nothing there. Then the mother is attacked by a figure, while the girl uses the time to hide. The figure that attacked the mother is revealed to be a demon. The demon injures the mother and takes the girl. Based on this action, we see a family separated by a demonic force, as the audience sees for the first time the girl, whose disappearance will be the subject of this season.

Theme Stated (12 min.): Father Ramiro goes to see the badly injured woman, who reveals to him that the girl is his daughter. Afterwards, the priest goes to the policemen in the hospital and tells them about the attack of the woman and the missing child, but they do not pay attention to him. Then, a nurse, Keta (Fátima Molina), approaches Father Ramiro and talks to him about Elvis, her brother who is a demon hunter. She explicitly says that this thing that took the girl away is not a human being. This phrase sums up the theme of the entire series. The center of the whole narrative is the clash of the human and the demonic worlds, and this scene is the first time it is clearly stated. Even if he is a priest, the protagonist of the narrative does not believe in demonic forces that can kidnap a child, so this scene encompasses the essence of the series' theme.

2. The Narrative Structure of the Complex Discovery Plot

Setup (1 min.–32 min.): The majority of the first episode of the series is dedicated to the introduction of the main characters and the creation of the fictional world, of the main situation and the events that will lead to the upcoming main conflict. In *Diablero*, the audience sees Elvis and how it is to be a demon hunter; learns about the eventual death of the attacked woman; and follows the priest, who is trying to save and meet Mariana, a daughter he was not aware existed. Moreover, Father Romero meets with Elvis, and even if he is a bit hesitant at the beginning, he ultimately sees demonic and paranormal activities and believes Elvis, something that leads him to open up to him about the deceased woman and the missing girl. After the first thirty-two minutes of the narrative, everything has been set up in order for the main conflict.

Catalyst (38 min.): The inciting incident of the overarching story takes place at the end of the first episode, right after the character of Nancy (Giselle Kuri), a modern-day, demonic super-hero, has been introduced. The characters take Nancy to Elvis's house and help her recover. Nancy has abilities that can help Elvis find the demons he wants, since she can be willingly possessed by demonic forces. Along with Keta, they eat together, and then Nancy agrees to help them find Mariana by going to the place the girl was attacked in order to find some paranormal evidence. This point of the narrative signals the completion of the main conflict and the commitment of the four main characters to fighting the evil forces. Also, it establishes the events that lead to the main dramatic question: will the main characters save Mariana from the demon?

Debate (28 min.–75 min.): The second episode is dedicated to the fifth beat, whose main purpose is to conclude the first act. This is the moment of the narrative before things will get more serious and the characters will go deep into the main conflict. In this beat, we see the girl in an underground location trying to hide from the demon, while at the same time the four main characters try to find the identity of the demon that kidnapped the girl. They all go to find Isaac "El Indio" (Humberto Busto) in a demon-fighting arena. Nancy senses that the demon they are looking for started from this arena, so they engage in demon fighting in order to find a lead in their case, but in vain. The fighting is interrupted by demons that were unintentionally released by Father Ramiro.

Break Into Two (75 min.): The first plot point, based on which the narrative enters its second act, is placed at the end of the second episode. Keta goes to see the dead body of the woman from the first scene,

The Netflix Vision of Horror

while she invites the other three characters to join her. The four characters look at the corpse, and Elvis recognizes a symbol on the body—the same symbol worn by Mayaken, a toddler who was lost years ago. This symbol is on other corpses too. Elvis wants to give up, but Nancy persuades him to continue. At the same time, Mariana is in a forest and tries to escape from the demon. The demon finds and chases her. After a few moments, Mamá Chabela (Dolores Heredia) finds and saves her. At this point, the narrative changes direction and the main dramatic question comes again to the fore, since the audience wonders if Mariana will be saved.

B Story (77 min.): While the narrative enters its the second act, a secondary storyline makes its appearance. In *Diablero*, the secondary story that helps the building of this act is the story around Mayaken, which starts right after the first plot point. Eight years before the main events of the narrative, we see how Mayaken, the child of Keta and Isaac, disappeared. The child had a strange birth sign, like the ones on the dead bodies. This story will be part of the narrative until the end of the season, leaving unanswered questions that will probably be part of the next season.

Fun and Games (77 min.–148 min.): The next two episodes are dedicated to the whole path of the narrative towards its midpoint, in which the stakes will get higher. At this point, things do not look so serious, and the audience believes that Mariana is going to be saved since she is in good hands. Chabela took Mariana to her house, where she has other kids that she has saved from this demon. At the same time, the four main characters try to find some clue that will lead them to Mariana. Father Ramiro goes to speak to Cardenal Morelo (Flavio Medina) and with the help of a potion gets the truth out of him. The church knew about Ramiro's child; the audience learns that there is a list of the illegitimate children of different priests. The main characters try to anticipate the next attack of the demon in order to find Mariana through him.

Midpoint (148 min.): In exactly the middle of the overarching story and of the second act, the narrative presents the events of the midpoint to the audience. After the main four characters save a mother and her son from the demon's attack, they bring them to Elvis's house in order to be safe. Ultimately, the demon possesses the mother and kidnaps the son. Afterwards, the demon gets the child to Chabela and she kills the mother with her own hands in order to keep the child. Mariana sees the whole interaction and decides to run away from Chabela's house. The audience thinks that even if the four main characters are not close to

2. The Narrative Structure of the Complex Discovery Plot

discovering Mariana, the girl has a positive figure protecting her. With the actions that occur at the midpoint at the end of the fourth episode, the stakes get higher, since the girl has two threats to face, while no one around her is protecting her anymore.

Bad Guys Close In (148 min.–199 min.): The rest of the second act seems more serious than ever, and the tenth beat of the narrative brings the evil and demonic forces closer to the main characters. More specifically, someone kidnaps Keta and tortures her in order to get some information from her, while the policemen that Mariana asked for help bring her back to Chabela's house. At the same time, Father Ramiro and Nancy seem to have feelings for one another, but then three unknown men take Ramiro with them to an undisclosed destination. Even though the four main characters were approaching Mariana, after the events of the midpoint leading to higher stakes, everything seems more difficult than before, while the main characters face different problems that keep them away from Mariana.

All Is Lost (199 min.): The next beat comes when the unknown men bring Father Ramiro to Cardenal Morelo, who offers him a new start. There, with the help of medical equipment, the church has kept alive the mother of Mariana from the first scene. Cardenal Morelo offers Ramiro the woman he loved in exchange for his daughter. Mariana is the key to something powerful that is approaching, and with the help of Ramiro, Morelo can proceed with the actions that will lead into a new era. After some thought, Father Ramiro does not take immediately the offer, and he leaves. The pressure on the protagonist is very strong and every hope starts to vanish.

Dark Night of the Soul (199 min.–230 min.): With many pressures on main characters, the twelfth beat concludes the second act and leads the narrative into its final part. Keta and Elvis go to a female demon hunter who is responsible for their mother's death. She manipulates and controls them, while everything seems lost. At the same time, Nancy has developed a connection with Wences (Quetzalli Cortés), the person who is possessed by the demon and follows the orders of Mamá Chabela. All of the main characters are in the worst positions yet, and things that seemed achievable now look impossible.

Break Into Three (230 min.): At the end of the sixth episode, there is the second plot point which changes the direction of the narrative and brings the main dramatic question back to viewers' minds. The four main characters are approaching Chabela's house because of Nancy's connection with Wences. At the same time, Chabela prepares the ritual of the sacrifice. The four characters arrive at the house, but they only find Wences, who is chained up, while Chabela has left with the four kids. This new information changes drastically the progression of the narrative, which enters the third and final act, in which the resolution of the conflict will be achieved. At this point, the dramatic question of if the main characters will manage to save Mariana is more relevant than ever.

Finale (230 min.–302 min.): Since it is the biggest beat of the third act, the finale takes place in the seventh and eighth episode of the series. At this point, the narrative progresses towards its climax, in which the main conflict of the narrative will be resolved and the dramatic question will be answered. The main characters are searching for Chabela in order to save Mariana and the other kids. They ultimately find her, but cannot stop the ritual. The kids are sacrificed, and they turn into demons that will call the mighty demonic force, which will bring the apocalypse. After the final confrontation of the main characters with the powerful demon, the protagonists win and Father Ramiro sacrifices himself in order for Mariana to be saved. The main conflict is resolved in favor of our characters, and Mariana is eventually saved by her own father.

Final Image (302 min.): After the victory of our main characters over the evil forces, the series closes with its final image. In the last scene of the season, all the characters are united and happy, like a big family, while there is no trace of any demon. Their happiness is so great that Elvis tries to check whether this is part of reality or an illusion. Of course, Father Ramiro is not there, since he was sacrificed in order for this happiness to be possible. This image is in total contradiction with the first image, in which a family is separated by evil forces. After the long journey of the narrative, the final image shows us the exact opposite, something that proves the big change that occurred. Finally, right before the end credits, there is another small scene in which the audience sees Mayaken in an undisclosed location, a connection that will lead us in the second season.

This thorough analysis is a hard proof that *Diablero* is in fact a concrete narrative that is structured under the norms of the three-act model. More specifically, the first act is 25 percent, the second act is 51 percent, while the third act is 24 percent of the total narration. From the numbers, it is clear that the narrative is working as if it were a unified filmic text and follows every norm of the classical model of narration. Every beat is placed at the right position of the story, while the function of each helps the progression of the narrative.

2. The Narrative Structure of the Complex Discovery Plot

Furthermore, the narrative has all of Carroll's four functions, making it part of the complex discovery plot category. The onset function is at the Setup beat, when the audience sees the demon but Father Ramiro and the other characters (apart from Elvis and Keta) are not aware of this metaphysical threat. The discovery function is from the Catalyst beat and on, when Father Ramiro receives proof that demons exist and starts to believe that their antagonistic forces are not human. The confirmation function is at the Fun and Games beat, where the main characters find the next potential victims and inform them about the demon. The confrontation function comprises all the actions against the demon, Chabela, and the powerful demonic force at the end. In conclusion, *Diablero* is a good example of a series that follow the three-act structure, while its narrative incorporates the four functions into its plot.

Ghoul—*A Structural Analysis*

Ghoul is an Indian horror mini-series written and directed by Patrick Graham and jointly produced by Blumhouse Productions, Phantom Films and Ivanhoe Pictures. The mini-series was released on August 24, 2018, by Netflix, but they held a screening premiere on August 22, 2018, in Mumbai.[14] The narrative of *Ghoul* is based on an Arabic folklore monster, and it is one of the two Netflix Originals from India that belong to the corpus of this study. The story is set in a dystopian India where fascism governs the country, and the story is centered around the interrogation of a notorious terrorist in a secret government internment camp that ignites a series of horrifying and supernatural events in the aftermath. Even if *Ghoul* takes place in a not-so-distant dystopian future, the series is an allegory of today's society of India. Regarding the nature of *Ghoul*'s narrative, Rahul Desai points out:

> The real horror of a show like *Ghoul*, or *The Handmaid's Tale*, or a film like *V for Vendetta*, lies in the viewer's willingness to recognize that their dystopian worlds—built on a structure of fear-mongering, military lockdowns, ideological reconditioning and religious/sexual discrimination—aren't so dystopian anymore. *Ghoul*, for instance, is based in an India in which minorities are tortured and exterminated. The terms "waapsi" and "adarsh nagrik" are tossed around. Books are burnt and intellectuals imprisoned by faceless "protection squads." Liberals are declared anti-national, seditious elements. The government has installed academies that propagate Islamophobia and brainwash citizens into becoming patriotic soldiers for whom country must trump family. Terrorism lies within, say their slogans.[15]

The Netflix Vision of Horror

This series is the shortest of the corpus under analysis, since it has only three episodes and a total duration of 127 minutes. Originally, this narrative was meant to be the first of three films in a deal between the three production houses, since in 2014 Blumhouse Productions, Phantom Films, and Ivanhoe Pictures announced a partnership deal for creating local-language horror films in India.[16] Eventually, in February 2018, Netflix acquired the production after Graham felt that a longer format would be better, and had it turned into a mini-series.[17] Manav Kaul, the actor who plays Colonel Sunil Dacunha, called this transformation of the film into a series a "blessing in disguise" as it gave them the breathing room to add a bit more backstory.[18] Even the creator himself stated that this transformation from a film to a mini-series helped him narrate better the story.[19]

From the length of the narrative to the production details, we can clearly see the connection of this audiovisual work with filmic and not television practices. As Rohan Naahar comments, "Watched in one go—which shouldn't be difficult—the episodes feel arbitrarily separated and not entirely episodic."[20] *Ghoul* is not a conventional TV series, and as expected, its narrative is structured in this manner. The series faithfully follows Snyder's beats approach and its narrative can be divided into three acts. More specifically, the beats are the following:

Opening Image (1 min.): The series starts with a prisoner who is cutting his hand and then performs some sort of a ritual. We do not see who he is, but he seems to be in a jail cell. Afterwards, the fictional world is established, since the series takes place in a dystopian and totalitarian regime. In this scene, we see policemen hunting down possible terrorists. The opening image of *Ghoul* is setting the tone in order for the audience to be able to appropriately interpret the invents that will follow. The series in not based on the present society, while it has metaphysical elements at its core. Both of these characteristics are present in the opening sequence.

Theme Stated (11 min.): As in the previous examples, the core of the series' theme is stated in a dialogue between the main characters minutes after the beginning of the narrative. Nida Rahim (Radhika Apte), the protagonist of the series, is in the car with her father (S. M. Zaheer) and going to an unknown location. The father drives while describes to Nida how the policemen took their books and burned them all. Inside the car, he has literature about the resistance. Nida seems hesitant and says that the regime does not capture innocent people. This dialogue reveals the true essence of the theme of the overarching

2. The Narrative Structure of the Complex Discovery Plot

story: on one hand we have characters that blindly follow the totalitarian regime, while on the other hand there are people who are willingly to resist by any means (even with metaphysical and paranormal actions). Based on this theme, the narrative is built around a deep political meaning.

Setup (1 min.–14 min.): The first minutes of the narrative are dedicated to the introduction to this dystopian parallel present in an India that is being ruled by a totalitarian regime. The first scene is the starting point of the metaphysical essence of the story, while the rest of the opening sequence is dedicated to establishing the main character, the key premise of her relationship with her father, and the rebellious nature of the father. At this beat, the narrative gives to the audience all the necessary information for the main conflict to be established, and therefore the main dramatic question to be shaped. Finally, in this beat of the narrative Nida is recognized as the primary protagonist, meaning that the story will be told from her point of view. This is important, since both the main conflict and the dramatic question will be formed around her actions.

Catalyst (17 min.): Then, after the audience has been introduced to the fictional world of the narrative, the inciting incident occurs. The Catalyst, the fourth beat of the overarching narrative, happens at the seventeenth minute, when Nida calls the authorities to give information about her father. After that, policemen go to father's house and arrest him. The main conflict arises, since Nida betrays her father and chooses the regime over him. She is so convinced that the intentions of the government are pure that she decides to give information about her father which will eventually even cost his life. But Nida does not believe that the regime will kill an innocent person, something that is fundamentally wrong. The central dramatic question that is being created at this beat of the narrative is about the relationship between Nida and the regime, which she blindly follows.

Debate (17 min.–32 min.): The rest of the first act is dedicated to the events that will lead Nida to the secret government internment camp where the metaphysical events of the narrative will take place. Nida's father is in the interrogation room, and the policeman says to him that he has no rights. Afterwards, Nida goes inside the room and tries to convince him to hear them out and tell the truth, but in vain. The policemen blindfold the father and take him away. Then, in the present, Nida goes to the internment camp to help with an interrogation. There, they have twelve prisoners whom they treat badly, but Nida helps one of them by giving him a blanket. Even if Nida follows the regime and puts it above her father, she seems hesitant and not entirely convinced about the current situation. This fact is the essence of this beat, since the main character is not certain about the journey she is called to take.

Break Into Two (32 min.): With the sixth beat of the narrative, we enter into the second act. The first plot point of *Ghoul* occurs at the thirty-second minute, when Nida meets for the first time with Colonel Sunil. Nida asks him about her sudden transfer to this camp, and the colonel says that they needed her for the upcoming interrogation of a famous terrorist, Ali Saeed (Mahesh Balraj). Then, Nida leaves and Laxmi (Ratnabali Bhattacharjee), an interrogation officer at the camp, says to Colonel Sunil that they should not trust her, because Nida belongs inside the prison cells. This scene changes the course of the narrative, as the audience learns that Nida's presence in this camp is not a coincidence and that the personnel of the camp distrust her because of her past. Nida is in danger and does not know it yet.

B Story (41 min.): At the beginning of the second act, a secondary storyline is introduced in accordance with the main plot. In *Ghoul*, the B story of the narrative is the interrogation of Ali Saeed, a notorious terrorist, according to the regime. As will be revealed later on, he is not who he seems to be. Inside the interrogation room, there is a supernatural entity with Ali Saeed's appearance that turns the tables on his interrogators, exposing their most shameful secrets. At the forty-first minute of the narrative, a chained Ali Saeed arrives at the secret government internment camp.

Fun and Games (41 min.–60 min.): The stakes are not high yet, and everything seems easy for the main protagonist. The soldiers take Ali Saeed inside the camp and lock him inside a prison cell, while the other prisoners shout in favor of him. Colonel Sunil says that they have only twenty-four hours to break him and made him talk. At night, everyone in the camp has nightmares, including Nida, who sees her father. The next day, the interrogation of Ali Saeed starts, and Nida watches the procedure from outside. Until this moment, in the eyes of the protagonist nothing seems difficult and the situation is under control. Also, until this beat of the narrative, every part of the story seems realistic and nothing betrays the metaphysical turn the narrative will have.

Midpoint (60 min.): At exactly the first hour of the narrative, the midpoint takes place. Ali Saeed whispers something to the soldiers who are interrogating him, and suddenly they start to fight. Nida watches from a CCTV monitor and hallucinates that Ali Saeed asks her about

2. The Narrative Structure of the Complex Discovery Plot

her father, while the cameras stop working. Before the other soldiers go to the interrogation room, one interrogator kills the other in the fight. Colonel Sunil approaches him before his last breath and he says to him that they are all guilty. This plot point raises the stakes and makes the situation more difficult and challenging than before. At this beat, which is at the middle of the second act and therefore the whole season, the metaphysical element enters the narrative and Nida is called to face a challenge she could not imagine, since Ali Saeed seems to know a lot about her father and her past.

Bad Guys Close In (60 min.–85 min.): After the midpoint, the antagonistic forces seem to come closer to the main characters and win. After the death of one of the soldiers, Colonel Sunil sits inside the interrogation room and decides to speak to Ali Saeed himself. Ali Saeed says something about the colonel's family, something that angers him. Colonel Sunil starts to electrocute Ali Saeed, but the power goes off. Nida enters the room and sees Ali Saeed as a demon who speaks to her as her father. When the lights turn on, the demon-like Saeed has disappeared from the room and her human body is on the ground. Colonel Sunil says that after that, Ali Saeed should be dead, but he sits there, smiling. Nida and the rest of the characters are trying to overcome the obstacles, but the main antagonist seems to have the upper hand at this point.

All Is Lost (85 min.): New information significantly alters the circumstances and the progress of the series. The eleventh beat of the narrative is at the eighty-fifth minute, when Nida goes inside the cell of a prisoner and asks him about that entity inside the interrogation room that looks like Ali Saeed. He says that this being is a ghoul—something like a genie, a monster, or a demon. When someone calls it, he sells his soul to it in exchange. The ghoul takes the form of the last person it has bitten, while it uses the sins of the people in order to exterminate them.

Dark Night of the Soul (85 min.–96 min.): In the last beat of the second act, Nida comes into contact for the first time with the ghoul. Now, Nida's main concern is to find out who called the ghoul. Colonel Sunil is informed that the dead body of Ali Saeed has been found, so this entity that is inside the camp is not him. At the same time, the ghoul attacks Faulad (Surender Thakur) and takes his form. At this point, everything seems pointless for the main characters and there in no hope on the horizon.

Break Into Three (96 min.): At the ninety-sixth minute of the narrative, the second plot point occurs. Laxmi leads an apostate group of soldiers who believe that Nida is responsible for Faulad's death, while

The Netflix Vision of Horror

they arrest her and Colonel Sunil for trying to protect her. They believe that Nida is a terrorist who has come to avenge her father's death. The situation for Nida has drastically changed, and her relationship with and faithfulness to the regime are at stake. For this reason, the dramatic question arises again and comes to the attention of the audience.

Finale (96 min.–127 min.): Afterwards, the narrative progresses towards the climax, in which the audience will get all the answers needed. The fortieth beat is the longest of the third act and incorporates the climax. At this beat, Nida is in the prison cell and realizes that they kill the prisoners—and so her father probably has been killed too. Nida is with the prisoners, while the soldiers find an unidentified body. They soon realize that one of the prisoners is the ghoul, and everyone tries to escape in a panic. It is revealed that the ghoul has assumed Maulvi's identity and attacks everyone. The ghoul bites Nida and takes her form. As the ghoul takes Nida's appearance, an injured Nida finds the remaining soldiers. Laxmi tries to torture Nida but gets shot and killed by the colonel. Nida soon realizes that these camps are actually places where people opposed to the regime are tortured and killed, once information is extracted from them. Her father was a victim, and before being executed, he summoned the ghoul to make his daughter realize the truth about the regime and see the atrocities it committed in the name of patriotism. After the ghoul is killed, Nida is taken into custody for killing her commanding officer. She reveals the truth about the camp, but nobody pays attention to her, since they all already know the truth. At this beat, all the answers are given and the narrative concludes. The main dramatic question about the relationship between Nida and the regime has been answered, and the main protagonist finally sees the truth.

Final Image (127 min.): The last beat is the final image of the narrative. In *Ghoul*, we see Nida in her prison cell taking a hidden razor from her mouth. She starts the ritual of calling the ghoul. As expected, the Final Image is contradictory to the Opening Image, since according to Snyder's approach, the first and the last beat are reserved to show the big change that has occurred in the narrative and the main characters. In the first scene, we saw Nida's father calling the ghoul because he was a victim of the regime, while Nida was the one that betrayed him. At the end, the last scene is Nida herself in exactly the same position, meaning that she now knows the truth about the totalitarian government she once blindly followed.

From analyzing the above fifteen beats, we can clearly see that

2. The Narrative Structure of the Complex Discovery Plot

Ghoul is a narrative that is structured according to the three-act model. More specifically, it has a first act of 25 percent, a second act of 50 percent, and a third act of 25 percent, a fact that means that this narrative follows the three-act structure by the book.

Moreover, the plot of the series incorporates all of the four functions, making it part of the complex discovery plot category. The onset function is at the first beat, the Opening Image, in which Nida's father starts the ritual to summon the ghoul. The discovery function is at the Fun and Games beat, when Nida starts suspecting that Ali Saeed is not who they really think he is, since some metaphysical actions are occurring (like the vision of her father, the nightmares, and Saeed's calling her like her father used to do). The confirmation function is at the All Is Lost beat, when Nida learns about the ghoul and then sees it with her own eyes. Afterwards, Nida shares this information with the rest of the characters, and the confrontation function starts, which includes all the attempts of the main characters to defeat the ghoul until the end of the narrative. Confrontation mostly takes place in the third act and more specifically in the Finale beat.

Ghoul has an unusually strong connection with the norms of a filmic narrative, since it was meant to be a feature film and not a mini-series. This is one of the many reasons the narrative of this text faithfully follows all of the conventions of the three-act model, and as with the rest of the case studies in this chapter, it constitutes a fine example of a complex discovery plot.

Hemlock Grove—*A Structural Analysis*

Hemlock Grove is an American horror series produced by Eli Roth, developed by Brian McGreevy and Lee Shipman, and based on McGreevy's 2012 novel of the same name. In December 2011, *Deadline Hollywood* reported that Netflix and Gaumont International Television were finalizing a deal for a 13-episode order for *Hemlock Grove*,[21] making it one of the first three Netflix Originals, since it premiered on April 19, 2013, with all the episodes of the season made immediately available for online viewing.

Even though Netflix usually keeps the ratings of its shows private for internal uses, sometimes it shares them for publicity reasons. One of these instances was after the opening weekend of *Hemlock Grove*, when Netflix announced that it was viewed by more members globally in its

The Netflix Vision of Horror

first weekend than *House of Cards*.[22] The series was a hit, in fact one of the first Primetime Emmy Award nominations for original online-only web series at the 65th Primetime Emmy Awards in 2013, along with *Arrested Development* (Fox, Netflix, 2003–present) and *House of Cards* (Netflix, 2013–2018), which also earned nominations.[23] The series went on for three consecutive seasons and end in 2015 when Netflix decided to conclude the narrative.[24]

The story is set in the small Pennsylvania town of Hemlock Grove, which is built around a mixture of extreme wealth and poverty. Peter Rumancek (Landon Liboiron), a 17–year-old Romani boy, is suspected of some brutal murders of local teenage girls based on the rumor that he is a werewolf. He is in fact a werewolf, but not the murderer. Along with the heir to the Godfrey estate, Roman Godfrey (Bill Skarsgård), he sets out to solve the mystery. *Hemlock Grove* has a mixture of fantastic and horror elements that create a hybrid narrative. Nevertheless, the series is a fine example of series horror. As Jack Wilhelmi observes, the executive producer, Eli Roth, became a big name with horror fans early on in his career with *Hostel* (Roth, 2005) and *Cabin Fever* (Roth, 2002), so Netflix took a chance on the genre with an experienced creator.[25] Even Alison Willmore recognizes the importance of having Roth's name attached to the series in order to attract genre fans.[26]

The first season of *Hemlock Grove* has thirteen episodes and a total duration of 656 minutes, which makes it the longest narrative of the corpus in both number of episodes and overall length. The narrative follows Snyder's approach and structures its story based on the fifteen beats. The fifteen beats of *Hemlock Grove* are the following:

Opening Image (1 min.): The series starts with one of the main characters, Roman. The audience sees Roman having sex with a girl in his car, then paying her in order to leave. While having sex, Roman plays with his blood on her body, something that turns him on. Of course, as we later see, Roman is an Upir, a kind of a vampire, so this scene establishes his real nature. Then Roman waves a girl at the school who, later on, is murdered by an unidentified creature. The first sequence of the narrative introduces to the audience two important elements of the story: one of the main characters who struggles with his mortal and supernatural nature, and the main storyline of murders that will develop through the entire season. This season will be based on both of these elements, and the opening image sets the tone for the rest of the narrative.

Theme Stated (37 min.): Later on, the narrative has a sequence that clearly states the theme and sets the tone for the whole season. A girl is

2. The Narrative Structure of the Complex Discovery Plot

jogging in the woods and finds the dead body of the girl from the first sequence. The police go to the scene, where they see Peter and start asking him questions. This raises some concerns about Peter and his possible connection with the murder, a rumor that hunts him at the school. Everybody thinks that he is a werewolf and responsible for the murder of this girl. This metaphysical identity of the main character and the suspicion of the community about his actions are in the core of the narrative and constitute the main theme of the story.

Setup (1 min.–86 min.): The first two episodes are dedicated to the presentation of the fictional world of *Hemlock Grove*: they introduce the main two characters, Peter and Roman, establish the town and the people that live there, and take the first steps towards the main conflict of the narrative. Both the main characters have a metaphysical nature, since we are talking about mythical creatures like werewolves and vampires. Moreover, the problem that arises in this small town and will eventually lead to the main conflict of the narrative is that another mythical creature is there, killing innocent girls. The Setup beat is meant to establish both the realistic and metaphysical aspects of the fictional world, while setting the tone of the entire narrative.

Catalyst (94 min.): At the end of the second episode, there is the inciting incident of the entire narrative. Peter invites Roman to his house, but his mother, Lynda (Lili Taylor), is against that since she is does not trust Roman's family. Peter convinces her by saying that Roman is the only one that believes that he is innocent. Roman arrives at their house and talks with Linda while Peter is getting ready. Afterwards, Peter transforms into a werewolf in front of Roman, who now seems speechless. This is the first time that Roman and the audience see Peter transform and get the validation that he is indeed a werewolf. This sequence establishes the main conflict, since we have two mythical entities that conflict with each other but are called to solve murder cases. The main dramatic question that is created in this narrative is about the relationship of these two characters and whether they will manage to get along.

Debate (94 min.–145 min.): The third episode is reserved for the fifth beat of the narrative. Clementine Chasseur (Kandyse McClure) arrives at Hemlock Grove and takes over the case of the girl's murder. At the same time, Peter says that the killing occurred by a vargulf, a sick person that transforms into a wolf, but refuses to cooperate with Roman to find the real killer of the girl. This beat of the narrative shows how the main character doubts the journey he is called to take and how the audience is uncertain about the characters' upcoming decisions. These are the steps towards the first plot point, where the main character will commit to the (internal and external) journey of the narrative.

Break Into Two (145 min.): At this beat, the narrative enters the second act. The first plot point takes place at the end of the third episode. Peter goes to Roman's house and wants to talk to him. He says that his uncle, who was a werewolf too, was a killer, and he is afraid that Chasseur will find out and lock him in a cage. Afterwards, Peter agrees to team up with Roman in order to find the vargulf and kill it. This is the point of no return for the main characters. They undertake the obligation to find the entity responsible for these killings and destroy it. Even if they are two different mythical creatures with dissimilar desires, Peter and Roman decide to ally in order to protect their beloved ones. As a main function of the first plot point, this action consolidates and restores the central dramatic question about the relationship of these two characters.

B Story (155 min.): In the second act, a key secondary storyline that is harmonized with the overarching story makes its appearance. In *Hemlock Grove*, the B Story is around Francis Pullman (Ted Dykstra), the man who witnessed the murders of the vargulf and knows of the existence of mythological creatures in this town. Norman Godfrey (Dougray Scott) and Chasseur are questioning Francis, who asserts that he saw the creature that killed the girls, describing it as an impossibly huge "demon dog" with black fur and yellow eyes. He tells them that he saw the monster "goes for her lady parts first." Chasseur and Norman admit that Francis's knowing that key detail about the case, when it has not been revealed to the public, makes his story a lot more credible than it sounds. Francis is a man who went insane after witnessing murders because he could not handle it, so at the end he kills himself by pushing a syringe deep into his skull. This is the leading B Story of the second act that constantly interacts with the main storyline.

Fun and Games (155 min.–319 min.): After the first plot point, the next three and a half episodes are dedicated to the Fun and Games beat. At this part of the narrative, the audience sees the efforts of the two main characters to solve the murders and kill the vargulf. Their first action is to dig up the girl's grave and take a sample of her intestines. Later on, Peter and Roman bring a jar of intestines to Destiny Rumancek (Kaniehtiio Horn), Peter's older cousin. She takes a worm, puts it into the jar and leaves it overnight. The next day, Destiny takes the worm out of the jar and summons the soul of the deceased girl. Peter asks her questions about the vargulf. These new leads make the two characters

2. The Narrative Structure of the Complex Discovery Plot

continue their search in the long abandoned and decrepit ruins of the Godfrey Steel Mill. At this beat, even if the main characters are committed to the journey that the narrative has brought them to, the obstacles and problems are not mighty enough.

Midpoint (319 min.): Later, around the middle of the narrative, the midpoint occurs. Peter and Roman's fight splits them, something that raises the stakes. While Peter is at his school locker, he notices a folded-up note containing a painting of a beheaded wolf. Peter takes this strange warning very seriously, and afterwards he meets with Roman to end their friendship because he is not going to be investigating with him anymore. Roman nearly begs Peter to change his mind, but in vain. When Roman realizes that Peter is not going to change his mind, he turns vicious, telling Peter that if he sleeps with Letha (Penelope Mitchell), he will kill him. This creates a tension between them and ends their partnership. The actions of the midpoint speed up the appearance of new problems that will eventually lead to the second plot point and the third act. But more importantly, they will make the rest of the second act more difficult for the main characters.

Bad Guys Close In (319 min.–449 min.): The rest of the seventh episode and the eighth and ninth episodes are dedicated to the tenth beat of the narrative. In this beat, we see how the characters continue on their separate paths, while external and internal pressure make the situation more difficult for both of them than before. The audience feels that the antagonistic forces are severely approaching the protagonists, who are not a team anymore. While Peter becomes a couple with Letha, Roman has a hard time that eventually leads him into a coma, caused by Dr. Pryce (Joel de la Fuente). Peter tries to find a solution by himself, and meanwhile Roman is in a coma and fights with his inner demons. Both characters seem to be losing against their own antagonistic forces.

All Is Lost (449 min.): Later, at the end of the ninth episode, another action makes the situation even worse and everything seems to be lost. Peter wants to keep Letha protected and makes her promise that she will stay in a safe location while he goes after the vargulf and tries to kill it. Letha does not agree, because she worries about Peter. They fight, and Letha says that this is not a game. Peter will not change his mind and is determined to find and kill the vargulf. This fight ends with Letha's leaving. After the midpoint, everything gets worse for the main two characters, but the only positive note in Peter's life was Letha. At the All Is Lost beat, even this small hope is gone, and the two main characters seem to be headed towards the worst point of the entire narrative.

The Netflix Vision of Horror

Dark Night of the Soul (449 min.–493 min.): The next beat of the narrative is the last of the second act, and the main characters are in their most difficult position. All the actions of the tenth episode towards the second plot point find Peter and Roman in weak situations, since Roman has just come out of the coma and Peter—according to Chasseur—is the main suspect in the murders. Both characters decide to leave their differences into the past and team up once again for the greater good. Peter and Roman go to the abandoned ruins of the Godfrey Steel Mill and Peter transforms into a wolf, since there is a foul moon. Chasseur is there too, a fact that complicates the situation.

Break Into Three (493 min.): Near the end of the tenth episode, the narrative enters its third and final act. During their meeting at the abandoned ruins of the Godfrey Steel Mill, Chasseur captures Peter, while he is in a form of a wolf, and Roman cannot do anything. At the same time, the sheriff's twin daughters end up getting attacked by the vargulf in their own home while the sheriff is outside investigating some weird noises. By the time he gets back, they're both dead. Back at the steel mill, Chasseur makes Roman leave by putting a knife to Peter's werewolf neck and threatening to kill him. During the second plot point, the two characters are in danger and once again split up, something that raises for one last time the narrative's central dramatic question about the relationship of Peter and Roman.

Finale (493 min.–656 min.): The fourteenth beat happens in the third act. In this part of the narrative, the audience sees the whole path of events that will lead to the solution of the main conflict and the upcoming separation of Peter and Roman. With the help of Olivia (Famke Janssen), Roman's mother, Chasseur is out of the way and Peter is free. Roman and Peter find out the real identity of the vargulf, which was Christina Wendell (Freya Tingley), a shy, inquisitive student at Hemlock Grove High School. The two characters team up and with the help of Shelley Godfrey (Madeleine Martin), Roman's sister, confront and defeat the vargulf. Afterwards, Letha dies during childbirth, and then Olivia reveals to Roman that the angel Letha thought she had been impregnated by was him all along. Roman embraces his Upir nature and attacks his mother, who said to him that he had to kill the baby. Finally, Peter with his mother are leaving Hemlock Grove. At this beat, the main conflict has been resolved and the audience sees how all of the main characters end up. Consequently, the central dramatic question is answered at the climax, since the two characters are driven apart, each of them fully embracing their true nature.

2. The Narrative Structure of the Complex Discovery Plot

Final Image (656 min.): In the final sequence of the entire narrative, the audience sees Peter with his mother driving away from Hemlock Grove, while Roman has fully embraced the metaphysical aspects of his true identity. In the first image, the narrative introduced Roman, who was in denial of his true nature, but in the last image we see the big differentiation that has occurred during the progression of the narrative. At the end of the last episode, the audience gets a glimpse of what is inside the ominous black box in the Institute's basement. We see a humanoid body that has just opened its eyes. In the ending credits, the camera zooms in slowly on Christina's tombstone and we hear screaming from underground, indicating she is still alive. So, in this beat, apart from the indication of the big change that has occurred during the whole narrative, the audience gets some first clues about the second season of the series.

Having analyzed all fifteen beats of the narrative of *Hemlock Grove*, we can see that this series is following the three-act structure. The first act is 22 percent, the second act is 53 percent, and the remaining 25 percent is reserved for the third and final act. As observed, the first act is slightly smaller than the third in order for the second act to have more space to develop all the necessary actions, but the narrative falls into the general outline of the three-act model.

Regarding the four functions of the series' plot, *Hemlock Grove* incorporates all of them, since the series follow the complex discovery plot. The onset takes place at the Opening Image, since the establishing of the Other and the first killings start in the first sequence of the narrative. The discovery function occurs at the Catalyst beat, when Roman learns that Peter is a werewolf, but not the one that is killing the innocent residents of the town. The confirmation function takes place mostly at the Fun and Games beat, when other characters, like Letha, are convinced of the existence of the vargulf. Finally, all the actions against the vargulf until the ultimate victory of our main characters are part of the confrontation function, which mostly takes place at the Finale beat.

Hemlock Grove is the first horror series under the label Netflix Originals, since it was one of the early series that constituted the inaugural content from the online streaming platform. This narrative is a concrete example of how a series can be structured like a long-form filmic text following the three-act model and based on the complex discovery plot category norms. Its legacy led to the creation of most of the series that are part of the corpus of this study.

The Netflix Vision of Horror

Marianne—*A Structural Analysis*

Marianne is a French horror series created and directed by Samuel Bodin and written by Bodin and Quoc Dang Tran. This series in the only European audiovisual work in this study. The series was released on September 13, 2019, but Netflix canceled it after only one season in January 2020.[27] The story of the series revolves around Emma Larsimon (Victoire Du Bois), a famous French author who is haunted by Marianne, the witch character that she created and that causes her sleepless nights. Having tired of the abnormal world she has created, Emma decides to retire from writing about Marianne, but a bizarre visit from a childhood friend forces her to go to her hometown, a place she had sworn she would never visit again.

This series is one of the corpus examples that are pure horror narratives with no hybrid features. A lot of critics praised the horror elements of the series, with Meagan Navarro stating that *Marianne* is a nightmare personified and declaring it the most terrifying Netflix Original horror yet.[28] Elena Nicolaou observes that the narrative of the series remains terrifying until its climactic, exorcism-filled end.[29] Even the king of horror himself, Stephen King, celebrated the horrors of *Marianne* and told his Twitter followers that its narrative had a "Stephen King vibe."[30]

Marianne has eight episodes with a total duration of 350 minutes. The series has a classical narration and follows faithfully the fifteen beats of Snyder's approach. The fifteen beats are the following:

Opening Image (1 min.): The narrative opens with a hole in the ground seen from the inside, a reference to Marianne's grave. Afterwards, Caroline (Aurore Broutin), calls for her mother, Madame Daugeron (Mireille Herbstmeyer), and finds her in the kitchen. There, Madame Daugeron puts a knife in her mouth and taking out a tooth, saying it's "for Emma." It is clear that something is wrong with Madame Daugeron, and later on it will be shown that she is possessed by the spirit of Marianne. We see Emma doing a reading of her latest book and telling everyone that this is the last book, since she is done writing about Marianne. The opening image of the narrative establishes the two main characters: the metaphysical entity of Marianne that has the power to possess other people, and the main protagonist of the series, Emma. These two have a peculiar connection between them, which will be the basis of the whole narrative.

Theme Stated (20 min.): Twenty minutes after the start of the series, there is a scene with Emma and Caroline that expresses the

2. The Narrative Structure of the Complex Discovery Plot

theme of the whole narrative. After Caroline has attended a book signing by Emma, she goes to find her at her office. There, moments before she commits suicide, Caroline says that Marianne wants Emma to keep writing about her and that she will not leave with empty hands. Afterwards, Caroline hangs herself in front of Emma. This dialogue states the theme and sets the tone of the narrative, since the foundation of the story is based on Marianne's need to force Emma keep writing about her and thus keep her alive.

Setup (1 min.–41 min.): The first episode of the series is dedicated to the Setup beat, in which the narrative establishes the main characters, the basic premise, and all the necessary elements to form the main conflict and the dramatic question. In these first minutes, we are introduced to Emma, a famous, self-created writer who is the creator of a famous book series about Lizzie Larck and Marianne. At the same time, the audience is familiarized with Marianne herself, a witch spirit in Emma's hometown. Caroline goes to Emma and sets in motion the first steps towards the main conflict of the narrative. After Caroline's suicide, Emma is forced to go back to Elden, her hometown, and face her past and her long-hidden fears. Emma does not go alone, though, as Camile (Lucie Boujenah), her assistant, goes with her.

Catalyst (51 min.): At the end of the first episode, the inciting incident of the narrative takes place. Camile and Emma arrive at Elden and they spent the night at Emma's parents' house. There, metaphysical events start to occur. Camile is sleepless; she goes to the bathroom, but someone is at the door and scares her. Emma's parents are naked and acting bizarre. They leave the house and Emma follows them. There, in the middle of the woods, a voice tells her to write. At this beat, the main conflict is established, since Marianne pushes Emma to write about her in every possible way. The dramatic question of the narrative is around the relationship between Emma and Marianne. More specifically, the question is what exactly is happening between them, why Marianne wants Emma to write about her, and how this situation is going to be resolved.

Debate (51 min.–97 min.): The second episode is dedicated to the Debate beat, since the actions indicate that Emma is not ready to commit to the journey that lies before her. At this beat, the city of Elden is established, while the audience is introduced to the characters from Emma's past. Her old friends from her school years are once again in her life. All of them meet at Caroline's funeral. Both Emma's parents have disappeared, but Emma is in denial regarding the existence of Marianne.

Even if all of the signs tell her to write again about Marianne in order to get back her parents in a safe condition, she does not obey them, and rejects this path. She does not believe that Marianne is anything more than a part of her imagination and does not want to engage in bizarre thoughts. Of course, all of these positions will change in the next beat and the transition of the narrative to the next act.

Break Into Two (97 min.): At the end of the second episode there is the first plot point, based on which the narrative enters the second act. Even if at the previous beat Emma was in denial, at this point of the narrative she accepts her fate and starts taking the journey that lies ahead of her. While drunk, Emma returns home and thinks about Marianne's commands. She starts writing a new piece about Marianne, and at the same time, the audience sees Madame Daugeron, the woman possessed by Marianne's spirit, getting stronger and more satisfied. The next morning, Emma's mother returns from the woods and walks completely naked in the streets. She has wounds on her body, but she safely returns to her house. This action changes the course of the narrative, since Emma is now engaging with Marianne's challenges, something that strengthens the main conflict and resurfaces the dramatic question of the narrative.

B Story (107 min.): While the second act begins to unfold, the narrative introduces a secondary storyline that is in accordance with the theme and the tone of the narrative. In *Marianne*, the B Story is about the relationship between Emma and her mother. This complicated relationship stems from the mother's complicated background and Emma's teenage years, developing until the present day and their multilayered interaction that followed Emma's return to her hometown. This storyline starts right after the appearance of Emma's mother that occurred at the first plot point and develops until the upcoming death of the mother and the events that will follow. Even if it is a secondary storyline, it interacts with the main story of the narrative, while it encompasses the main theme of the series, since the mother represents the past that Emma wanted to leave behind after her departure from Elden.

Fun and Games (107 min.–190 min.): The first part of the second act is exactly what the name of this beat states: the actions are perceived by the main characters, and more specifically by Emma, as fun and games. Although Emma starts to realize the existence of Marianne, she does not fully understand how dangerous she is. At this beat, which takes place in the third and the fourth episodes of the series, Emma tries to confront Marianne who is speaking through Madame Daugeron. This

2. The Narrative Structure of the Complex Discovery Plot

action shows that Emma does not seem to understand the full and true nature of this antagonistic force, since Marianne is the spirit of a witch and not a real person. The conflict of the narrative escalates quickly, but Emma is unaware of how things could easily be turned around and how some of her closest people could be in real danger—not from a real person, but from a metaphysical entity that has haunted this city for decades.

Midpoint (190 min.): At the end of the fourth episode and a couple of minutes after the exact middle of the whole narrative, we can spot the midpoint beat. As Emma starts to realize the importance of her actions, she stops writing about Marianne. At night, Emma wakes up and sees some figures inside her room. The voice of Marianne says to her that because she is not writing anymore, Marianne wants to play with her. Emma's friends get a visit from Marianne that night. Tonio (Mehdi Meskar), who took over a shift at the port, is captured by Marianne. Aurore (Tiphaine Daviot) is visited by her dead little sister, Lucie (Romane Libert), who appears evil, while at a hospital, Seby's newborn son is taken by Marianne, with a witch charm left in his cradle. At the midpoint beat, everyone is affected by Marianne and the stakes get higher, making Emma reconsider her previous actions.

Bad Guys Close In (190 min.–248 min.): The fifth episode and the beginning of the sixth episode are devoted to the tenth beat. The narrative boldly dedicates a big part of this beat to a flashback sequence from fifteen years earlier in which the audience sees how Emma and her friends gather at their old school at the lighthouse for a ritual that changed their lives. This sequence breaks the linearity of time, a basic characteristic of the classical narration. Nevertheless, it is conceived as a flashback that aims to enrich the background of the main characters, a tactic that is also used in classical films that follow the three-act structure.[31] Based on this observation, it is clear that *Marianne*'s narrative is still a classical model that fits into the three-act structure. At this beat, we see the first contact of Emma's friends with Marianne and the reason Emma decided to leave forever from Elden. The audience now having all this information from the flashback sequence, in the present Emma and the rest of the characters decide to confront Marianne. At this beat, we see that Marianne has a lot of influence against the group of the main characters and her power seems to be increasing.

All is Lost (248 min.): After the main characters decide to confront Marianne, they go to their old school at the lighthouse in order to recreate the ritual and call Marianne's spirit. The group of old friends,

The Netflix Vision of Horror

with Inspector Raunan (Alban Lenoir), gather at their old classroom and start the ritual, but in vain. The spirit invocation is not successful, and there is no indication of Marianne's presence. Everything seems lost for the main characters, who cannot do anything to prevent the cruel things that are happening to them. Marianne has gained power and they seem helpless in the face of the events that are happening to them.

Dark Night of the Soul (248 min.–263 min.): The rest of the sixth episode is dedicated to the twelfth beat, in which the main characters are at their lowest position and everything seems to be pointless. After the unsuccessful ritual, the characters do not know what to do next or how to face Marianne. They decide to stay at the school all night to find a solution. This is how the second act was supposed to end, since it is part of this beat's identity. With all the characters being at their weakest, the narrative has placed all the elements at the right position in order for the second plot point to happen.

Break Into Three (263 min.): The second plot point occurs at the end of the sixth episode, and the narrative enters its final act. All the characters are at the old school at the lighthouse, and most try to get some sleep. Inspector Raunan is awake at the classroom, while Emma and Seby (Ralph Amoussou) are asleep. The inspector senses the presence of Marianne. All of the characters are gathered in the classroom, and the inspector informs them that the ritual was successful after all and Marianne is there. The inspector realizes that Marianne is inside him, and in order to prevent her from doing something bad to the other characters, he commits suicide with his gun in front of the others. Before he shoots himself, the inspector says that Marianne will take the other characters, one after the other. This course of action changes the status and direction of the narrative, since the stakes are high and no one is safe anymore. As this is a plot point, it strengthens the main conflict and reasserts the narrative's dramatic question about the relationship between Emma and Marianne.

Finale (263 min.–350 min.): Following the second plot point, the narrative progresses, and the third act leads to the climax of the series and the conclusion of the main conflict. After Inspector Raunan's suicide, Marianne's spirit flees his dead body as the others escape: Arnaud (Bellamine Abdelmalek) runs to the beach where he sees Tonio, who tells him that he's a prisoner and that Emma must write by Tuesday; Emma goes to the car; and Aurore and Seby return to the lighthouse, where Lucie shows herself and tells Aurore that Emma was there when she died, something Emma has never told her. They all end up back at

2. The Narrative Structure of the Complex Discovery Plot

the lighthouse and confirm that no one is Marianne, but the pressure on Emma to write is getting stronger. Emma starts writing, and Seby's son is returned to him. This leads to the Marianne's final confrontation with Emma and her ultimate victory with the help of Father Xavier (Patrick d'Assumçao), who lights Marianne's grave on fire. The dramatic question is finally answered, with Emma being the winner of the main conflict.

Final Image (350 min.): The final image of the narrative is of Emma leaving Elden with Camile, who feels better. Emma feels sick and vomits a couple of times on the way home. At one of their stops, Camile buys a pregnancy test and gives it to Emma, who eventually takes it and finds that she is pregnant. In the seventh episode, Seby showed up at Emma's house and the two proceeded to have simple, one-time sex, to make up for what they never did as teens, but in the last episode Seby denied ever having slept with Emma and got angry at her, meaning that the person who slept with Emma was really Marianne in Seby's body. This means that Emma is carrying Marianne's offspring. The final image contrasts with the opening sequence, in which we saw for the first time the two characters. Now, as the narrative comes to an end, we see how their peculiar connection got even stronger and Emma is doomed to be followed by Marianne.

After this thorough, beat by beat analysis, we can see that Marianne is another fine example of how the three-act structure fits perfectly in a complex-discovery-plot series. The first act is 28 percent, the second act is 47 percent, and the third act is 25 percent of the whole narrative. We can observe that the first act takes some narrative time away from the second act, but it is a slightly difference that still falls within the standard spectrum of this model.

Furthermore, the narrative incorporates all of the four plot functions. The onset takes place at the Opening Image, when the audience sees the possessed Madame Daugeron and hears for the first time about Marianne. The discovery function occurs at the Fun and Games beat, when Emma realizes that Marianne is real and not only part of her fictional books. The confirmation function is at the Bad Guys Close In beat, when all of the main characters accept that Marianne is real, while every confrontation between Marianne and the main characters until the eventual victory of Emma is part of the confrontation function.

Marianne is a satisfactory sample of how a foreign audiovisual text can exist in the global market of a SVOD platform like Netflix. While one of the four foreign texts, and the only European one, of the corpus, this series is a sufficient example of a complex discovery plot that is structured under the norms of the three-act model of narration.

The Netflix Vision of Horror

Stranger Things—*A Structural Analysis*

Stranger Things is an American hybrid fantasy horror series with science fiction elements, created by the Duffer brothers. The series premiered on Netflix on July 15, 2016, and it already includes four seasons. Initially, the series was meant to be called *Montauk*, and it was going to be set in the real Long Island town of Montauk, New York, since the creators originally wanted *Stranger Things* to take place in a coastal town, like the film *Jaws* (Spielberg, 1975).[32] Even though the location changed, a lot of references to other classical films and television shows made it to the narrative of *Stanger Things*, creating a nostalgic tone for the entire series.

Nostalgia has a central role on this narrative. Phillip Mlynar points out that *Stranger Things* "comes off like a brilliantly nostalgic ode to the '80s, as it blends horror, sci-fi and supernatural elements and affectionately nods to movies like *The Goonies*, *E.T.* and *The Thing*."[33] It is worth mentioning that in their initial review of the first season, the *New York Times* compared the series to Rob Reiner's *Stand by Me* (1986), relating their nostalgic feel by "finding that timeless moment where everything seemed tantalizingly, scarily new."[34] Even the Duffer frothers had *Stand by Me* as a point of reference in the whole creation process; actors auditioning for the children's roles were given lines from this film to read.[35]

Regarding the overarching story of the series, *Stranger Things* is set in the fictional rural town of Hawkins, Indiana, during the early 1980s. The National Laboratory of the town supposedly performs scientific research, but secretly does experiments into the paranormal and supernatural, including those that involve human test subjects. During these experiments, they have created a portal to an alternate dimension, "the Upside Down," which starts to affect the residents of Hawkins in several ways.

The first season, which is part of the corpus of this research and consists of eight episodes with a total time of 383 minutes, begins in November 1983, when Will Byers (Noah Schnapp) is forced into the Upside Down by a monstrous creature. His mother, Joyce (Winona Ryder), the town's police chief, Jim Hopper (David Harbour), and Will's friends, Mike (Finn Wolfhard), Dustin (Gaten Matarazzo), and Lucas (Caleb McLaughlin) all search for Will in their own way. At the same time, a young psychokinetic girl called Eleven (Millie Bobby Brown) escapes from the laboratory and suddenly appears in the lives of Will's friends.

2. The Narrative Structure of the Complex Discovery Plot

At first glance, the overall story of the series follows faithfully the three-act structure and behaves as a unified narrative. Based on interviews with the creators, this was their intention from the beginning of this project. According to Joseph Sirianni, "For their network pitch, the Duffers explicitly indicated that the entire series would be structured like one, long film similar to the Hollywood three-act structure with a definitive beginning, middle, and end to allow for complete character arcs and satisfactory storytelling."[36]

According to Sirianni, since the series is a tribute to classical Hollywood films from the 1970s and 1980s that follow the three-act structure, it seemed natural to the creators to use the same technique and treat the entire season as a unified long-form filmic text, like the ones it pays homage to. Therefore, it not only creates a concrete narrative that follows the three-act model but also incorporates all of the fifteen beats of Snyder's approach. The fifteen beats of *Stranger Things* are:

Opening Image (1 min.): In the opening image of the series, the narrative establishes the main characters and the central premise of the story. The audience sees a scientist getting attacked inside the lab by an unidentified creature, while at the same time Will, Mike, Dustin, and Lucas are playing Dungeons and Dragons in Mike's basement. This sequence concludes with Will's disappearance while going back to his house. From the opening image, the audience gets familiar with the metaphysical nature of the narrative, the portal to the Upside Down, and the group of friends who will constitute the main characters of our story. Will's disappearance in the opening sequence will be the core of the entire narrative, since every character is searching for him.

Theme Stated (19 min.): As in most of the previous case studies, *Stranger Things* reveals the theme of its narrative in a dialogue between two of its main characters. When Joyce goes to the town's police station to see Hopper, they talk about Will's disappearance. Hopper says to her that 99 percent kids who disappear are found safe and alive. Joyce responds to him with the question, "What about that 1 percent?," expressing her agony about her kid's fate. This dialogue sets the tone for the entire narrative and encompasses the theme of the first season of the series. The entire overarching story will be structured around Will's disappearance and Joyce's persistence in searching for him. The theme of the narrative is the strong love of a mother and a group of friends who are willing to overcome metaphysical and realistic obstacles in order to find their beloved one.

Setup (1 min.–40 min.): The entire first episode is dedicated to

The Netflix Vision of Horror

the Setup beat, in which the audience is introduced to the main cast of characters, the premise of the narrative, the fictional world of Hawkins, the first attack of an unseen creature, the group of friends that are playing together, the eventual disappearance of Will, Joyce's first actions after the disappearance, Hooper's investigation, and the introduction of Eleven, a nervous young girl with a shaved head wearing a hospital gown, as she wanders into a local diner. There, the owner takes care of Eleven, but soon secret agents arrive and kill him. Eleven manages to escape using telekinetic abilities. Lastly, Joyce's phone short circuits after she believes she can hear Will breathing on a phone call. In this beat, the audience starts to feel the tone that the narrative will follow. From pure realism to science fiction elements, the first episode makes the viewer understand what will follow next in the overarching narrative.

Catalyst (46 min.): The first episode of the season ends with the inciting incident of the entire narrative. The group of friends wander into the woods looking for clues regarding Will's disappearance, and they find Eleven. This point of the story is crucial in the progression of the narrative, since the main characters who will be the subject of the whole series are met. On one hand, we have Will's friends representing the real world, while on the other hand, we have Eleven, living proof of the existence of metaphysical aspects of this world. Their meeting completes the components of the main conflict, which is the struggle between the real world and the Upside Down, while it clearly states the central dramatic question that is around finding Will and the possible victorious outcome of the main conflict.

Debate (46 min.–100 min.): The rest of the first act takes place in the second episode of the series and represents the main characters' denial of the metaphysical aspect of the conflict they are called to resolve. Mike, Dustin and Lucas bring Eleven to Mike's house, where they disagree on how to deal with her. Eventually, Mike agrees to let her sleep in his basement that night, and Eleven reveals to him that "bad people" are looking for her. After recognizing Will in a picture and demonstrating her telekinesis, Eleven convinces the group of friends to trust her, while they believe that she could help them find Will. Eleven suggests that Will is in the Upside Down and is being hunted by the creature from the first scene, known as Demogorgon. At the same time, the rest of the characters are approaching Will's disappearance realistically and ignore the metaphysical features around it.

Break Into Two (100 min.): At the end of the second episode the

2. The Narrative Structure of the Complex Discovery Plot

first plot point takes place. Mike's sister, Nancy Wheeler (Natalia Dyer), and her friend Barbara "Barb" Holland (Shannon Purser) go to a party with Nancy's boyfriend Steve Harrington (Joe Keery). Nancy gets drunk and has sex with Steve, leaving her friend alone. After some moments alone by the swimming pool, Barb is attacked by the Demogorgon and disappears. This collision of the real world and the Upside Down starts to have real victims, while the main characters are unaware of what is coming. As a plot point, this scene strengthens the main conflict of the narrative, while reasserting the central dramatic question of the series regarding the struggle between the real world and the Upside Down. Since there are no witnesses, but the audience knows exactly what happened, Barb's killing creates a more suspenseful progression of the narrative by leaving the main characters in ignorance.

B Story (110 min.): The first plot point sets the basis for the secondary storyline that will be developed in the second act of the narrative. Since the main characters do not know Barbara's fate, their parents, the police and Nancy herself start to search for her. This storyline is in accordance with the main story of the series and had a powerful impact on the fan community. After Barb's killing, the fans created a viral campaign under the name "Justice for Barb,"[37] demanding justice for a character they believed died in vain. The campaign not only gave more exposure to this secondary storyline, it even resulted in an Emmy nomination for the actress who portrayed Barb. Even if this B Story remains part of the first season, which is analyzed in this book, it is worth mentioning that this viral campaign resulted in an additional final closure of this storyline in the second season, as the creators decided to give justice by punishing the culprit and divulging the truth about her murder.[38]

Fun and Games (110 min.–196 min.): The first part of the second act is dedicated to the Fun and Games beat, the part of the narrative in which the characters confront the antagonistic force, but the risks are low. In the third and fourth episodes, which constitute this beat of the narrative, the main characters have not yet discovered the involvement of metaphysical elements in the main conflict, and the approach the situation in a realistic manner. Will's apparent body is found by a search party, but Joyce refuses to believe that this body is Will's. Mike feels betrayed by Eleven until she proves to him that Will is still alive, channeling his voice through Mike's walkie-talkie. Joyce hears Will's voice in her living room wall and by tearing away the wallpaper, she sees him. Eleven uses the radio to channel Will talking to his mother. Finally, Hopper has suspicions regarding the authenticity of the body found in the

The Netflix Vision of Horror

quarry and confronts the state trooper who found it, who admits that he was ordered to lie.

Midpoint (196 min.): At the middle of the total duration of the narrative, the midpoint occurs, and its action sets the stakes at the highest level yet. In this beat, Hopper goes to the morgue and finds that the apparent Will's body is a plastic mannequin filled with cotton. Hopper suspects that the lab's director, Dr. Martin Brenner (Matthew Modine), is responsible for this and decides to break into the lab in order to find some hard proof. Until this beat, Hooper was represented as the more realistic character of the narrative. After this new information at the midpoint, Hooper gets the evidence he wanted in order to believe Joyce's claims. Afterwards, nothing remains the same, and the characters start to fully embrace the metaphysical aspects of the main conflict.

Bad Guys Close In (196 min.–241 min.): After the midpoint, the narrative progresses towards the empowerment of the antagonistic forces. The fifth episode is dedicated to the tenth beat, in which Hopper searches the lab but is discovered and knocked out by the lab's guards. Hopper awakens at his house and finds a hidden microphone, leading him to realize that Joyce was right the whole time. At the same time, Lucas misinterprets Eleven's actions as acts of treason, leading Mike and Lucas to fight and Eleven to telekinetically defend Mike. These events force Eleven to run away. Both internally and externally, the pressure against our main characters seems stronger than ever before. The characters face their biggest challenges and are heading towards a potential catastrophe.

All Is Lost (241 min.): Near the end of the fifth episode, everything seems lost for the main characters. The group of friends are splitting up. Lucas blames Eleven and Mike for trusting her; Eleven defends herself and Mike, something that forces her to escape from this situation immediately; and the only ones still speaking to each other are Mike and Dustin. Everyone gets their own way, and everything now seems hopeless and impossible to achieve.

Dark Night of the Soul (241 min.–291 min.): The second act concludes with the twelfth beat of the narrative, the darkest period for the main characters. Nancy and Jonathan (Charlie Heaton), Will's brother, formulate a plan to kill the Demogorgon. They start searching for it in the woods. Eventually they find it, and Nancy follows it through a gate to the Upside Down, drawing its attention to her. Jonathan pulls Nancy back through the gate, saving her from the Demogorgon, but Nancy, visibly fragile, is afraid to be alone and asks Jonathan to stay with her at

2. The Narrative Structure of the Complex Discovery Plot

her house. Joyce and Hopper track down Eleven's mother and get all the information they can from her sister. At the same time, while searching for Eleven, Mike and Dustin are ambushed by bullies, but are rescued by Eleven, who breaks one of the bullies' arms. Eleven tearfully admits to Mike that she is responsible for allowing the Demogorgon to enter the real world.

Break Into Three (291 min.): At the end of the sixth episode, the second plot point occurs and the narrative enters its third and final act. Lucas is outside the lab and tries to find some clues, while Dustin, Mike and Eleven are together and someone is watching them. This man informs the lab about the three kids, and reinforcements head towards them. Lucas sees this movement and notifies his friends that they are after them. The course of events takes a turn that pushes the narrative in a new direction that resets and reinforces the main conflict, since the protagonists are facing a real threat. Therefore, for the third and final time, the dramatic question comes again to the fore, because with the new turn of events, the audience wonders how the narrative will conclude regarding the struggle between the real world and the Upside Down.

Finale (291 min.–383 min.): The rest of the narrative is dedicated to the third act, the resolution of the main conflict, and the answer to the central dramatic question. After Lucas warns Mike that agents are searching for Eleven, Mike, Dustin, and Eleven flee the house. With the help of Eleven's telekinetical powers, the kids escape and reunite with Luke. Nancy and Jonathan reveal everything they know about the Demogorgon to Joyce and Hopper. The group meets the kids, and everyone asks Eleven to search for Will and Barb. To strengthen Eleven's powers, they break into the middle school and build a makeshift sensory-deprivation tank. Using her telepathy, Eleven finds Barb's corpse, and with Joyce's help, she finds Will alive, hiding in the Upside Down version of his backyard fort. Realizing that the gate is in the basement of the lab, Hopper and Joyce break into the lab, but they are captured by security guards. Hopper gives Eleven's location to Brenner in exchange for letting them enter the Upside Down to rescue Will, whom they eventually find and save. The Demogorgon locates the kids, and Eleven sacrifices herself in order to disintegrate it. The climax is over, since Will has been saved and the struggle between the real world and the Upside Down is over.

Final Image (383 min.): The narrative concludes with its final image, in which the group of the kids are playing Dungeons and Dragons like in the first sequence of the overarching story, and then Will returns home and eats dinner with his mother and his brother. This final beat is the proof of the big change that has occurred to the fictional world, since it totally contradicts the first sequence of the narrative. Of course, since we are talking about a series with other seasons that followed, the final image sets some cliffhangers in order to start the next season (and consequently the next three-act structured narrative). So in this beat, we also see that Will coughs up a slug-like creature and has a vision of the Upside Down, but when he returns to the dinner, he hides these events from his family.

Based on this beat analysis, the narrative of the first season of *Stranger Things* follows all the norms of the three-act structure. The first act is 26 percent, the second act is 50 percent, and the remaining 24 percent is reserved for the third and final act. The percentages of each act are very similar to the standard classical model of narration, a fact that is linked with the complex discovery plot that *Stranger Things* incorporates.

Stranger Things has all of the four functions in its plot. The onset function is at the Opening Image, when the creature attacks the scientist and afterwards Will disappears. The discovery function is at the Fun and Games beat, when Joyce sees the Demogorgon in the wall, while Jonathan and Nancy see it in Jonathan's pictures. The confirmation function is at the Dark Night of the Soul beat, where Nancy and Jonathan see the Demogorgon for the first time and verify its existence, while every clash between the main characters and the Demogorgon in the third act constitutes the confrontation function.

Stranger Things is one of the most popular Netflix Originals and a fine example of how a series can be considered a long-form film that fully obeys the norms of the three-act structure, while incorporating all of the four plot functions in its story. Fitting well into the complex discovery plot category, this series structures its story according to the classical model and ultimately creates a concrete narrative that does not rely on an episodic unfolding of events.

Typewriter—*A Structural Analysis*

Typewriter is an Indian horror series directed by Sujoy Ghosh. It premiered on Netflix on July 19, 2019. The series is the second Indian—and the fourth and final foreign—audiovisual text that will be analyzed

2. The Narrative Structure of the Complex Discovery Plot

in this study. The story follows a group of school children, Sameera (Aarnaa Sharma), Satyajit (Mikhail Gandhi), and Devraj (Palash Kamble), who live in Bardez, Goa. The group of friends form a ghost club, and as their first mission, they decide to search for a ghost at an old, haunted villa in their neighborhood. However, before the children are able to start their search, a new family moves in and the legend of the villa resurfaces. The story revolves around the mystery behind the typewriter that is in this villa, one which seems to be possessed by an evil force.

Netflix local productions in India are not something new, since the platform enjoyed early success in that country, where the long-form series format is relatively new.[39] The show was praised for combining meaningful Indian representations with strong scares,[40] meaning that this production was faithful to both the local and the horror elements of its narrative. As Aditya Shrikrishna observes, the series goes through several genre shifts,[41] from horror to mystery and to an action-adventure mixture, but ultimately the series is clearly a pure horror narrative that invokes the audience's reflections of fear.

Typewriter consists of five episodes and has a total duration of 234 minutes, making it the second-shortest narrative of the corpus behind the other Indian series, *Ghoul*. If we analyze its narrative based on Snyder's approach, we will see that *Typewriter* faithfully follows all fifteen beats, divided into three acts. The fifteen beats of the series are the following:

Opening Image (1 min.): The series starts with a flashback wherein a young Jenny (Tvisha Jain) is put in bed by her grandfather Madhav Matthews (Kanwaljit Singh) in Bardez Villa, in Goa. She runs to her grandpa because she's afraid there's a ghost in her room, and he tries to calm her down. After looking throughout her room for the ghost and finding nothing, Madhav places Jenny in her bed, to only realize that the "real" Jenny is actually under her bed, hiding. The Jenny under the bed tells Madhav that there is something on her bed. This opening image sets the tone of the entire narrative, introduces the horror element that will be the basis of the series, and establishes the main character and the villa in which the events will occur at the present.

Theme Stated (17 min.): At the seventeenth minute of the narrative, there is a scene which clearly sets the theme of the entire narrative. In this scene, the audience sees the three children who are the main protagonists and have form the ghost club as they visit the villa, accompanied by Ravi Anand (Purab Kohli), the father of Sami. In the villa, they meet the new family that just moved there, the family of Jenny (Palomi Ghosh). While everybody says that this villa is haunted, nobody truly believes it. At the same time, a strange figure from inside the house is watching them. The dialogue of this scene and the parallel action of the bizarre figure sets the tone of the narrative and introduces the audience to the main theme of the series, which is the collision of the real world and the paranormal nature of the villa. This distinction between reality and the metaphysical world is at the core of many narratives of the corpus of this analysis, since it is an element of the true identity of the horror genre.

Setup (1 min.–22 min.): The first twenty-two minutes of the narrative are dedicated to introducing the fictional world and the main characters who live in it. The villa, a big part of the metaphysical world of the narrative, is established, while the protagonists are linked with it in various ways. Finally, the audience gets a first glance at the typewriter, an element of the narrative which is so important that it gives its name to the entire series. Since the overall narrative is shorter than other audiovisual texts of the corpus and the number of episodes is only five, the setup beat is relatively small and takes place in the first half of the first episode. But the time is long enough to establish all the necessary elements of the narrative that will be used in order to build the main conflict.

Catalyst (27 min.): At around the middle of the first episode, the narrative introduces the catalyst that will accelerate the progression of the narrative. In this inciting incident, Amit Roy (Jisshu Sengupta), the mysterious man who will later be revealed to be Fakeer's son, kills the man who did not succeed in bringing him the typewriter from the villa. This action creates an enigmatic condition around the typewriter, while it launches the antagonistic force that will oppose the main characters. Some of the protagonists live inside the villa, where the typewriter is, so they are potentially in danger. Therefore, this action creates the main conflict, the struggle between the real and the metaphysical world, and raises the central dramatic question around the possibilities of the typewriter and its importance.

Debate (27 min.–48 min.): The rest of the episode is dedicated to the Debate beat, in which the main characters are not ready to take the journey that is before them. Characteristically, apart from the members of the ghost club, the main characters deny the existence of ghosts and every paranormal act that is linked with the villa. Even if there are proofs around them, the characters are not ready to accept them or the ultimate

2. The Narrative Structure of the Complex Discovery Plot

confrontation with this metaphysical world. Of course, the three kids of the ghost club are willing to take this journey, and the narrative shows glimpses of their backgrounds in order to explain their motivation.

Break Into Two (48 min.): At the end of the first episode, the narrative enters its second act with the actions of the first plot point. In this scene, we see that the villa has a metaphysical identity and that paranormal actions surround the main characters who live there. While it is night and everybody is sleeping, the typewriter starts to write on its own the phrase, "ghosts do exist," as an answer to the characters' denial in the Debate beat. We see Jenny asleep at her bed, while the "demonic" Jenny is in front of her, staring at her threateningly. This scene reminds the watcher of the opening image of the series, when the narrative established the existence of the real Jenny and her identical ghost. The second act begins with the materialization of the metaphysical world and the real danger our characters are facing without even knowing it yet.

B Story (55 min.): The second act introduces the secondary storyline, which will support the structure of the narrative. The B Story of the series is centered on the "demonic" Jenny and her evil actions. While Jenny is an actual person who interacts with the rest of the protagonists, "demonic" Jenny is a ghost that complicates the situation, since it looks identical to the real character. This entity commits murders and does evil actions that are not compatible with real Jenny, a fact that creates a confusion for some of the main characters and, in some scenes, even for the audience. This storyline is in accordance with the overarching story, since they share the same theme and are established in the same manner and tone. Both the main and the secondary storylines are tangled. Together they constitute the second act, while some of the actions continue into the final act, when the main conflict is resolved.

Fun and Games (55 min.–100 min.): The second episode of the narrative is dedicated to the Fun and Games beat, in which the second act establishes the first complications around the main conflict, but when the main characters perceive all these as some sort of a game and not as real threats. The protagonists have not fully understood the importance of the situation, and the obstacles around them allow them to keep an innocent way of thinking. The four kids who constitute the ghost club want to exploit Maria's death in order to see a real ghost, while the policemen are ignoring the metaphysical elements around her death and investigate the case as a real murder. On one hand we have the characters of the ghost club, who believe in the existence of the paranormal, but see it as a game, while on the other hand, the adults in the

The Netflix Vision of Horror

narrative persist in focusing on aspects of the real world and fully ignore the metaphysical danger.

Midpoint (100 min.): Just before the middle of the narrative, the midpoint occurs and raises the degree of the danger around the main characters. At the one hundredth minute of the whole narrative, "demonic" Jenny is outdoors and kills James (Masood Akhtar), while Sam sees the whole action. As expected, Sam is terrified and runs away. She ultimately goes to the church, where real Jenny is. Jenny sees Sam and brings her to sit next to her, but Sam is frightened. At this point, which takes place at the end of the second episode, our main character sees a course of deeds that reveals to her the real danger that the whole community is facing. With the events of the Midpoint beat, the stakes are higher than before and the characters' understanding of events has irrevocably changed.

Bad Guys Close In (100 min.–136 min.): After the dramatic midpoint, every action that follows seems more substantial than the previous ones. The stakes are higher and the pressure against the main characters is growing. Sam is now afraid of Jenny, but Sam goes to her with the hope of getting help in speaking to her dead mother. The main reason Sam believes in the metaphysical world and wants to meet a ghost is because her mother died and Sam wants to talk to her. By believing that ghosts exist, she can imagine that she could talk again with her deceased mother. This is why Sam approaches Jenny: so that she could see if her dream can come true. At the same time, the audience sees a flashback sequence from 1950, where Fakeer's mother is being pressured because of her paranormal activities. Finally, in the present, Jenny is linked with the three murders that have been committed by her identical ghost. The antagonistic forces seem to win, and the main characters face one obstacle after another.

All Is Lost (136 min.): At the end of the third episode, the actions of the eleventh beat take away every hope that existed. Ravi forces Sam to apologize to Jenny, even if Sam still believes what she saw. Sam believes in the metaphysical world and that ghosts are real, but her father forces her to act otherwise. From the beginning of the narrative, the adults ignore the paranormal signs and, in this beat, their actions push the only character who sees the real truth to abandon her beliefs. Sam is represented as defeated, and everything seems lost for her, and also for the resolution of the main conflict between the real and the metaphysical worlds.

Dark Night of the Soul (136 min.–178 min.): As was the case with the previous case studies, the last part of the second act finds the main characters in their worst possible positions, and hope has vanished

2. The Narrative Structure of the Complex Discovery Plot

once and for all. So, at the twelfth beat of the narrative, Nick (Aaryansh Malviya) fights with Sam, because she accused his mother about James's murder, while both Jenny and Sam learn from different sources about Fakeer. More specifically, Jenny goes to her nanny in order to collect some information about the past and the villa's history, while Sam learns about the long-ago events from Moses (Harish Khanna). While the characters are in their weakest positions, the narrative sets the new story elements and prepares the transition into the third and final act.

Break Into Three (178 min.): Just before the end of the fourth episode, the second plot point occurs and the narrative enters its final act. In this scene, Sam tells her two friends what she has learned from Moses about Fakeer. By processing the new information along with what James said before his murder, the members of the ghost club conclude that Fakeer's soul is trapped inside the typewriter at the villa. As with all the plot points, this scene changes the course of the narrative, while at the same time it repeats the dramatic question, since it strengthens the main conflict between the real and the metaphysical worlds. The main protagonists are ready to face the antagonistic forces of the narrative and resolve the main conflict.

Finale (178 min.–234 min.): The rest of the narrative is dedicated to the third act. The end of the fourth episode and the entire fifth episode set the path towards the climax, in which the final resolution will be established and the audience will get all the answers needed. The episodes include the abduction and removal of the typewriter from the villa and the efforts by Fakeer's son to make a sacrifice and bring his father back to life. Eventually, the typewriter returns inside the villa and Fakeer's son has the upper hand. With the help of the adult main characters, the ghost club manages to conquer the antagonistic forces and prevent the return of Fakeer. This point is the climax of the narrative, because the audience feels that the story they have been watching for almost two hundred and thirty minutes is ending. The dramatic question is answered, and the real world prevails over the metaphysical entities that threatened it.

Final Image (234 min.): The final scene of the narrative is when Fakeer's son sacrifices his own soul in order to save the typewriter and, therefore, his father's soul. His eyes starting to bleed, and Fakeer's son's blood starts to fall on the typewriter, which was damaged. He ultimately dies, but the typewriter starts to heal itself. The closing image is of typewriter looking like a brand new one, meaning that the sacrifice was successful and Fakeer's soul is still inside the typewriter. In the opening image, the paranormal aspects of the narrative were introduced while

Madhav was writing at this very same typewriter. In the final image these paranormal aspects have partially concluded, while the same typewriter is still there, giving a sense of an endless evil that will always haunt the real world.

After this thorough, beat by beat analysis, we can conclude that *Typewriter* is another fine example of a three-act structure. Its first act is 21 percent of the length, its second act is 55 percent, and the remaining 24 percent of the narrative is dedicated to the third and final act. The percentages of the acts are almost the same as in the standardized three-act structure, with a slightly longer second act. Step by step, the narrative of *Typewriter* follows Snyder's approach and fulfills each of the fifteen beats in a manner that creates the sense of a unified audiovisual work and not an episodic narration.

The series is also a part of the complex discovery plot category, with all of the four functions described by Carroll. The onset function occurs at the Opening Image, when the metaphysical danger is being established and "demonic" Jenny is threatening the main character. The discovery function takes place at the Midpoint, when Sam witnesses the murder of James by the "demonic" Jenny. The confirmation function is at the Dark Night of the Soul beat, when Sam and Jenny both learn about the past misdeeds that led to the present metaphysical threat, while from that point on, every battle towards the main characters' victory is part of the confrontation function.

After the study of *Typewriter*, we can clearly state that it follows the three-act model of narration regarding its overarching story, while at the same time obeying the norms of the complex discovery plot. This series, like the rest of the case studies of this chapter, is an excellent example of how a three-act structure is combined with complex discovery plot techniques and creates a long-form, unified narrative. The narrative of *Typewriter* has many similarities to the other case studies of the complex discovery plot, because it shares the same pattern of structuring and plot functioning. The series has all of the four functions in the right places, and therefore its action distribution is well-balanced and in accordance with the norms of the classical model of narration.

V Wars—*A Structural Analysis*

V Wars is an American horror series with a plethora of science fiction elements. It was created by William Laurin and Glenn Davis, based

2. The Narrative Structure of the Complex Discovery Plot

on the homonymous graphic novel of Jonathan Maberry. The series centers on an ancient virus that made its appearance due to climate change and transforms humans into bloodthirsty predators, setting the stage for a conflict between the infected and the healthy people. The two main protagonists of the narrative are the scientist Dr. Luther Swann (Ian Somerhalder) and his best friend Michael Fayne (Adrian Holmes), who face the developing emergency of this deadly outbreak that splits society into opposing groups, potentially escalating to a future war between humans and vampires. The story of the series is based on a viral outbreak, a fact that made a lot of fans, including the protagonist of *V Wars*, Ian Somerhalder, claim that the series predicted the level of unpreparedness of the world regarding the coronavirus outbreak.[42]

V Wars premiered on Netflix on December 5, 2019, making it the most recent audiovisual text in the corpus of this study, while the second season is expected in late 2020.[43] The series has ten episodes and a total duration of 395 minutes. It is worth mentioning that this series is the only one of the eight audiovisual texts with complex discovery plots that belongs to the Horror of Armageddon category, since the other seven series all are part of the Horror of the Demonic category. As the last case study of a three-act narrative with a complex discovery plot, *V Wars* is undoubtedly a classical narration that follows all the norms stated below. Isaac Feldberg compared its narrative to a B movie that was stretched out to series' length.[44] Regarding Snyder's approach, the structure of *V Wars* too follows all the beats and creates a unified narrative that does not rely on episodic installments. The fifteen beats of the narrative are the following:

Opening Image (1 min.): The series opens at a remote, snowy area. A man goes out of a facility and seems to suffer. After a few moments, he commits suicide. The sequence continues with Luther giving a lecture about how the ice's melting can bring to life some kind of ancient microorganisms that can wipe all of humanity out. Afterwards, Dr. Lansing (Nigel Bennett) tells him that they lost contact with their scientist in the Arctic (from the first scene) and that before his disappearance, he wanted to talk to Luther. Luther is asked to go to the Artic to see what happened, and he calls Michael in order to meet up and go together. The Opening Image is straightforward, since it establishes the central premise of the series, the fictional world of the narrative, and the main characters that live inside it. From the very first sequence, the narrative establishes the tone of the story, and the audience becomes part of this fictitious community.

The Netflix Vision of Horror

Theme Stated (19 min.): As a continuation of the Opening Image, at the nineteenth minute of the narrative, the audience is familiarized with the principal theme of the story. Luther is at the laboratory and talks with his assistant, Teresa Tangorra (Samantha Cole). He has not found any microorganisms yet in the samples, but he is certain that something is not right. His exact phrase is "the search goes on," a key line that gives the theme of the narrative. The theme of the series is centered on the humanity's research and its possible evolution into a new species. On one hand, we have this rapid evolution that is represented by Michael, while on the other hand we have Luther, who represents the science of humanity. As in all of the previous case studies of this chapter, this beat encompasses the true meaning, theme, and tone of the overarching story.

Setup (1 min.–49 min.): The first episode of the series is dedicated to establishing of the fictional world and introducing to the main characters, while it sets the stage for the forthcoming main conflict, Luther's and Michael's trip to the Arctic, their sickness, and their unavoidable isolation that occurred due to their infection. Though Luther gets better, Michael's condition gets worse and, ultimately, he commits a murder. This disease altered his behavior and made him violent. The police arrest Michael and take him to the hospital, where he turns into a vampire. He kills people and runs away, while Luther watches the whole situation. Also, a key character to the rest of the narrative, reporter Kaylee (Jacky Lai), sees and covers these events of Michael's transformation. The establishing events of this fictional world are the first steps in an epidemic outbreak that will threaten the existence of the modern society, but so far, no one knows that this may be a contagious disease. In order for the narrative to keep developing, a conflict must be established.

Catalyst (53 min.): At the end of the first episode, the inciting incident occurs and establishes the main conflict, while creating the central dramatic question. After the events at the hospital, Luther arrives at his home. There, his wife has turned into a vampire and attacks his son from another marriage. Luther tries to defend his child, and he kills his wife. Afterwards, the police arrest him for killing her. The first episode ends with new evidence that creates the core of the narrative. At the previous beat, we had the routine of a modern-day community in its moments before the outbreak. At the Catalyst beat, we have the confirmation that it is contagious. Luther's wife did not travel to Arctic, but nonetheless, she was infected and transformed into a vampire who threatened the

2. The Narrative Structure of the Complex Discovery Plot

life of her own family. With these actions, the main conflict between the infected and the healthy people is established, while the question that arises is whether the healthy people can survive this enormous threat.

Debate (53 min.–90 min.): The second episode is dedicated to the Debate beat. Luther stands out as the main character from the side of the uninfected, while Michael is the protagonist of the vampires. The progression of the narrative shows both characters in denial about the upcoming journey they have been called to take. Luther is accused of his wife's murder, but the DNS asks him to help with his knowledge on the outbreak of this crisis in exchange for helping him and his son. Eventually, Luther accepts the deal. At the same time, Michael hides and tries to cope with this new situation. The ending of the first act is reserved for the final questioning of the commitment the main characters are called to take, and *V Wars* is no exception to this rule. Both characters face a dilemma that they have to resolve quickly, because the progression of the narrative jumps quickly into the second act.

Break Into Two (90 min.): Later, at the ending of the second episode and at the beginning of the third episode, the first plot point takes place. Calix Niklos (Peter Outerbridge), the person from DNS who first approached Luther, is speaking on the phone and says that even though Luther believes that the infected people are victims and need help, he does not believe that—he will use Luther in order to defeat the vampires, and then he will get rid of him. Calix has even access to hidden cameras inside Luther's room, so he can spy on him whenever he needs to. Then, despite Luther's suggestions, in a televised statement DNS declares Michael to be a public danger. With these actions, the narrative changes its course dramatically, and both main characters become committed to their path, since there is no turning back. Both Luther and Michael are in danger for different reasons, and the main conflict has been much strengthened. Lastly, as the second act starts, the dramatic question arises again, since the facts have been substantially altered and the audience wonders about the fate of this struggle.

B Story (97 min.): While the second act begins at the start of the third episode, two storylines make their appearance; they will, ultimately, jointly create the B Story of the narrative. Bobby (Greg Bryk) and some motorcyclists start to hunt down and kill vampires, while Danika Dubov (Kimberly-Sue Murray), who had a past relationship with Michael, starts to have symptoms indicating that she will transform into a vampire. These two stories are actually one secondary storyline, since

The Netflix Vision of Horror

Danika will become a vampire and Bobby's gang will be after her and her servants. The B Story of *V Wars* is in accordance with the main plot and is built around the central theme of the series, the struggle between humans and vampires in the midst of this epidemic. As expected, this secondary story has a lot of interaction points with the main storyline and the central protagonists of the narrative.

Fun and Games (97 min.–207 min.): The first part of the second act treats the main characters with sympathy, because the obstacles are still manageable. Luther talks about a new species that has arisen from DNA mutation, while the vampire population is growing more and more. The DNS is getting closer to capturing and killing Michael, but Luther warns them with a call. Luther finds Michael in order to talk, but an undercover sniper who followed Luther abruptly interrupts their conversation. Vampires start to organize as a community under the name "Bloods" and elect Michael, their patient zero, as their leader. Danika is also part of this community, since she went to find Michael. Finally, Teresa finds a gene that every infected person possesses, but Luther tells her that they must keep it a secret, because he does not trust the DNS anymore. As the narrative progresses, the condition starts to get complicated, and step by step, the characters get themselves into increasingly difficult situations.

Midpoint (207 min.): Several minutes after the exact middle of the narrative and at the end of the fifth episode, the Midpoint beat occurs. Before now, the main characters faced obstacles, but the situations were manageable. Now, with the actions of the midpoint, the stakes are higher than before, and the protagonists are called to face a new, terrifying fact that reinforces the main conflict. Luther and other DNS members watch the video of Michael in which he declares war against humans in order for his species to prevail. Luther gets back to his room and finds his son with symptoms of infection. In just one sequence, the stakes get much higher for both the main characters, since Michael leads a war against humanity while Luther faces a potential tragedy, since his son could become a vampire. Luther knows what the government wants to do to these people, and the possibility that his son could be one of them is devastating for him.

Bad Guys Close In (207 min.–254 min.): The second half of the second act seems more serious and dangerous for the main characters. In the tenth beat of the narrative, which takes place in the sixth episode, the pressure from the antagonistic forces increases greatly. At this point of the narrative, Luther tries to protect his child by hiding the fact that

2. The Narrative Structure of the Complex Discovery Plot

he is ill and by sending him away with the help of his assistant. Luther tells Teresa to take the child and go to one of his friends and that he will follow them afterwards. At the same time, Calix learns everything from the hidden cameras, even about the discovery of the gene in the infected people. Luther tries to run away, but he is arrested. Calix takes him out of there, but Calix is plotting a trap in order to find the child too. The conflict is getting stronger since the antagonistic forces are frighteningly approaching the protagonist of the narrative.

All Is Lost (254 min.): At the beginning of the seventh episode, the All Is Lost beat takes place. Everything seems hopeless now for the main character. After Calix sets him free, Luther walks into the woods in order to go to his son, while a vampire follows him. He arrives at his friend's office, where he finds Teresa murdered. His son, Desmond (Kyle Breitkopf), walks alone and calls someone from a telephone booth for help. Luther is under attack by a vampire and ultimately, he kills it. At the same time, Desmond's birth mother picks him up. In this sequence, we see that the protagonist is both externally and internally under attack, while every hope for his reconnection with his child seems to have vanished. Luther is now all alone, with a lot of enemies and far away from resolving the main conflict of the narrative: the battle against the new species.

Dark Night of the Soul (254 min.–290 min.): The rest of the seventh episode is the last part of the second act. Since this act is reserved for complications regarding the main conflict, the twelfth beat of the narrative finds the main characters in their worst possible spot. While Luther is being chased, he is saved by Jimmy (Michael Greyeyes), an undercover agent. Luther wants to find his child, but Jimmy is hesitant. After an argument, Jimmy is convinced to help Luther. They go to the house of Luther's ex-wife, Rachel (Nikki Reed), and find the dead body of the policeman Rachel killed. Afterwards, they find Desmond in a concentration camp for infected people. Every action of this beat represents the desperate situation Luther is in. From the life-threatening conditions he experiences to the search for his son, the main protagonist is at his lowest point and the narrative is ready to move to the final act and the resolution of the conflict.

Break Into Three (290 min.): At the beginning of the eighth episode, the narrative enters the third and final act, in which the main conflict has to be resolved. The thirteenth beat is the second plot point, which will change the course of the narrative. Luther enters the camp and tries to save his son. At the same time, Jimmy calls the senator he is working for and tells her to do something, or else Luther will be murdered. Luther finds the child, but the policemen are ready to shoot him. At the last minute, Jimmy intervenes and with the help of the FBI, takes Luther and Desmond in order to go with them to the senator. At this point of the narrative, the specifics are once again changing, and the main conflict arises again. No matter what the facts are about the main character, the narrative is structured around the struggle between humans and vampires, and the new direction of the narrative reasserts the dramatic question regarding who will eventually win.

Finale (290 min.–395 min.): The fourteenth beat is the longest part of the third act, since it spans almost its entire duration. The eighth, ninth, and tenth episodes are dedicated to narrative's progression towards the resolution of the conflict in the climax. The two sides of this war discuss a possible truce, and after negotiations they achieve it. After the poisoned BludSubs, supplements of blood for the vampires, the truce breaks and the Bloods want revenge. The senator is being punished for this, even if it is not her fault, and the new events force Luther to be away from his son again. The climax occurs when the main conflict is resolved in favor of the Bloods and Calix, who changed sides, while the dramatic question is finally answered.

Final Image (395 min.): The final sequence of the narrative finds Luther watching the televised statement of Ava (Sydney Meyer), in which she tells about the execution of Michael and the election of Calix as the new leader of Bloods. Calix has poisoned the water of many big cities to infect a great part of the human population. Finally, Calix has Desmond as a hostage, since he is the only person who is immune to the transformation. The audience sees Luther four months later, when Mila Dubov (Laura Vandervoort) visits him and tell him that she knows where his son is. In the Opening Image, the audience witnessed the outbreak of this disease, while in the Final Image we see how the fictional world developed and changed based on the new facts. The narrative leaves some indications and develops some actions that will lead to the second season of the series, which will be about Luther's search for his son.

Like the seven previous case studies, it is clear that *V Wars*, too, is a fine example of a unified narrative that is closely related to filmic norms rather than episodic conventions. The narrative is based on the three-act model, and the percentages of each act are very similar to the standardized model. The first act of *V Wars* is 23 percent, the second act

2. The Narrative Structure of the Complex Discovery Plot

is 51 percent, while the third act is 26 percent. From the numbers, it is clear that this series has an appropriate and well-adjusted structure that obeys the rules of classical narration.

Under the conventions of the three-act structure, *V Wars* incorporates all of the four functions in its plot, making it part of the complex discovery plot category. The onset function occurs at the Opening Image beat, when the audience is first introduced to the virus. The discovery plot takes place at the Catalyst beat, when Luther finds out that his wife has turned into a vampire and, therefore, that the virus is transmitted. The confirmation function occurs at the Fun and Games beat, when Luther informs and convinces the members of the DNS about the DNA mutation and the creation of a new species, while the confrontation function includes every possible effort for this conflict to be over— from the truce to the killings of Bloods.

V Wars, the most recent example of a horror series that is part of the corpus of this study, verifies the consistency of the way Netflix structures its original content. The series acts like a long-form film that relies on the beats of its narrative and not on the episodic structuring that is based on unnecessary cliffhangers that serve extra-narrational elements of the industry.

Structuring Norms of the Complex Discovery Plot

The biggest part of the corpus under analysis has two main characteristics: firstly, each of these series follows the three-act structure and the norms of the classical narration, while secondly, each incorporates all of the four functions into its plot. Therefore, 61 percent of the series in this corpus belong to the complex discovery plot category and transform the rules of the classical narration to their needs.

The above eight case studies prove that when a narrative has all of the four plot functions, its operation is highly similar to the standardized three-act structure and does not rely on episodic narration like a conventional TV series. Since their plots follow the pattern of establishing the Other for the audience and then for some characters, who have to convince the rest of the protagonists, and then to confront the Other, these series' structures are very similar to the harmonized percentages of the three-act model. Based on Snyder's description of every part of a classical narrative, here is a concrete table with all the percentages of each beat:

The Netflix Vision of Horror

Table 3. Standardized 15-Beat Sheet

Beat	Occurs At
Opening Image	1%
Theme Stated	5%
Setup	<9%
Catalyst	11%
Debate	11%–25%
Break Into Two	25%
B Story	27%
Fun and Games	27%–50%
Midpoint	50%
Bad Guys Close In	50%–68%
All Is Lost	68%
Dark Night of the Soul	68%–75%
Break Into Three	75%
Finale	75%–100%
Final Image	100%

According to these data, the initial five beats constitute the first act (25 percent), the next seven beats are the second act (50 percent), while the remaining three beats are the third and final act (25 percent). Even if Snyder talks about fifteen different narrative units, his examination is a more analytical approach of the standardized three-act model. The analysis of all of the case studies of this chapter was made according to this theoretical tool, and each series faithfully follows this pattern and incorporates all of the fifteen beats in its narrative.

Even if this tool was created for filmic texts with a unified narrative and is reserved for the film industry, the new distribution method of an SVOD platform like Netflix made this approach appropriate for contemporary series. Based on the above analysis of every series of the corpus under examination that belong to the complex discovery plot category, here is a table with the average percentages of this model of narration:

2. The Narrative Structure of the Complex Discovery Plot

Table 4. Complex Discovery Plot 15-Beat Sheet

Beat	Occurs At
Opening Image	1%
Theme Stated	6%
Setup	<11%
Catalyst	12%
Debate	12%–24%
Break Into Two	24%
B Story	27%
Fun and Games	27%–50%
Midpoint	50%
Bad Guys Close In	50%–66%
All Is Lost	66%
Dark Night of the Soul	66%–75%
Break Into Three	75%
Finale	75%–100%
Final Image	100%>

If we compare the two tables, we see that each beat has almost the same duration as the standard version of Snyder's approach. These series not only adapt every beat of the analytical three-act structure approach but also keep the percentages of each unit appropriately the same. Hence, they create narratives that are closely related to filmic conventions. Based on the data extracted from the case studies, the complex discovery plot has a three-act structure that has a first act of approximately 24 percent, a second act of approximately 51 percent, and a third act of approximately 25 percent, meaning that apart from 1 percent that is taken from the first act to be given to the second, everything seems to be in the right place.

Regarding the first act, the majority of the case studies tend to have a slightly smaller percentage than the standard 25 percent, with the exception of *Marianne* and *Stranger Things*, which have slightly longer openings. Here is a table with the percentages of each beat of the first acts of the case studies:

The Netflix Vision of Horror

Table 5. The Beats of the First Act

	Opening Image	Theme Stated	Setup	Catalyst	Debate
Chilling Adventures of Sabrina	1%	6%	<9%	10%	10–21%
Diablero	1%	4%	<10%	12%	12–25%
Ghoul	1%	8%	<11%	13%	13–25%
Hemlock Grove	1%	6%	<13%	14%	14–22%
Marianne	1%	6%	<12%	15%	14–28%
Stranger Things	1%	5%	<10%	12%	12–26%
Typewriter	1%	7%	<9%	11%	11–21%
V Wars	1%	5%	<12%	13%	13–23%

Even if the first act in this category is usually smaller, we can see that every beat tends to be marginally later than Snyder's approach states. Five out of the eight series have their Theme Stated after the 5 percent mark (at approx. 6 percent), six of the eight series tend to have a longer Setup (at approx. 11 percent instead of 9 percent), while six series have their inciting incident (Catalyst) after the 11 percent that Snyder states (at approx. 12 percent). Consequently, with the exception of *Stranger Things*, the Debate is smaller than usual. Even though these narratives follow filmic conventions, they are still delivered as series and most of them have extensive lengths. This means that the narrative needs more time to introduce the fictional world and the main characters, because there is much more information to be given to the audience than in the usual two-hour film. This is why these narratives borrow time from the further act one development that follows the inciting incident and give it to the setup of the fictional world. But even with this slightly change,

2. The Narrative Structure of the Complex Discovery Plot

the first acts of the complex discovery plot series behave as expected according to the narrative theory.

As mentioned above, the second act is marginally longer than in the standard three-act model, with the exception only of *Marianne*, which has a slightly shorter second act. The average size of the second act in the complex discovery plot category is 51 percent instead of 50 percent. Here is a table with the percentages of each beat of the second acts of the series:

Table 6. The Beats of the Second Act

	Break Into Two	B Story	Fun and Games	Midpoint	Bad Guys Close In	All Is Lost	Dark Night of the Soul
Chilling Adventures of Sabrina	21%	22%	22–51%	51%	51–68%	68%	68–76%
Diablero	25%	26%	26–49%	49%	49–66%	66%	66–76%
Ghoul	25%	32%	32–47%	47%	47–67%	67%	67–75%
Hemlock Grove	22%	24%	24–49%	49%	49–68%	68%	68–75%
Marianne	28%	31%	31–54%	54%	54–71%	71%	71–75%
Stranger Things	26%	29%	29–51%	51%	51–63%	63%	63–76%
Typewriter	21%	24%	24–43%	43%	43–58%	58%	58–76%
V Wars	23%	25%	25–52%	52%	52–64%	64%	64–74%

The Netflix Vision of Horror

From this table, we can clearly see that on average, every beat that belongs to the second act is nearly the same as in the filmic approach. The only alteration, which does not cause any difference in the functioning of the second act, is the fact that the majority of the series tend to have the All Is Lost beat earlier, which that makes the Bad Guys Close In beat shorter and the Dark Night of the Soul beat longer. But this difference is approximately only 2 percent of the entire narrative, so it has no substantial impact on the functioning of the second act.

Then there is the third act, which behaves just like the prototype narrative descripted by Snyder. Of course, the third act has only three beats, while the Finale beat is in fact the whole act (the thirteenth beat is the action that begins the events of the third act, while the fifteenth beat is the last image/scene of the narrative). In the table, we can see the percentages of each beat of the third acts of the series:

Table 7. The Beats of the Third Act

	Break Into Three	**Finale**	**Final Image**
Chilling Adventures of Sabrina	76%	76–100%	100%
Diablero	76%	76–100%	100%
Ghoul	75%	75–100%	100%
Hemlock Grove	75%	75–100%	100%
Marianne	75%	75–100%	100%
Stranger Things	76%	76–100%	100%
Typewriter	76%	76–100%	100%
V Wars	74%	74–100%	100%

2. The Narrative Structure of the Complex Discovery Plot

The data make it clear that the ending of each series that belongs to the complex discovery plot category is structured like the third act of a film that follows the classical narration model. In this act, the percentage of difference in comparison to the prototype is in the margin of error (1 percent or less), and each series has a well-crafted final part that has a total duration of 25 percent of the whole narrative.

Apart from some minor changes that are in fact modifications to suit the needs of each audiovisual work, we can see that all of the three acts are performing like the narrative is a film and not a TV series. Each act has a beginning, a middle, and an end structured around a key conflict between the main characters and the antagonistic forces, which ultimately creates the central dramatic question. Each of these series hooks the audience with a question that arises in the beginning and is answered at the end of the narrative. Thus, every viewer consumes this product as a whole and not based on individual units, like the episodes of a conventional TV series.

Now, regarding the essential functions of these plots, we can easily detect and analyze a pattern. Each function is closely connected with a specific portion of the narrative and usually is linked with a particular act. Therefore, the structure of these series is not only affected by the three-act model of classical narration but is also being influenced by the four essential plot functions.

The first of the four functions, the onset, is strictly connected with the first act. Onset is reserved to introduce and establish the Other of the narrative to the audience, because it will be vital to the creation of the main conflict. Of course, the Other is part of the fictional world, while at the same time a big percentage of the first act is needed for the introduction to this specific world. So it is highly normal for the onset function to be located in the first act of each narrative. Out of the eight case studies, six of them—*Ghoul, Hemlock Grove, Marianne, Stranger Things, Typewriter*, and *V Wars*—have their onset function at the first beat of their narratives, the Opening Image. The other two case studies, *Chilling Adventures of Sabrina* and *Diablero*, place the onset function at their Setup beat (<9 percent and <10 percent, respectively). We see that a large percentage of the series introduce their antagonistic force to the audience as early as possible, placing it in their first sequence, while no case study places the onset function later than the first 10 percent of the entire narrative. Thus, the onset function is not only located in the first act, but it is positioned in the opening part of this act. Each narrative tries to introduce its Other to the audience as early as possible in order

The Netflix Vision of Horror

to create the tension between the antagonistic force and the main characters of the overarching story.

The discovery function is an irregular case, since it is the only function that, depending on the narrative, can be located in two different acts. Five case studies (*Chilling Adventures of Sabrina, Ghoul, Marianne, Stranger Things*, and *Typewriter*) place the discovery function in their second act, while the other three case studies (*Diablero, Hemlock Grove*, and *V Wars*) place it in the first act. But even in these different groups, we can locate other patterns that could be useful in this analysis. Three out of the five series that have the discovery function in their second act place it at the Fun and Games beat (*Ghoul, Marianne* and *Stranger Things*), whereas the other two case studies place it at the Break Into Two beat (*Chilling Adventures of Sabrina*) and the Midpoint (*Typewriter*). Regarding the three case studies that incorporate the discovery function in their first act, all of them have it at the Catalyst beat. We see that more than 62 percent of the case studies prefer to incorporate the discovery function in the first half of the second act, while the rest of the series place it in the second half of the first act. Overall, this function is located between the 12 percent and 43 percent marks of each narrative. While every narrative has established the presence of the Other for the audience, this function in important since it communicates the existence of the Other to some of the main characters. If the narrative chooses to place this action in the first act, the best possible beat is the one in which the main conflict is being formed. But the majority of the series choose the second act and the beats that still have lower stakes for the main characters.

The confirmation function has a more stable presence in each of the case studies than its predecessor, because every series places it exclusively in its second act. However, we can observe a scattering in different beats, and the confirmation function can be found either at the beginning or at the end of the second act. Three series (*Diablero, Hemlock Grove*, and *V Wars*) place the confirmation function in the Fun and Games beat, while two case studies (*Stranger Things* and *Typewriter*) incorporate this function in the Dark Night of the Soul beat. The rest of the series place the confirmation function in different beats: *Chilling Adventures of Sabrina* links this function with its B Story, *Ghoul* places it at the All Is Lost beat, and *Marianne* incorporates it in the Bad Guys Close In beat. According to the performance of the confirmation function, at this point all of the main characters are convinced about the existence of the Other and, naturally, they have to take appropriate actions in order to weaken or even defeat this antagonistic force. Thus,

2. The Narrative Structure of the Complex Discovery Plot

depending on the series and its overarching story, the confirmation function is placed at the point from which the narrative wants to start the confrontation of the Other by the main characters. In simple words, the more confrontation scenes a series wants, the earlier the confirmation function will be placed. In *Typewriter* and *Stranger Things*, where the confirmation function is placed at the last beat of the second act, we do not have many conflict scenes between the main characters and the Other, while in *Chilling Adventures of Sabrina*, where the confirmation function is established at the second beat of the act, we have a plethora of several types of confrontation.

The last function of the complex discovery plot category is the confrontation. This function is reserved for all the actions in which the main characters try to overthrow the Other and be the winners of the main conflict. Having in mind the aforementioned analysis, the confrontation starts immediately after the confirmation function. The operation of the confrontation function is more complicated than the previous three, since it is not located in a single scene or a sequence. Every confrontation after the confirmation between the main characters and the Other is part of this function. Nevertheless, the core of the confrontation function is always located in the third act. Even if the confirmation function takes place at the beginning of the second act, every confrontation scene or action that takes place until the second plot point has minor impact on the main conflict. We should not forget that the first half of the second act has low stakes and insignificant conflicts in comparison with the ending of the act and more specifically the third act.

Having all that in mind, it is clear that the primary and most important part of the confrontation function is in the third act, which is reserved for the resolution of the main conflict, and specifically at the Finale beat. All of the eight case studies place the center of the confrontation function at the Finale beat, because it is almost the entire third act; the thirteenth beat is the second plot point, which helps the narrative enter into the act, while the fifteenth beat is the final scene or sequence of the narrative, making both beats small. Thus, it is clear that even if this function has roots in other beats, it is closely connected to the Finale beat of the third act. Finally, since we are talking about series that usually desire to have another season, the confrontation function is usually not fully resolved, and the narrative leaves some of its aspects unsettled in order to create some questions that will be the basis of the next installment of the series (or in other words, another three-act structure narrative that is based on the same fictional world).

The Netflix Vision of Horror

In conclusion, it is obvious that the main four functions of each series are linked with specific portions of the narrative. The onset function is placed at the beginning of the first act, the discovery function can be found either at the end of the first act or at the beginning of the second act, the confirmation function is located in the second act, and the confrontation function is mainly developed and concluded in the third act. This uniform distribution of the four functions creates a balanced sharing of the portions of the narrative to its three acts. In other words, the narratives of the case studies of this chapter have a similar distribution of their action to the 25 percent–50 percent–25 percent of the standardized classical model because they all incorporate all of the four functions into their overarching stories. Hence, it is clear that these series are based on unified narratives with a beginning, a middle, and an end, while they do not rely on an episodic narration that pays more attention to the units than the entire construction.

The question that arises is what happens if we remove one or even two of the plot functions. As stated in the first chapter, some of the audiovisual works of the corpus of this study do not follow the complex discovery plot and chose different categories of plots with three or two functions. These case studies have an unbalanced distribution of the percentages of each act and adapt their narratives to the needs of their overarching stories. Hence, the next chapter of this book will deeply and thoroughly analyze the other plot categories that can be found in the corpus: the discovery plot, which incorporates the onset, discovery, and confrontation functions; the discovery/confirmation/confrontation plot; and the discovery/confrontation plot. Each of these categories have different plot functions, and therefore their narratives adapt to different norms.

Chapter Three

The Narrative Structures of Triple and Double Function Plots

The complex discovery plot is the most common category among the Netflix Original series that belong to the horror genre. As seen in the previous chapter, these series incorporate all of the four functions (onset, discovery, confirmation, and confrontation) in their plots, while they faithfully follow the three-act structure. Since they have all four of the functions, their acts have similar percentages to the standard 25 percent–50 percent–25 percent model. Of course, there are other plot categories that can be identified. As Noel Carroll writes, "Often one observes that one can arrive at the characterization of the plot structure of a given horror story by subtracting various of the functions or plot movements from the complex discovery plot."[1] Consequently, there are narratives that are part of the corpus which do not have all of the four function. Therefore, we have series that follow triple- and double-function plots.

Since every function is highly connected with a specific part of the narrative, the absence of one or two functions will inevitably cause some disturbance in the distribution of the action among the three acts. This chapter will analyze the case studies of every other plot category that is part of the corpus and will define their structuring conventions in order to outline the construction of each type of narration.

More specifically, in this chapter I will analyze the discovery plot with the series *Chambers* (Netflix, 2019) and *The Haunting of Hill House* (Netflix, 2018), the discovery/confirmation/confrontation plot with the series *Santa Clarita Diet* (Netflix, 2017–2019) and *The Order* (Netflix, 2019–present), and the discovery/confrontation plot with the series *Black Summer* (Netflix, 2019–present), the only double-function plot of the entire corpus. Based on these five case studies, I will define the characteristics and the narrative structures of the three plot categories, and I will compare them with the complex discovery plot, the prototype model of this analysis.

The Narrative Structure of the Discovery Plot

According to Carroll, one quite common alternative plot category among the horror genre, as opposed to the complex discovery plot, is the discovery plot. This category incorporates three of the main functions: the onset, the discovery, and the confrontation. In other words, this category is the complex discovery plot minus the confirmation function.

These narratives are structured so that the Other is established for the audience, then the main characters learn about the danger that is before them, and then all the actions around the struggle between the protagonists and the antagonistic forces start to occur. The main difference between the discovery plot and the complex discovery plot is that in the first category, there is no need for confirmation of the existence of the Other, since in the discovery function all of the main characters learn about this antagonistic force. The discovery plot merges the purpose of the confirmation into the discovery function.

As expected, this difference in the incorporated functions of the discovery plot has a huge impact on the narrative structuring of these series and alters the distribution of the action into the acts. While in the complex discovery plot we have a balanced distribution of the acts that is similar to the standard three-act model, in the discovery plot this is not the case. In order to thoroughly study this category, first we have to investigate the structuring methods of the two series that belong to this category.

Chambers—A Structural Analysis

Chambers is an American fantasy horror series with supernatural elements, created by Leah Rachel. The first season premiered on Netflix on April 26, 2019, but one month earlier, the series had its official premiere with the screening of the first two episodes at the Series Mania International Festival in Lille, France.[2] Although *Chambers* was supposed to continue for more than one season, on June 18, 2019, Netflix cancelled the series.[3]

3. The Narrative Structures of Triple and Double Function Plots

The story of the series centers on Sasha Yazzie (Sivan Alyra Rose), a teenager who, after receiving a heart transplant, begins to develop different personality traits and have peculiar visions about the deceased girl who was the donor of the heart. As the visions increase, Sasha begins to unravel the horrifying circumstances and conspiracy that led to the donor's mysterious death. The premise of the narrative reproduces several stereotypes that are connected with this kind of audiovisual work,[4] and it was highly criticized, with Lucy Mangan observing, "Sex equals death in any TV or film venture involving teenagers and the supernatural. *Chambers* takes the trope literally, giving its sullen 16-year-old protagonist Sasha a heart attack as she tries to lose her virginity to her boyfriend."[5]

The series has ten episodes and a total duration of 412 minutes. *Chambers* follows the three-act structure, but the percentages of every act are not in accordance with the harmonized rule of the classical model. Nevertheless, the series follows every beat of Blake Snyder's approach, and a relevant analysis can help us extract some useful data regarding the norms of the structuring methods of this narrative. The fifteen beats of the series are the following:

Opening Image (1 min.): The series opens with Sasha in her house getting ready, while her boyfriend, TJ Locklear (Griffin Powell-Arcand), comes to pick her up. Sasha is a virgin, and the couple is getting ready to have sex for the first time. TJ takes her in his car to a closed mattress store, and they start making love. Suddenly, Sasha seems to suffer from a seizure, and her boyfriend takes her immediately to the hospital. The first scene of the narrative establishes the main premise of the series, since it introduces to the audience the beginning of Sasha's health problem and subsequently the start of the upcoming main conflict. Furthermore, this scene introduces the main character, Sasha, who will be the center of the entire narrative. This series is primarily based on this particular character, and every step of the narrative concerns her actions.

Theme Stated (24 min.): At the twenty-fourth minute of the narrative, there is a dialogue scene which establishes the theme of the series. As we saw in the second chapter, this tactic is very common, since the majority of the audiovisual works incorporate and state their theme through a dialogue scene. In this particular narrative, we have a dinner with the family of Becky (Lilliya Scarlett Reid), Sasha, and her uncle, Frank (Marcus LaVoi). Both Becky's mother and the father ask intrusive questions of Sasha and want to give her a scholarship in order to study at Becky's school. As observed in this vital scene, the theme of the narrative

The Netflix Vision of Horror

is the family's attempt to replace their dead daughter with Sasha. On a second level, this attempt hides a controlling attitude towards Sasha and her metaphysical reflection, Becky. The theme and the tone of the narrative pave the way for the main conflict of the narrative.

Setup (1 min.–40 min.): The first forty minutes of the narrative are dedicated to the Setup beat. In this part of the narrative, there is the introduction to all the aspects of the fictional world, including the central premise of the series and the main characters, but also a first glimpse into the antagonistic forces that will eventually create the main conflict of the narrative. The audience sees Sasha—and her medical problem that will be the foundation of this narrative—and learns about her friends and family, while the narrative establishes their low-income status. We also have Becky's family, which consists of her mother, Nancy Lefevre (Uma Thurman), her father, Ben Lefevre (Tony Goldwyn), and her brother, Elliott Lefevre (Nicholas Galitzine). This family is the exact opposite of Sasha's world, since they belong to the upper class. Consequently, it is logical that Sasha accepts the scholarship from the family and tolerates their interference with her life.

Catalyst (46 min.): At the end of the first episode, the narrative establishes the main conflict during the inciting incident. At this beat, Sasha talks with her best friend, Yvonne (Kyanna Simone Simpson), about Becky's family and all of the things that happened during the Setup beat. Yvonne informs her that if someone dies from electrocution, they are not eligible to be an organ donor. Becky's family did not tell Sasha the truth about how Becky died. Then, late at night, Sasha sees Becky in the mirror instead of her own reflection. This sequence establishes both antagonistic forces that will come into conflict with the main character of the series: the Other of the narrative is Becky's environment, which will cause major problems for Sasha, while Becky herself works as an antagonistic force to Sasha, since in a manner she possesses her. Through these actions, both the main conflict and the central dramatic question arise, and the narrative's progression will lead to their resolution.

Debate (46 min.–132 min.): The second and the third episodes are dedicated to the Debate beat, which constitutes the last part of the first act. In this beat, the main character is in denial about the journey that lies before her and does not want to engage in the main conflict of the overarching story. After Sasha accepts the scholarship, and even though Becky's family lied to her, she starts going to her new school and meeting Becky's friends. Her new life begins to develop, while Becky's family,

3. The Narrative Structures of Triple and Double Function Plots

and most explicitly her mother, continue to be intrusive and controlling. Sasha and Yvonne go to Becky's house in order to attend a ceremony for Becky. There, they hack a hidden camera that Sasha found in Becky's room in order to see who put it there. Through the camera, they see a burned hand place it in the room. The rest of the Debate beat consists of Sasha's efforts to find whose hand is that on the camera, while her visions about Becky are increasing dramatically.

Break Into Two (132 min.): After the aforementioned events, the narrative is ready to enter its second act and complicate the aspects around the main conflict. Therefore, at the end of the third episode, there is the first plot point. At this scene, while Sasha makes dinner, a friendly mouse (whose connection and friendship with Sasha were established earlier) approaches her. She starts feeding it, but suddenly Sasha becomes vicious with no reason and attacks the friendly mouse with the knife. She goes into her room in a panic and sees a picture that she had taken earlier (at a shop) of her aura. Becky appears inside the picture instead of Sasha, and the picture bursts into flames. This scene is very important and changes the course of the narrative, since it establishes that Becky's spirit has an enormous impact on Sasha's behavior, making her extremely violent even towards a friendly presence. This scene reasserts the main conflict and the central dramatic question, because the new events that change the progression of the narrative make the audience wonder about the possible outcome of the main protagonist's struggle with the antagonistic forces of the overarching story.

B Story (146 min.): While the second act starts, a secondary storyline is introduced that is in complete harmony with the main story, the theme, and the tone of the narrative. At this particular series, this B Story is about the aggressiveness Sasha has developed and showed at the first plot point. At the starting point of this storyline, Sasha goes to Yvonne's house and looks at a knife weirdly, as she wants to harm someone again, like in the Break Into Two beat. While the visions and the paranormal events are increasing, Sasha's violent behavior becomes a problem for her and a possible threat to others. This secondary storyline develops throughout the second act and ends with the overarching story at the climax of the narrative.

Fun and Games (146 min.–215 min.): The second act begins, whose main purpose is to complicate the circumstances around the main conflict. The first part of this act, though, is meant to have lower stakes, and the events are perceived by the characters as something normal and manageable. In *Chambers*, at this beat Sasha tries to discover

The Netflix Vision of Horror

the truth while not knowing how serious the situation is. This condition of not knowing the truth highly influences Sasha herself and her attitude towards everyone. There is even some indication that this might have a physical impact to her, since she ends up at the hospital, while some of her hair starts to be blond, just like Becky's. Sasha thinks that Becky was murdered, and that if she finds the killer, Becky will rest in peace and the visions will stop. By making this assumption, Sasha asks Yvonne to help her find the killer so everything will go back to normal. Yvonne agrees, and they both start looking for suspects who would have been able to kill Becky.

Midpoint (215 min.): Around the middle of the narrative, there is the Midpoint beat. Here, there are some actions that suddenly raise the stakes too high for the main characters, and the conflict gets stronger than before. At this series, the midpoint occurs at the end of the fifth episode: while Yvonne and Sasha are talking in the street, Yvonne's mother, Tracey (Patrice Johnson), who suffers from Alzheimer's disease, approaches them and tells Sasha that this white girl will never leave them alone—meaning Becky. Tracey grabs her hand and removes the bandage. Sasha's hand is now white around the wound. Until the previous beat, everything had been developing in a realistic manner, in which Sasha's main influence was her mental state. Now, the dangers increase and give the main character another critical problem to be concerned about, because Becky is now taking control of her body too.

Bad Guys Close In (215 min.–264 min.): The rest of the second act seems more serious, and the main character now faces precarious situations that can be life-threatening. The sixth episode of *Chambers* is dedicated to the tenth beat of the narrative, in which Sasha's body starts to change because of the strong influence Becky's spirit has on her, since her skin and hair start to change in accordance with the physical traits of Becky. At the same time, Sasha continues trying to find Becky's killer. She speaks with Nancy, who acts weird, and asks her if she feels a connection with her daughter. Sasha continues to have these strange visions, and the connection with Becky is getting even stronger every day. As the name of this beat indicates, the antagonistic forces seem to gain power over the main character, who now feels that she has the lower hand in the situation around the main conflict. Something that seemed manageable and achievable at the start of the second act now seems impossible.

All Is Lost (264 min.): At the end of the sixth episode, there is the All Is Lost beat, according to which the main character loses every hope about the eventual outcome of the conflict. In this series, we see

3. The Narrative Structures of Triple and Double Function Plots

Sasha going to her house, where Frank waits for her. They speak, and Sasha accuses him, saying that it is his fault that her mother—and his sister—died. Sasha leaves the house and seeks a shelter for the night at her best friend's home, but Yvonne refuses to let her stay because of their intense relationship. Feeling that there is no hope left, Sasha calls Becky's mother, who picks her up and brings her to their house. Sasha is going to live with Becky's family. After everything falls apart in her life, Sasha is forced by events to live with the family that caused all this pressure in her life.

Dark Night of the Soul (264 min.–305 min.): The last part of the second act finds the main character at her lowest. At the beginning of the second act, everything seemed under control and the protagonist had the upper hand regarding the outcome of the main conflict. At the twelfth beat of the overarching story and just before the narrative enters its third and final act, the protagonist has lost the control of the situation and nothing is in her favor. Sasha has lost contact with everyone from her previous everyday life who loves her—including her uncle Frank, her best friend and her boyfriend. At the same time, she lives with Becky's family, who are the ones that caused her all this paranoia and brought the paranormal aspects into her life. At this point, the main character has lost everything, and the series is ready to change its narrative course and incorporate new elements that will help in the construction of the ultimate resolution.

Break Into Three (305 min.): With the conclusion of the second act, the second plot point takes place and transfers the fictional world into the third act, which is reserved for the resolution of the main conflict and the answer to the central dramatic question. At this beat, the audience sees Sasha and Elliot going together to the spring equinox ceremony, which is the same place Becky takes the narcotic substance. Sasha wants to take this drug too in order to better connect with Becky and see what has really happened to her. So, Sasha and Elliot are at the exact same place Becky was, and Sasha takes the narcotic substance. This is the starting point of the new direction the narrative takes, which ultimately will lead to the climax of the series. After the defeats that took place in the last part of the second act, Sasha now is ready to take control of the action and solve this problem once and for all.

Finale (305 min.–412 min.): The fourteenth beat of the narrative is the largest part of the third act and also incorporates the climax. In this beat, the audience witnesses the final part of the narrative, in which the resolution of the main conflict will occur and the dramatic question

The Netflix Vision of Horror

will ultimately be answered. In this series, we see that the person who is responsible for Becky's fate is Coach Jones (Michael Stahl-David), a school counselor and member of Annex. He is the one who took Becky to the ritual, while Annex is also involved in this situation. Even Becky's father knew about Becky's real fate, but he did not do or say anything. At the same time, while Sasha is battling to overcome Becky's influence on her mind and body, Yvonne and TJ are trying to save her while she is unconscious. Ultimately, Sasha is declared the undisputed winner of the narrative, since she prevails over Becky. This beat takes place in the last three episodes of the series and helps conclude the overarching story.

Final Image (412 min.): In the last scene of the narrative, Sasha is inside her house and people from Annex have gathered outside, holding candles and waiting for her. Sasha walks out of the house and a woman from the crowd approaches her. She tells her that since Becky is now out of the way, Sasha can finally fulfill the coming of Lilith. As Ariana Romero explains, this Final Image "confirms Becky wasn't exactly ruining Sasha's life at all. Instead, Becky was Sasha's final line of defense against Lilith, the ancient, dangerous supernatural being the Southwest Annex Foundation funneled into Becky's heart, which now lives inside of Sasha."[6] The ending of this scene finds Sasha refusing to follow the group and killing all of them with a single gaze. The final scene works as a proof of the big change that occurred in the main character during the progression of the narrative. At the first beat, we had a virgin girl, ready to have sex for the first time, but her body was so fragile that this led her to a heart transplant. At this final beat, we see a fearsome character who kills people with a glance. At the same time, this final image sets the tone for the next season, which, after Netflix's decision to cancel the series, never happened.

From the above analysis, we see that *Chambers* follows every beat of Snyder's approach regarding the three-act structure. The most notable thing, though, is that it does not fully obey the timeframe of this theory or therefore that of the general three-act structure. The series has three acts that use 32 percent, 42 percent, and 26 percent of the total narrative duration. It is clear that the second act is substantially shorter than in the standard approach, and most of the narrative time that was supposed to be part of this act goes to the beginning of the series. So, even though the series has a three-act structure, the division of the percentages of each act does not follow the norm of the classical narrative.

Regarding the plot functions, as the series is part of the discovery plot category, in this case study we have the onset, the discovery, and the confrontation functions. The onset takes place at the Catalyst beat, when the audience sees Becky through Sasha's mirror. The discovery function occurs at the Debate beat, when Sasha realizes that Becky is inside her, causing all these paranormal experiences. Finally, every part of the story in which Sasha tries to oppose Becky is part of the confrontation function. It is clear that there is no confirmation function, because from the moment Sasha understands that she is possessed by Becky, she starts to confront her, and she does not have to convince anyone else. In other words, the narrative goes from the discovery straight to the confrontation function without any more actions in between.

Chambers is an example of how a narrative can follow the three-act structure but at the same time adapt it to its unique needs. The acts do not have the duration they are supposed to have; however, the narrative functions as a classical model and incorporates all of the fifteen beats into its overarching story.

The Haunting of Hill House—*A Structural Analysis*

On October 12, 2018, a new original horror series appeared on Netflix. *The Haunting of Hill House* is an American supernatural horror series created and directed by Mike Flanagan, and loosely based on the 1959 homonymous novel written by Shirley Jackson. Since it was announced that the second season would have a completely different story and set of characters, this study will treat this audiovisual work as a mini-series. The story is about the members of the Crain family, who confront haunting memories of their old house and the terrifying events that led them abandon it. The plot alternates between two timelines, following the five adult Crain siblings—Steven (Michiel Huisman), Shirley (Elizabeth Reaser), Luke (Oliver Jackson-Cohen), Theodora (Kate Siegel), and Nell (Victoria Pedretti)—whose paranormal experiences at Hill House continue to haunt them in the present day, and flashbacks depicting events leading up to the eventful night in 1992 when the family escaped from the house. As Melanie Robson comments, "The hauntings experienced by the Crain children figure as a metaphor for their losses, anxieties, addictions, and instabilities that later plague them as adults."[7]

The first remark regarding the plot of the series is about the constructing of time. One of the main features of classical narrative, and consequently the three-act structure, is linear time.[8] From a first look at the story of *The Haunting of Hill House*, it seems that its structuring of time is based on non-linear techniques, but this is far from the truth. The narrative is structured in a linear manner with both past and present coexisting. In the last episode of the series, the ghost of Nell says to her four siblings: "I thought for so long that time was like a line, that our moments were laid out like dominoes, and that they fell, one into another and on it went, just days tipping, one into the next, into the next, in a long line between the beginning and the end. But I was wrong. It's not like that at all. Our moments fall around us like rain. Or ... snow. Or confetti."

This is exactly how the narrative of the series treats time. The past is synchronized with the present and both of them interact with each other. An example that strengthens this argument is the revelation that the bent-neck lady, the ghost that haunted Nell as a child, is basically her after her suicide, while the bent neck was how her ghost appeared after the violent hanging from the staircase. Another example of how the narrative is organized in a linear manner of events by embracing the coexistence of past and present is in the ninth episode, when Olivia (Carla Gugino), the mother of the family, sees the future of her twin children, Nell and Luke, in the form of a dream brought to her by the house in order to manipulate her. So, even if the story of the series is non-linear, the plot uses the elements of past and present in a linear manner, which allows the narrative to be considered as a three-act structure.

The Haunting of Hill House has ten episodes and a total duration of 555 minutes. From a first reading, the narrative of the series obeys most of the rules of the three-act structure. Despite its uniqueness in the way it handles and assembles time, the overarching story of *The Haunting of Hill House* can be divided into three acts.[9] Moreover, the series incorporates all of the fifteen beats of Snyder's approach, but with some minor adjustments regarding the timeframe. More specifically, the fifteen beats of *The Haunting of Hill House* are these:

Opening Image (1 min.): The opening scene of the series sets the tone of the narrative and introduces the main component of the series: the house itself and the main protagonists. The first image is of the Hill House itself in the night. There are some external shots of the house surrounded by fog, and then we see the inside of the mansion—empty corridors, imposing spaces, and some frames with pictures of the Crain family. The introduction of the house is full of mystery, which indicates that it is not just some ordinary set, but an integral component

3. The Narrative Structures of Triple and Double Function Plots

of the narrative. Then there is an introductory scene of the family, in which Nell is scared of the bent-neck lady and her father tries to calm her down. Hence, in the first image of the narrative, there is an establishment of the house, the main characters, and the initial impression of the audiovisual work. Finally, the horror element is present in the entire beat and gives the viewer a small sample of what will follow.

Theme Stated (30 min.): The theme of the narrative is about a dysfunctional family and how they manage to live in the shadow of a haunted house. The "heart" of the narrative is the interpersonal relationships between the five siblings, the father and their past, which is full of ghosts—literally and figuratively. After the first minutes of the narrative and the introduction to the main characters of the overarching story, the theme is clearly stated in a phone call between Nell and her father, in which she tells him that the bent-neck lady is back. As we saw in all of the previous case studies, the theme is usually stated in a dialogue scene, and this is the case for *The Haunting of Hill House*, since we have a dialogue scene over the phone. One of the main characters states to another that the paranormal activity has returned, and this action disturbs the core and the relationships of the family.

Setup (1 min.–56 min.): From the beginning of the series until the 56th minute of the entire narrative, we have the setup of the fictional world, in which the audience is introduced to the main characters and the location of the action—a key element for the tone and the premise of the narrative. Thus, the whole first episode except the last scene is working as the Setup beat of the overarching story and the whole narrative. There is an introduction to the Crain family, to the main antagonistic force, even to the Hill House itself. Due to how time is structured, the characters are introduced to the audience both in their present and in their past forms. Even with non-linear time, the narrative works as a unified structure with three acts, and the setup establishes even this trait of time.

Catalyst (58 min): After the narrative successfully introduces all the integral parts of the story, the main conflict has to be established. The last scene of the first episode is the Catalyst beat of the whole narrative. After seeing Luke in the front door of his building trying to steal his things, Steven returns to his apartment, only to find Nell inside. Even though she is not talking at all, Steven does not suspect anything and talks to her casually. After some moments, their father talks to Steven and tells him that Nell has committed suicide, meaning that the entity next to him is his sister's ghost. This event attracts the viewer's attention and creates the central dramatic question, which is whether the Crain family will manage to overcome the metaphysical powers of the Hill House. The main conflict is created based on the collision between the real world and the metaphysical world.

Debate (58 min.–209 min.): Following the events of the inciting incident, the main characters must have doubts before their journey becomes inevitable, and so the second, third, and fourth episodes of the series are dedicated to the fears of each of the main characters about engaging in this conflict that is before them. After focusing on Steven, the audience sees Shirley, Theodora and Luke living their lives in the present and with the ghosts of their past. Each of the siblings has negative thoughts about the Hill House, but not all of them accept the metaphysical aspects of their past. Their adult selves have transformed these paranormal experiences into bad memories of their childhood. These events and their denial are the closing part of the first act, and the narrative's progression will shift towards another direction. All of the four siblings are questioning the journey they are called upon to take, until the forthcoming first plot point.

Break Into Two (209 min.): As the first act closes, the second act begins with the first plot point of the overarching story, with which the narrative develops a number of complications in connection with the main conflict of the series. The sixth beat happens at the end of the fourth episode, in the scene where Luke meets Steven. There, Luke says that Nell's death was not a suicide. Since the inciting incident was the fact that Nell is dead, the first plot point changes the course of the narrative to a new direction and raises the dramatic question once more. Again, we see how the metaphysical world comes in contrast with reality and the everyday life of the main characters. Luke believes in this metaphysical world and in the connection of Nell's death with paranormal entities, while Steven is in denial and considers only the real world to be an aspect of their lives.

B Story (210 min.): As the narrative enters its the second act, the audience witnesses the beginning of a secondary story, which is in line with the narrative's theme, tone, and premise. So, at the beginning of the fifth episode, the audience is introduced to the multifaceted relationship of Nell with Hill House and its complicated existence in time and space. This subplot incorporates and highlights the fact that Nell was the bent-neck lady all along. The B Story starts at the beginning of the second act and goes beyond the fifth episode, while it covers almost the entire second act of the overarching story. Apart from that, this beat

3. The Narrative Structures of Triple and Double Function Plots

has another function, since it familiarizes the audience with the complicated use of time. This series is structured as a non-linear story, but the narrative uses conventions that indicate that past and present co-exist. The B Story of the narrative is the one that establishes this convention and gives the opportunity for the series to be considered a three-act structure.

Fun and Games (210 min.–277 min.): The fifth episode of the series functions as the eighth beat of the overarching story. As the narrative progresses towards its Midpoint, the difficulties are perceived as Fun and Games, while the main characters do not realize the importance and the seriousness of the situation. Thus, Nell's path to suicide is the part of the second act where stakes are not high, but the audience already knows most of the facts of this situation. Even if we already know that Nell will die, the narrative has not given us enough information in order to understand how difficult this situation is. Apart from that (and as already mentioned), the main characters do not fully understand how dangerous and powerful Hill House is in relation to their family and to themselves, since some of them do not believe in its metaphysical aspects.

Midpoint (277 min.): Exactly at the middle of the whole narrative, the stakes start to rise, and both the audience and the protagonists understand that the situation is far more difficult than perceived at the previous beat of the overarching story. The Midpoint beat of the narrative is when the audience learns that the ghost of the bent-neck lady was Nell all along. The fact that the ghost that was haunting Nell as a child was her adult version changes the fundamental facts of the story and complicates even more the progression of the narrative. This part of the narrative creates a tension that was never before seen in the narrative, while it establishes the significance and power of the metaphysical aspects of the Hill House. From this beat and on, nothing can be taken for granted by the audience, while the situation has risen to a whole new level of seriousness.

Bad Guys Close In (277 min.–380 min.): The next two episodes of the series constitute the tenth beat of the narrative. In this part of the overarching story, the main characters seem both internally and externally to be approaching dangerous territories. After the Midpoint beat, in which was established the supremacy of the Hill House, the antagonistic forces seem to gain ground and the protagonists look desperate and weak. More specifically, in this beat of the series we see the members of the Crain family gather for Nell's funeral. There are several conflicts and revelations about the past and the family's relationship with the house and its ghosts. After a long period of time, all the main characters of this family meet in the same place for an unpleasant situation, while their complicated relationships reveal a tension among them that gives the upper hand to their antagonistic forces.

All Is Lost (380 min.): At the end of the seventh episode, after the big pressure that occurred in the previous beats, the Crain family is separated when, after the funeral, Luke walks away without saying anything to anyone. After the big tension during the revelations and conflicts of the previous part, it seems like everything is lost for the members of the family. The family has already experienced the loss of one of its members, so the disappearance of Luke is more alarming than usual. Here, the Crain family has lost every hope, and something that looked manageable back in the beginning of the second act now seems impossible. The antagonistic forces and the Hill House, which serves as the Other of the narrative, appear to be the possible winners of the narrative. Of course, nothing is final yet, and the narrative has another act before it ends.

Dark Night of the Soul (380 min.–430 min.): At the twelfth beat of the narrative, the main characters have lost all hope and are almost ready to give up. This part of the narrative, which consists of the last segment of the seventh episode until the ending of the eighth episode, is the last portion of the second act, and it is logical that the complications will be at their highest level, since this is the true nature and purpose of this act. The Crain family has been divided into two groups: Steven and their father are driving around and looking for Luke, while Shirley and Theodora are left behind at the funeral home. The two groups of characters are fighting between them, and the hope for all of them has been lost. After a lot of obstacles, the Crain family seems more divided than ever, while there is no sign of Luke. Their victory over the antagonistic forces looks unachievable since they are not united.

Break Into Three (430 min.): These events lead to the beginning of the third act and the second plot point. At the end of the eighth episode, Luke is determined to confront Hill House and to put an end to all of this. The second plot point is when Luke goes to the house with five cans of gasoline and tries to burn the house down. The house resists and the ghosts overpower him. Luke's fate is in the hands of the Hill House, and the metaphysical world seems to have taken over the progression of the narrative. At this point, the main conflict is reestablished

3. The Narrative Structures of Triple and Double Function Plots

and reinforced, since the real world is in danger from the actions of the metaphysical world. Therefore, the central dramatic question once again comes to the fore, and the audience wonders about the fate of the Crain family.

Finale (430 min.–555 min.): Then, the fourteenth beat of the narrative takes place, which is the biggest part of the third act. Here, the main conflict has to be resolved and the dramatic question has to be answered, since the climax is at the end of this beat. The last two episodes of the series are dedicated to this objective. Luke is trapped and unconscious inside the house, while the rest of the family goes there to rescue him. This is the final clash of the narrative, since the Crain family goes back to Hill House to confront its past. After a multilayered confrontation of the Crain family with the Hill House, the real world manages to overcome the obstacles and prevail over the metaphysical entities of the house. During this effort, the father of the family sacrifices his life to save his kids, while this action makes Steven believe in the existence of this metaphysical world.

Final Image (555 min.): After the resolution of the main conflict and the answer to the central dramatic question, the only beat left is the Final Image of the audiovisual work. After seeing that each member of the Crane family that survived has finally found the peace that everyone was searching for, the last image of the narrative is the house itself. Hill House seems empty, deserted, and ruined. Then, its lights are turned off. The final beat is the exact opposite of the opening image and works as proof that change has taken place both to the characters and to the narrative itself. In the first image of the narrative we saw a powerful house, a scared family, and a metaphysical world that had the upper hand. In the closing scene, we witness the exact opposite, since the family is happy and has the upper hand, while the house is metaphorically and literally abandoned.

Even if the series has peculiarities regarding the structuring of time, it is clear that it follows every beat of the three-act structure and can be divided into three major acts with the characteristics that indicate the classical model of narration.

As was the case with *Chambers*, *The Haunting of Hill House* does not have a balanced distribution of the action into acts. We see that the first act is 37 percent, the second act is 40 percent, while the third and final act is 23 percent. In this case study too, the second act is substantially smaller and the first act enormously bigger than usual. As a matter of fact, these two acts are almost the same length, while the third act is the only one that has the expected percentage based on the classical model.

Regarding the plot of the series, since it is part of the discovery plot category, it has three out of the four functions. More specifically, the onset function takes place at the Opening Image beat, where the metaphysical aspects of the Hill House, which serves as the Other of the narrative, are established. The discovery function takes place at the Break Into Two beat, in which, after the main characters were denying the existence of metaphysical aspects of their story, a main character starts to believe again after seeing a ghost. Then starts the battle between the Crane family and the Hill House that will lead to the climax and the final confrontation of the narrative. It is clear that there is no confirmation function, since each of the main characters discovers the existence of the Other and then starts the confrontation.

The Haunting of Hill House is a pure horror narrative which shows that a series can have a unified narrative that follows the three-act structure norms, while it does not have to follow the convention regarding the distribution of the action into acts. Of course, as a discovery plot, this series follows the norms of its category and adapts the classical model of narration into its needs.

* * *

After analyzing the two case studies of the discovery plot category, we can make some useful observations. The plots of this category follow an outline in which first there is the establishing of the Other for the audience, then the main characters learn about the existence of the Other, and finally the main characters confront the Other. If we compare this with the pattern of the complex discovery plot that was analyzed in the second chapter, we will see that the step in which the main characters have to convince the rest of the protagonists is missing. All of the main characters learn about the existence of the Other and do not have to do anything but confront the Other directly, so this category misses one major plot function.

Furthermore, in both cases, there is a pattern in which the second act is significantly shorter than the usual, while there is a need for longer first acts. The only act that behaves as expected is the third and final act. Since Snyder's approach is more thorough and exposes the useful details of each structure, it will be more fruitful to study the percentages of each beat. Therefore, here is a concrete table with the percentages of each beat:

3. The Narrative Structures of Triple and Double Function Plots

Table 8. 15-Beat Sheet

Beats	Snyder's Approach	*Chambers*	*The Haunting of Hill House*
Opening Image	1%	1%	1%
Theme Stated	5%	6%	5%
Setup	<9%	<10%	<10%
Catalyst	11%	11%	11%
Debate	11%–25%	11%–32%	11%–37%
Break Into Two	25%	32%	37%
B Story	27%	35%	38%
Fun and Games	27%–50%	35%–52%	38%–50%
Midpoint	50%	52%	50%
Bad Guys Close In	50%–68%	52%–64%	50%–68%
All Is Lost	68%	64%	68%
Dark Night of the Soul	68%–75%	64%–74%	68%–77%
Break Into Three	75%	74%	77%
Finale	75%–100%	75%–100%	77%–100%
Final Image	100%	100%	100%

With this detailed, beat-by-beat percentage breakdown, it is obvious that the durations of each portion are similar in the two series. Until the Catalyst beat, both narratives follow a similar path to the original Snyder's approach, while from the Midpoint beat till the Final Image, again the series respect the norms of the detailed three-structure model of narration. The substantial difference starts to occur at the Debate beat, which in both series is considerably longer than expected. This is because the first plot point is slow to appear, and even if the Debate starts at the

The Netflix Vision of Horror

right time, it ends later than anticipated. Then, until the Midpoint, every beat is late and therefore is not in the portion of the narrative where Snyder places it in his timeframe. The narrative goes back into the right track at the Fun and Games beat, which is noticeably shorter. Hence, even though this beat starts later, it has a shorter duration and ends early, something that gives the Midpoint beat the right place in the overarching story, which is the middle of the whole narrative.

Apart from the relationship between the percentages of the Snyder's approach and the distribution of the action into beats in the two case studies, another important comparison is between the categories of complex discovery plot and the discovery plot. In the first category, which has similar beat sizes to the general model of classical narration, there are all of the four plot functions, while the discovery plot misses one function, which consequently disturbs the balance of the acts. In the next table, there is a detailed comparison of the average percentages between the two plot categories:

Table 9. Plot Categories Comparison

	Complex Discovery Plot	Discovery Plot
Opening Image	1%	1%
Theme Stated	6%	6%
Setup	<11%	<10%
Catalyst	12%	11%
Debate	12%–24%	11%–34%
Break Into Two	24%	34%
B Story	27%	37%
Fun and Games	27%–50%	37%–51%
Midpoint	50%	51%
Bad Guys Close In	50%–66%	51%–66%
All Is Lost	66%	66%
Dark Night of the Soul	66%–75%	66%–75%
Break Into Three	75%	75%
Finale	75%–100%	75%–100%
Final Image	100%	100%

3. The Narrative Structures of Triple and Double Function Plots

These data come as a continuation of the previous table. The initial parts of the first acts almost match, while the second halves of the narratives are identical. The two beats that disturb the balance of the acts are the Debate, which in the discovery plot is 11 percent longer than usual, and the Fun and Games beat, which is 9 percent smaller than in the complex discovery plot. In brief, based on the data from the two case studies of this analysis and the eight series of the second chapter, the discovery plot differentiates itself in the second part of the first act (after the inciting incident) and in the first half of the second act (until the midpoint).

In order to see why this is happening, we have to see the plot categories and the functions that are incorporated into theses series' plots. In the second chapter, it was established that each of the four functions are linked with specific parts of the narrative. The onset function is at the beginning of the first act, the discovery function can be placed either at the end of the first act or in the beginning of the second act, the confirmation function is part of the second act, and the confrontation function is mainly placed in the third act. Since the complex discovery plot incorporates all of the four functions into its narratives, there is a balanced distribution of the action, and the acts have similar percentages to the generalized classical model of narration. This is not the case with the discovery plot. In the following table are the placements of each essential plot function in these series:

Table 10. Placement of Plot Functions for *Chambers* and *The Haunting of Hill House*

Plot Functions	*Chambers*	*The Haunting of Hill House*
Onset	Catalyst	Opening Image
Discovery	Debate	Break Into Two
Confirmation	—	—
Confrontation	Finale	Finale

In both case studies of this plot category, we do not have all of the four functions, since the confirmation function is absent. The onset function is again placed at the beginning of the first act, the discovery function is around the first plot point, just like in the complex discovery plot, and the confrontation takes place and concludes at the Finale beat of the third act. The three functions follow the same outline as in the complex discovery plot, so the nonexistence of the confirmation function is the essential reason the narratives of the discovery plot do not have a balanced percentage distribution.

While the discovery plot has the onset and the discovery functions, it is absolutely normal that the first act stays almost intact, because these functions are highly connected with the beginning of a narrative. Following the same pattern, the third act is identical to the complex discovery plot regarding the existence of the confrontation function. The big difference in this plot category is the substantially shorter second act, and this is because of the lack of the confirmation function. Confirmation is strictly connected with the second act, so its nonappearance gives more space to the other functions to be developed. Since the absence of confirmation allows a big part of the action to be incorporated into the discovery function, it is logical that this missing percentage of the second act goes to the ending of the first act, in which this function occurs.

In conclusion, the discovery plot follows the same narrative structure norms as the complex discovery plot, but it adapts it to its own needs and based on the plot functions its narratives possess. More specifically, it abandons the 25 percent–50 percent–25 percent distribution rule regarding the acts and follows the percentage distribution of 34 percent–41 percent–25 percent, more convenient for this category. As is the case with the rest of the series that are part of the corpus under analysis, this category is considered a three-act structure that is based on a unified narrative and not on episodic storytelling, but it alters the classical model of narration and creates some new conventions that are more suitable to its plots.

The Narrative Structure of the Discovery/ Confirmation/Confrontation Plot

Another plot category that can be found in the corpus of this study is the discovery/confirmation/confrontation plot. The name of this category is self-explanatory, since these narratives incorporate three functions in their plots: the discovery, the confirmation, and the confrontation functions. As Carroll observes, this sort of plot might occur

3. The Narrative Structures of Triple and Double Function Plots

where there is no available evidence of the onset of the Other until the moment of discovery.[10] In other words, when the audience learns about the existence of the Other at the same time as some of the main characters of the narrative do, then this audiovisual work is part of the discovery/confirmation/confrontation plot.

These narratives are structured so that the main characters learn about the danger that is before them, they convince the rest of the protagonists about the existence of the Other, and then all together confront the antagonistic force that puts them and the community in great danger. The foremost difference between the discovery/confirmation/confrontation plot and the complex discovery plot is that in the first category there is no need for establishing the Other for the audience, since this happens at the discovery function.

As was also the case with the discovery plot, this divergence in the plot functions of the discovery/confirmation/confrontation plot alters the structuring methods of the narratives in a manner that disturbs the distribution of the action into acts. In the complex discovery plot we have a balanced distribution of the acts that is similar to the classical model of narration, in the discovery plot we have a considerably shorter second act that gives more space to the introduction of the narrative, while in this category we will see that we have the exact opposite. Of course, in order to see how this category works regarding its structuring methods, we first have to thoroughly analyze the two case studies that are part of the discovery/confirmation/confrontation plot.

Santa Clarita Diet—*A Structural Analysis*

Santa Clarita Diet is an American horror-comedy series created by Victor Fresco. The first season premiered on February 3, 2017, while on March 29, 2017, it was announced that Netflix had renewed the series for a second season, which premiered on March 23, 2018.[11] The series was renewed for a third season, which premiered on March 29, 2019, but the show was cancelled on April 26, 2019.[12]

The story of the series is centered on Sheila Hammond (Drew Barrymore) and her husband, Joel (Timothy Olyphant), a couple of everyday suburban real estate agents in Santa Clarita, California, who face a series of obstacles when Sheila becomes undead and starts craving human flesh. As Joel tries to help Sheila through her transformation, they have to deal with neighbors, cultural norms, and a potentially

The Netflix Vision of Horror

mythological mystery. *Santa Clarita Diet* is an unconventional series, since it is structured as a comedy narrative that has a horror element at its core. Fresco, the creator of the show, stated that he came up with the premise of the series because he wanted to make "a family show with an interesting approach that we haven't seen before," and at the same time he desired to explore the concept of narcissism, so this is why he put the horror element at the heart of the narrative. Fresco specified, "The undead are the ultimate narcissists. They want what they want when they want it and will do anything to just have what they want and don't care about other people's needs."[13]

The series has ten episodes and a total duration of 262 minutes. It is a part of the Horror of Armageddon category, making it one of only three series in the corpus that follow this type of horror. Even if the series does not have a balanced distribution of action into acts according to the standardized classical model of narration, nevertheless it is a fine example of a three-act structure that follows each of the fifteen beats of Snyder's approach. More specifically, the beats are the following:

Opening Image (1 min.): The series opens with a middle-class couple walking up in bed. They are a typical husband and wife with a teenage daughter, or in other words, a happy family living in the suburbs. With the opening image we have the establishing of the main characters, the location that will take place the story, and the tone of the narrative. This audiovisual work is a unique case in the corpus, since its hybrid narrative moves between comedy and horror. Even though the series qualifies for being a part of the corpus of this study, nevertheless it has a plethora of comedic elements, and the opening sequence sets the tone of this peculiarity. Regarding the location of the series that is established in the very first image of the narrative, Fresco chose Santa Clarita because of its middle-class residents, since this was something that he wanted to be at the heart of the narrative, while the Hammonds' profession as realtors was chosen because "it gets them out into the world" and because of the "forced friendliness" inherent to the profession.[14]

Theme Stated (14 min.): At the fourteenth minute of the narrative, the series introduces its main theme to the audience. In this scene, Sheila's heart stops beating, a very strange turn of events. She cuts her hand, but no blood comes out of the wound. Sheila starts acting weird, while Joel and their daughter, Abby (Liv Hewson), pass out from the sight of these strange actions. Apart from the first shock, the family stays together, strong and united against this abnormal situation. This is the heart of the series, a united family against a strange threat that

3. The Narrative Structures of Triple and Double Function Plots

could break them apart. The narrative shows, however, that the love of the family prevails, and all together face this bizarre adjustment that will change their lives forever. Even if the mother transforms into a zombie that wants to eat human flesh, the love of the family makes them stay together.

Setup (1 min.–25 min.): The first twenty-five minutes of the whole narrative, or in other words the first episode of the series, is dedicated to the Setup beat, which is meant to introduce the audience to the fictional world of the overarching story. In this part of the narrative, we see the main characters and all the aspects of their lives. The center of the narrative is a distinctive family in a typical suburban area of California. Then, the main premise of the series is established, since Sheila is suddenly transformed into an undead person. Her vital functions abruptly stop, and this new condition gives her the desire to eat raw meat. The family learns the new facts, and they try to overcome this new situation by staying united. According to the action that takes place in this beat, the audience has all the necessary information that is needed in order to have a global view of this fictional world, the theme of the narrative, and the tone of the overarching story.

Catalyst (27 min.): After the fictional world has been established, the narrative is ready to introduce to the audience the story's main conflict. So, at the fourth beat, the inciting incident of the overarching story occurs. At this point of the narrative, Sheila for the first time eats human meat when she eats her coworker Gary (Nathan Fillion) alive. In the Setup beat, the narrative was building the routine of this fictional world. Even if Sheila had turned into a zombie, this was part of the routine, since her deeds did not change her status in the community. In the Catalyst beat and with the inciting incident that takes place there, the narrative introduces the main conflict of the series and therefore the central dramatic question. Sheila starts killing and eating humans, so the main question is how she and her family will manage to cope with this new turn of events.

Debate (27 min.–54 min.): The second episode is dedicated to the main characters' refusal to accept the new facts and commit to the journey that is before them. In the Debate beat, none of the main characters want to engage with the main conflict, and they try to disconnect with the events of the story. In *Santa Clarita Diet*, the married couple is in denial about the cannibalistic nature of the undead Sheila, and they believe that they could find another viable solution. They try raw animal meat, live animals, and even dead human bodies from the morgue, but nothing works for Sheila, who covets fresh human meat. The last part of the first act is a desperate move of the main characters, who try to escape from the journey of the narrative. Of course, they are bound to follow their inner calling, so Sheila will eventually understand that this is her new nature, which she cannot avoid.

Break Into Two (54 min.): At the end of the second episode we have the first plot point, in which the narrative enters its second act. After many unsuccessful attempts to deny Sheila's new nature, Joel promises his wife that he will stand beside her and help her be her true self. Since there is no alternative and it is not done otherwise, Joel says that he will help her to kill people and have something to eat. Their daughter enters the room, and even though they do not tell her anything about this decision, they all lie on the bed, united against the conflict of the narrative. Since this action is part of a plot point, it reestablishes the main conflict and reasserts the dramatic question. With these events, the audience wonders again about the fate of the family that is in danger because of Sheila's new undead nature.

B Story (59 min.): After the beginning of the second act, the narrative introduces a secondary storyline that is in accordance with the overarching story, the theme, and the tone of the series. In this case study, the B Story is centered on the family's neighbor, Dan Palmer (Ricardo Chavira), a sheriff's deputy and the stepfather of Eric (Skyler Gisondo). Dan starts to suspect that something is not right about Sheila and Joel and, after several ineffective attempts and some coverups by the couple, he partially finds out the truth. This secondary storyline starts at the fifty-ninth minute of the whole narrative, when Dan asks the couple about the previous day when they were cleaning up their garden after Gary's murder. Of course, they lie to him and tell that they were doing disinfestation. The B Story is closely connected with the main storyline and has the same narrative tone that combines comedy and horror elements.

Fun and Games (59 min.–130 min.): After the commitment of the main characters to their journey, which occurred at the first plot point, the beginning of the second act finds them dedicated to their cause, but with a number of minor obstacles and problems. In the Fun and Games beat, we witness the start of Sheila's cannibalism, but before the stakes get higher. The couple searches for someone to kill in order for Sheila to have food, and they decide to kill someone who causes bad consequences for society. Accordingly, they agree to try to kill a drug dealer, but they fail. On their way back home, they fight with someone on the

3. The Narrative Structures of Triple and Double Function Plots

street, and Sheila kills him and eats his flesh. Sheila's uncanny reactions continue, while Dan discovers Gary's finger on the couple's lawn, a lead that makes him realize Gary's death. Dan starts to blackmail Joel and wants him to kill Loki (DeObia Oparei), a convicted felon. The couple agrees to kill him in order for Sheila to eat him, but they fail. This part of the narrative takes place during the third, fourth, and fifth episodes of the series.

Midpoint (130 min.): At the end of the fifth episode and the middle of the whole narrative, the midpoint occurs. After the establishment of the second act with the Fun and Games beat, the narrative changes course and raises the degree of danger to the maximum level. When the couple attacked Loki at his own house, in her effort to kill him, Sheila bit him. At the midpoint, we see that after this attack, Loki too has transformed into a zombie. This action has a dual functionality that interferes with the progression and the course of the narrative: first, it creates an antagonistic force that is as powerful as the undead protagonist of the narrative, while second, it complicates things because Sheila can transmit the undead nature to others. Based on these two functions of this scene, the stakes now are higher than before, and the characters start to face more difficult and complicated obstacles.

Bad Guys Close In (130 min.–156 min.): The rest of the second act creates a more serious sense regarding the position of the main characters in the narrative. Even the characters themselves realize that the stakes are high now, since they understand that someone they attacked has seen their faces. Moreover, they lost an advertising pen engraved with their real names at Loki's house, where the attack took place. At the same time, Dan threatens Joel regarding Gary's murder, and he tries to force him to kill another person (apart from Loki, whom Dan thinks is dead). The couple is facing two major problems: on one hand, they must close Loki's case and take back the pen before someone finds out about them, while on the other hand they have to kill another person in order to satisfy Dan's commands. The antagonistic forces seem to gain ground and the pressure on the main characters is growing.

All Is Lost (156 min.): The antagonistic forces seem to be closer to the characters, and the pressure is high. The couple did not manage to kill the person Dan commanded, since they discovered he was having an affair with Lisa (Mary Elizabeth Ellis), Dan's wife, and was not a criminal as they were told by Dan. This creates tension with Dan, who continues to blackmail Joel. At the end of the sixth episode, the narrative establishes the All Is Lost beat, in which every possible hope for the main characters has vanished. More specifically, in this beat, after a conversation that included threats, Joel kills Dan by hitting him with a shovel. This has a huge impact on the characters, since it is the first killing of a person so close to their everyday lives, and also it is vital for the course of the narrative that Dan was a sheriff's deputy, a fact that complicates the situation even more.

Dark Night of the Soul (156 min.–183 min.): The seventh episode is dedicated to the conclusion of the second act and to the twelfth beat of the narrative. At this part of the overarching story, the characters are at their lowest point, with no hope and being fully pressured by the antagonistic forces. Something that looked manageable at the first plot point now seems extremely complicated and not achievable. After the disappearance of Dan, the whole police department is at his house, searching for him. The main characters have Dan's body at their house, while they are surrounded by the police. Sheila and Joel try to find a way to move the body away from their house, but it is impossible. The next morning, the police will bring trained dogs to the area, a fact that further complicates the condition of the main characters.

Break Into Three (183 min.): At the end of the seventh episode, the narrative enters the third act, since the second plot point occurs. After the complications of the second act, now it is time for the narrative to resolve the main conflict. The course of the narrative changes once again with the second plot point, which brings to the fore the dramatic question regarding the fate of this family. At this beat and after the family manages to get rid of Dan's dead body, Sheila is taking a bath and sees her little toe fall off her body. This means that her body is decaying, since she is considered a living dead. This brings another major problem to the family, because their plan to kill and feed Sheila has an expiration date. This condition cannot last permanently, and the main characters are forced to find another solution to the problem of the narrative.

Finale (183 min.–262 min.): The fourteenth beat is the longest of the third act and incorporates the climax of the narrative, meaning that in this part of the overarching story the main conflict will be resolved and the dramatic question will be answered. The next three and final episodes of the series are dedicated to this objective. In this beat, the storyline of Loki is solved, since the main characters connect with him and eventually destroy him, while at the same time the couple tries to find a solution that will reverse the undead nature of Sheila, because decay is rapidly spreading through her body. Eventually, they communicate with Dr. Wolf (Portia de Rossi), a scientist focused on the undead,

3. The Narrative Structures of Triple and Double Function Plots

who promises to help them find the cure. Wolf tells Sheila that as her condition progresses, she will become uncontrollably violent and could harm her family and others. Sheila gets Abby to chain her up in the basement to prevent her from harming anyone, while at the same time Joel is arrested and committed to a mental institution. The family did not manage to stay together, and the conflict broke them apart.

Final Image (262 min.): The last beat of the narrative shows the great impact the conflict had on the main characters, who underwent radical transformations—internally and externally. In the last image of the series, the audience sees the once happy family finally being broken apart. Joel is seeing a psychiatrist, because no one believed him about Sheila's condition; Sheila is chained in her own basement, since she is afraid she might do something bad to her family; while Abby with her friend Eric is at the family's house, trying desperately to find the cure that will solve the main problem of the overarching story. In conjunction with the Opening Image, in which we witnessed a happy and united family, the Final Image shows us how the course of action has drastically altered the main characters. Moreover, the Final Image of the narrative sets the tone for the actions that will be developed in the second season, as the main problem has not completely resolved.

After this beat-by-beat analysis of the narrative of *Santa Clarita Diet*, it is clear that we are talking once again about a detailed three-act structure that obeys the norms of classical narration as a whole. However, the series does not have a balanced distribution of the action among its acts, and we can observe an anomaly in the percentages. The first act is 20 percent, the second act is 50 percent, and the third act is 30 percent. It is clear that the first act is substantially smaller than usual and gives more space to the third act for further development, while the second act is faithful to the general model.

Apart from the percentages of each act, in this analysis we must observe the utility and placement of each of the plot functions that the series incorporates in its narrative. As the series is part of the discovery/confirmation/confrontation plot category, we can spot in the overarching story these three specific functions. The discovery function is at the Setup beat, when the three members of the family come to understand the situation around Sheila and her new undead nature. The confirmation function takes place at the Fun and Games beat, when there is hard proof that Sheila is now a zombie who wants to eat only human meat. Finally, the confrontation function is fully developed at the Finale beat, in which the family tries to find the cure in order to reverse Sheila's undead status and her rapidly developing decay. Since the Other of the narrative is the protagonist herself, there is no need for the onset function, since the audience learns about the undead nature of Sheila at the same time that she discovers it. At this point, it is worth mentioning the fact that horror has a long tradition of connecting the female protagonist with the existence of the Other. Linda Williams states in her analysis of the female gaze that the woman "not only sees a monster, she sees a monster that offers a distorted reflection of her own image."[15]

Even if *Santa Clarita Diet* is mostly based on hybrid conventions that integrate horror and comedy elements, it still qualifies as a horror narrative and has all the essential characteristics that were thoroughly analyzed in the first chapter. The series is a fine example of a discovery/confirmation/confrontation plot that follows the three-act structure and adapts it into its own needs.

The Order—*A Structural Analysis*

The Order is an American fantasy horror series created by Dennis Heaton. It premiered on Netflix on March 7, 2019, and after its premiere the series was renewed for a 10-episode second season that will be released in 2020.[16] The series follows a college student, Jack Morton (Jake Manley), as he joins the Hermetic Order of the Blue Rose, a secret society that teaches and practices magic. While Jack goes deeper into the organization's hierarchy and learns about its movements, he uncovers dark secrets and an underground battle between werewolves and the practitioners of magic.

This series, too, sets the hybrid notion at the core of its narrative, since it blends several genre norms.[17] As in the case of *Santa Clarita Diet*, this show sets a different tone than a pure horror narrative does, since it includes fantasy and teen drama conventions. Michael Ahr describes it as a college-campus drama,[18] and Samantha Nelson observes that it is a horror series with pretty straightforward supernatural drama and a touch of dark humor.[19] Nevertheless, the series is an audiovisual horror work with hybrid elements and meets all of the criteria that were used for the creation of the corpus under analysis.

The Order has ten episodes and a total duration of 445 minutes. The overarching story of this case study follows the three-act structure and adapts it into its own needs. Nevertheless, the whole narrative

3. The Narrative Structures of Triple and Double Function Plots

incorporates all of the fifteen beats of Snyder's approach with all their vital functions. The fifteen beats of the narrative are the following:

Opening Image (1 min.): The series open with a scene of Jack, the main character of the narrative, who is at his mother's grave. He opens a letter from Belgrave University, the institution he needs to go to because he wants to be a member of the Order. The letter says that he has been rejected. At the same time, two women argue about Jack's acceptance or rejection. These women are high members of the Order; one of them is Vera Stone (Katharine Isabelle), the chancellor of the university and a temple magus of the Hermetic Order of the Blue Rose. While the letter stated that Jack was rejected, Vera uses magic and changes it into an acceptance letter. In this very first image of the narrative, we see the main character while we learn about his primary goal. Based on that, the audience is introduced to the basic premise of the narrative, as the tone of the series is established.

Theme Stated (19 min.): At the nineteenth minute of the overarching story, the narrative introduces the main theme of the series. As is common, the series presents its theme through a dialogue scene that takes place between two main characters. Jack is getting acquainted with Randall Carpio (Adam DiMarco), one of the resident advisors at Belgrave University and later to be revealed as a member of the Knights of Saint Christopher. Jack is trying to convey information about the Order, but Randall says that they want followers without will. This statement encompasses the subtext of the narrative, since the overarching story will be about Jack's struggle to penetrate the mystical hierarchy of the manipulative Order, and at the same time to be a secret member of the Knights of Saint Christopher and, therefore, a werewolf.

Setup (1 min.–42 min.): The majority of the first episode is dedicated to the Setup beat and the introduction to the fictional world of the series. The narrative establishes the main characters, the basic objective of the protagonist, the magical world of the Order, and the antagonistic forces that may step into its path. The audience sees Jack's acceptance to Belgrave University and his desperate moves to find a connection with the Order. The Hermetic Order of the Blue Rose is a secretive club, and potential members are selected by its leaders, a fact that makes Jack's situation even more difficult. Eventually, the Order gets in touch with Jack and other potential members, who then start different types of tests that will determine the selection outcome. Therefore, Jack starts these assessments by the members of the Order, determined that he will succeed.

The Netflix Vision of Horror

Catalyst (48 min.): At the end of the first episode, the narrative establishes the inciting incident of the overarching story. At this part of the narrative, while he tries to succeed in his assessments by the Order, Jack is at his mother's grave, digging it. Then, Kyle (Jedidiah Goodacre), a member of the Order who tries to create obstacles for Jack and leave him out of the selection process, goes there and videorecords Jack's action with his phone. Kyle sets up a trap to Jack to make him resign from the selection process. While the two boys are fighting, a werewolf emerges from the woods, attacks Jack and then disappears. With this action, the main conflict of the narrative develops, since the overarching story concerns the battle between magicians and werewolves, or in other words the fight between the Hermetic Order of the Blue Rose and the Knights of Saint Christopher. Even the protagonist of the narrative, Jack, will ultimately face this dilemma and will have to choose between those two groups. Based on this major conflict, the dramatic question of who will eventually win this war arises in the minds of the viewers.

Debate (48 min.–96 min.): After the inciting incident that occurs in the Catalyst beat, the next part of the narrative that takes place in the second episode is dedicated to Jack's course until he engages in the main conflict. The last part of the first act finds the main character in denial about the situation that has developed, and negative about engaging in the journey the narrative has brought in front of him. The Order tries to dismiss Jack, while at the same time Amir (Ajay Friese), one of the neophytes of the Order who was taking part in the selection process, dies. Jack tries to help and solve the mystery behind Amir's death, eventually finding the responsible golem in the face of his roommate Clayton "Clay" Turner (Dylan Playfair). With this new information, the Order takes Jack back, and everything is heading back on a normal track, but then, Jack is again attacked by a werewolf in the woods. In this course of events, we see that Jack denies the existence of other forces and tries to stay committed to his main objective.

Break Into Two (96 min.): The narrative enters its second act and the character now faces new events, after which there is no return to the previous carefree condition for him. The first plot point of the whole narrative is at the ninety-sixth minute when, after the werewolf attack, Jack finds refuge at a remote house into the woods in which he discovers a hide that possesses him. Jack wakes up in this house and finds Randall there with other two persons, Lilith (Devery Jacobs) and Hamish (Thomas Elms), who are all members of the Knights of Saint Christopher. All of the members of the Knights have existed for many years;

3. The Narrative Structures of Triple and Double Function Plots

they are chosen by one of the six hides to become werewolves and fight against evil magic. The first plot point finds Jack to be a member of both groups that are in a war, a fact that radically changes his plans. Jack refuses to be part of the Knights, but he is already a werewolf. This plot point restores the main conflict between these two groups and restores the dramatic question of the narrative.

B Story (117 min.): At the beginning of the second act, the narrative introduces the B Story, which is in accordance with the tone of the series, the theme of the narrative, and the main storyline of the overarching story. In this series, the secondary storyline concerns the interaction of Jack with Gabrielle Dupres (Louriza Tronco), an acolyte in the Hermetic Order of the Blue Rose, who start to make spells and practice magic for their own interest. Jack will ultimately discover that every spell has a price and that the practice of magic for one's own purposes has consequences. Since the protagonist of the series is the center of the B Story, it is clear that this secondary storyline is tangled with the main overarching story and that both interact in many aspects and layers. Nevertheless, it constitutes a separate storyline that boosts the actions of the second act and helps the structuring of the whole narrative from this point and on.

Fun and Games (117 min.–222 min.): After the entrance into the second act and the establishment of the secondary storyline, the narrative dedicates the third and the fourth episodes to the Fun and Games beat. At this part of the narrative, the audience sees Jack's actions as a member of both the Order and the Knights of Saint Christopher, while everything is under control. Since these two groups are in a war, Jack has not revealed the truth to any of the members of the Order, and this helps him to face the situation with no major problems and obstacles. At the same time, Alyssa (Sarah Grey), a college student and a Meddicum of the Hermetic Order of the Blue Rose, becomes one of four magical students under special assignment from Edward (Max Martini), Jack's estranged father and the grand magus of the Order, to unlock an ancient obsidian block that magically protects a hidden prize inside. It is clear that the beginning of the second act to a small degree complicates the obstacles around the main characters, but at the same time the stakes are not high enough.

Midpoint (222 min.): At the middle of the whole narrative, the Midpoint beat takes place, and its events help increase the risks and dangers for the main characters. While Jack gets even more committed to the actions of the Knights, he goes with Alyssa in a mission for the Order. More specifically, Renee Marand (Jewel Staite), a necromancer and former member of the Order, makes a proposal to help Edward's search for more missing pages to the Vade Maecum Infernal, in return for a lifesaving favor. The Knights prevent the five human sacrifices that will conclude the favor of removing Renee's terminal illness. While Jack and Alyssa are sleeping together in a hotel room, the illness returns and kills Renee. At this point, Jack's dual memberships in both the Order and the Knights are in great conflict, since he is technically responsible for this outcome. Therefore, the actions at this beat complicate Jack's condition even more and raise the stakes to a higher level.

Bad Guys Close In (222 min.–265 min.): The circumstances having become extremely unsafe for the main characters during the Midpoint, the second act dedicates the tenth beat to actions that will give precedence to the antagonistic forces and make the protagonists seem powerless. The Bad Guys Close In beat is committed to this objective, and the main characters feel the possibility of losing the battle. Renee's unnamed sister tries to avenge Renee's death by chasing Jack and Alyssa in order to take back her sister's "necrophone." During the course of these events, Alysa learns the true nature of Jack and the fact that he is a werewolf and a member of the Knights of Saint Christopher. Alyssa gets injured, while Jack manages to take back the necrophone from Renee's sister. It is clear that the midpoint changes the progression of the narrative in a manner that brings the main characters, and more specifically Jack, the protagonist of the series, into a more complicated and difficult situation.

All Is Lost (265 min.): At the eleventh beat of the narrative, which takes place at the end of the sixth episode, everything seems lost for the main character. Jack takes the unconscious Alyssa to his grandfather's house. Jack talks with his grandfather, Pete (Matt Frewer), who seems obsessed with taking down Edward Coventry, because he believes he is the reason his daughter (and Jack's mother) died. They connect the necrophone in order to talk to Jack's mother, who tell them that she wants to be with Edward and she is in love with him. This makes Pete so angry that he slams the necrophone and destroys it. In the meantime, Alyssa became conscious again and saw the entire incident, something that led her to leave. Jack has lost everything—from Alyssa, who now knows the truth, to his previously clear objective to take revenge on Edward. The protagonist of the narrative is at his lowest point ever and nothing seems to be hopeful anymore.

Dark Night of the Soul (265 min.–320 min.): The rest of the

3. The Narrative Structures of Triple and Double Function Plots

second act is dedicated to the twelfth beat of the narrative, in which the main characters have given up, since there is no hope anymore. Something that seemed achievable at the beginning of this act now seems impossible. In the Order, Vera tasks Gabrielle with finding out any truths about werewolves on campus, a power and authority that quickly Gabrielle abuses, as she follows Vera's strong suggestion to use a magical glove that detects and punishes lies. At the same time, Alyssa is afraid for Jack's fate, so she does not reveal his secret to anyone. Gabrielle interrogates all the members of the Order who might know something, but Alyssa tries to hide what she knows. Finally, Randall is captured by some scientists who want to experiment on him and create werewolves. Everything seems lost for the main characters, and the war between these two groups is in its most tense phase.

Break Into Three (320 min.): The overarching narrative enters in its third act by establishing the second plot point at the beginning of the eighth episode of the series. While their relationship is still complicated after his secret is revealed, Jack takes Alyssa to the house of the Knights of Saint Christopher in order to assist them locate and help Randall. At the beginning, the other two werewolves are hesitant, but since their friend is in danger, they accept Alyssa's aid. Alyssa makes a spell in order to find Randall's exact location, and all together go to this building to help him. While the war between the Order and the Knights is tense and at its highest, Jack and Alyssa are in contact again, with the latter helping the werewolves save a member of their group. This action brings the main conflict to the fore and reestablishes the central dramatic question of the narrative regarding the clash between these two groups.

Finale (320 min.–445 min.): The eighth, ninth, and tenth episodes are part of the Finale beat, the biggest portion of the third act. Alyssa's help in finding Randall, who was trapped in an unethical witch experiment, is successful. Jack and Alyssa face the question of their mutual attraction for each other versus allegiances to dangerously opposing organizations. The book that Edward wants desperately, Vade Maecum Infernal, delivers a fatal paper cut that separates Silverback (the werewolf that chose Jack) from Jack, who now has an afterlife experience. As Pete heads out for revenge over Jack's death, Edward kills him. Jack gets back on his feet, but after the news about his grandfather, he wants to take revenge. Alyssa brings Vera to the Knights in order to help, and eventually the werewolves win the war against the Order. The climax occurs, the main conflict is now resolved, and therefore the dramatic question is finally answered.

The Netflix Vision of Horror

Final Image (445 min.): The final scene of the narrative is indicative of the change that has taken place—both internally and externally—for the main characters. Jack is at his mother's grave, just like in the Opening Image, but now next to it is his grandfather's grave. Jack recounts the events that have occurred, and afterwards Alyssa approaches him. They talk and kiss and then Alyssa uses a magical powder to erase Jack's memory. Vera and other members of the Order use this powder on the other werewolves too, and they take every valuable artifact from their house. Jack wakes up in the cemetery, and he does not remember anything, not Alyssa or even his own name. In the first scene of the narrative we had the protagonist of the series establishing his main objective and the premise of the narrative. In the last sequence, we see the protagonist after the long journey of the narrative, while the last beat leaves an open window for the second season (which will probably be another three-act narrative).

The Order is an example of a three-act structure that obeys the fifteen beats of Snyder's approach and simultaneously adapts them to its own needs. From the above analysis, we can clearly see that the first act is 22 percent, the second act is 50 percent, and the third and final act is 28 percent. Again, this series seems to have a shorter first act and a longer third act, while the second act keeps the standard duration according to the classical model of narration and constitutes half of the entire narrative.

Apart from the structuring of the narrative, the plot of the series follows the norms of its plot category and incorporates three main functions. The Other of the narrative that works as an antagonistic force is Edward, his father, who is also responsible for his mother's death. There is no need for an onset function, since the audience already knows this information. The other three functions are chronologically placed in the narrative and create all the necessary norms of the discovery/confirmation/confrontation plot. The discovery function is at the Fun and Games beat, when Jack sees Edward and realizes he is the grand magus of the Order. The confirmation function is at the Dark Night of the Soul beat, when Alyssa is convinced that the Order, and therefore Edward, has impure intentions and tries to protect Jack. The confrontation function mostly takes place at the Finale beat, in which the main characters confront and defeat the Other.

From this case study, we can clearly see the interconnection of the narrative structure and the plot functions of a long-form audiovisual work. *The Order* follows the classical model of narration but adjusts the

3. The Narrative Structures of Triple and Double Function Plots

distribution of the action into acts based on the plot functions it uses. Therefore, this series is a fine example of the discovery/confirmation/confrontation plot category and also validates the main argument of the present study that the audiovisual works of the corpus work like unified narratives, not relying on episodic storytelling but reminiscent of filmic narratives.

***

As was the case with the discovery plot, from the above two case studies we can extract some valuable data regarding the discovery/confirmation/confrontation plot category. In both series, we can observe a tendency to shorter introductions of the narrative, a fact that helps the development of bigger final acts with a more detailed and thorough resolution of the main conflict. In other words, these audiovisual works create quickly the central dramatic question but dedicate more narrative time to answering it. The second act of each of these narratives has the standard length based on the classical model of narration and does not deviate from the convention of the three-act structure. The second act is dedicated to the complications around the main conflict, so it performs as a bridge between the introduction of the dramatic question and its resolution.

This pattern is faithfully followed by each of the fifteen beats of the analytical approach. Since it is more productive to see and compare the percentages of each beat in Snyder's approach and in both series of the discovery/confirmation/confrontation plot, here is a table with these data that will shed light on the subject:

Table 11. 15-Beat Sheet

Discovery/Confirmation/ Confrontation Plot	Snyder's Approach	*Santa Clarita Diet*	*The Order*
Opening Image	1%	1%	1%
Theme Stated	5%	5%	4%
Setup	<9%	<9%	<9%
Catalyst	11%	10%	11%
Debate	11%–25%	10%–20%	11%–22%

The Netflix Vision of Horror

Discovery/Confirmation/ Confrontation Plot	Snyder's Approach	*Santa Clarita Diet*	*The Order*
Break Into Two	25%	20%	22%
B Story	27%	23%	26%
Fun and Games	27%–50%	23%–50%	26%–50%
Midpoint	50%	50%	50%
Bad Guys Close In	50%–68%	50%–60%	50%–60%
All Is Lost	68%	60%	60%
Dark Night of the Soul	68%–75%	60%–70%	60%–72%
Break Into Three	75%	70%	72%
Finale	75%–100%	70%–100%	72%–100%
Final Image	100%	100%	100%

From the above table, it is clear that the middle act is almost identical to Snyder's approach, while individual beats in the first and third acts create the peculiarity of the discovery/confirmation/confrontation plot category. More precisely, the first four beats faithfully follow the percentages of the theoretical tool, while the Debate beat, the last of the first act, is considerably reduced, making the first act shorter than usual. This slightly affects the second act too, since it starts a little earlier than expected. In order for the Midpoint to be placed at the exact middle of the narrative, the Fun and Games beat is longer than in Snyder's approach, while after the Midpoint, the Bad Guys Close In beat is smaller by 8 percent, making the Dark Night of the Soul beat approximately the same percentage as the one Snyder described.

Even if the second act has the same duration as the classical model of narration, it nevertheless adjusts based on the new conventions of this plot category and rearranges its seven beats. It is also worth mentioning the fact that in the classical model of the three-act structure, the midpoint is placed at the middle of both the entire narrative and the second act, because of the symmetrical arrangement of the action into acts

3. The Narrative Structures of Triple and Double Function Plots

and the faithful structure rule of 25 percent–50 percent–25 percent. In the discovery/confirmation/confrontation plot category this is not the case, since the midpoint is placed at around the 45 percent mark of the second act.

Regarding the third act and its three beats, we can clearly see that the Finale beat is longer than in Snyder's approach, as it is technically the entire final act. The percentage of the narrative that was not part of the first act it is placed in the third act, making it almost 4 percent longer. This means that the audiovisual works that follow the discovery/confirmation/confrontation plot need less time to introduce the fictional world and more time to resolve the main conflict.

Apart from comparing Snyder's approach and the classical model of narration with the discovery/confirmation/confrontation plot category, it will be fruitful to examine the association with the data from the complex discovery plot. Let us not forget that the structuring method of this plot category, incorporating all of the four plot functions, works as a prototype for the horror narratives of the corpus of this study. In the following table, there is a comprehensive comparison of the average percentages between the two plot categories.

Table 12. Plot Categories Comparison

	Complex Discovery Plot	Discovery/Confirmation/ Confrontation Plot
Opening Image	1%	1%
Theme Stated	6%	5%
Setup	<11%	<9%
Catalyst	12%	11%
Debate	12%–24%	11%–21%
Break Into Two	24%	21%
B Story	27%	25%

The Netflix Vision of Horror

	Complex Discovery Plot	Discovery/Confirmation/Confrontation Plot
Fun and Games	27%–50%	25%–50%
Midpoint	50%	50%
Bad Guys Close In	50%–66%	50%–60%
All Is Lost	66%	60%
Dark Night of the Soul	66%–75%	60%–71%
Break Into Three	75%	71%
Finale	75%–100%	71%–100%
Final Image	100%	100%

Since the complex discovery plot has a lot of similarities to the classical model of narration based on Snyder's approach for filmic texts, it is clear that the differences previously analyzed between the discovery/confirmation/confrontation plot category and the classical model are still present. But the percentage differentiations in the individual beats are slightly smaller, since, as studied in the second chapter of the book, the complex discovery plot has adapted the norms of Snyder's approach based on the long-form nature of television narratives. Therefore, the first four beats are almost identical, the Debate beat ends earlier and is 2 percent shorter in the discovery/confirmation/confrontation plot, the first part of the second act works similarly in both categories, while the Bad Guys Close In beat is longer by 6 percent, which leads to the variation of the longer third act at the discovery/confirmation/confrontation plot category.

As was the case in the previous categories, there is a strong connection between the structuring methods of these narratives and the plot functions each type incorporates. Thus, it is crucial to examine the plot functions and their placements in the two case studies of the discovery/confirmation/confrontation plot and determine why this category has this distinctive distribution of the action into its three acts. The

3. The Narrative Structures of Triple and Double Function Plots

table below summarizes the plot functions of *Santa Clarita Diet* and *The Order*.

Table 13. Plot Functions of *Santa Clarita Diet* and *The Order*

Plot Functions	Santa Clarita Diet	The Order
Onset	—	—
Discovery	Setup	Fun and Games
Confirmation	Fun and Games	Dark Night of the Soul
Confrontation	Finale	Finale

It has been already established that the onset function is linked with the beginning of the first act, the discovery function is connected with the ending of the first act and the first part of the second act, the confirmation function is strictly connected with the second act, and the confrontation function is linked with the third act, since the point of the narrative is that the main conflict be resolved. Since the present category lacks the onset function, it is reasonable that the first acts of these case studies are noticeably shorter. Since the narratives do not have to separately introduce the Other to the audience and then to the characters, the introduction to the fictional world can be shorter than in the classical model, which incorporates all of the four functions.

Regarding discovery, it is placed in portions of the narrative that are highly associated with this particular plot function. More specifically, both the Setup and the Fun and Games beats that are the parts of the narratives in which the case studies incorporate their discovery functions comply with the aforementioned rule. The confirmation function, too, is placed in the expected portion of the narrative, since it is placed in the second act in both case studies. Finally, confrontation is reserved once again for the final act, which is longer than in the classical model, a fact that affects the function too, since it lasts longer.

In conclusion, the discovery/confirmation/confrontation plot category is an example that ultimately proves the hypothesis of this book: that Netflix Original horror series are structured like long-form films with unified narratives that obey the three-act structure model but nevertheless it adapts its norms to the specific needs of every series. In this category, since the audiovisual works do not have the onset function, it adjusts the classical model of narration to these requirements and modifies the action distribution rule of 25 percent–50 percent–25 percent to 21 percent–50 percent–29 percent, more convenient for this category. This approach of the discovery/confirmation/confrontation plot category rearranges the percentages of each beat, too, in order to create the desirable duration of each act, but the three plot functions of the category are still associated with the portions of the narrative where they are typically placed. Like the discovery plot, the discovery/confirmation/confrontation plot is another fine example of a triple-function plot that removes an essential function from the prototype complex discovery plot and redefines the rules of the three-act structure in its favor.

The Narrative Structure of the Discovery/Confrontation Plot

Apart from the triple-function plot categories, Carroll described the possibility of categories that incorporate only two functions, the so-called double-function plots. Carroll states on that matter,

> "By subtracting functions from the complex discovery plot, I have sketched a series of tri-function horror stories. Further subtractions suggest a range of dual function narratives, including: onset/confrontation; onset/discovery; onset/confirmation; discovery/confrontation; discovery/confirmation; and confirmation/confrontation."[20]

Carroll describes in great detail these six categories that belong the family of the double-function plot. In the present analysis, the case studies are long-form audiovisual narratives that have complicated and extensive plots that are capable of creating hours of content. This is the main reason double-function plots are not common in television series. In the corpus of this study, more than 61 percent of the series follow the complex discovery plot and incorporate all four of the essential functions, 31 percent of the series follow triple-function plot categories that were analyzed above, while only one series follows a double-function plot and places in its narrative only two of the four essential functions.

This category is the discovery/confrontation plot, and the series that follows it is *Black Summer*. The last part of this chapter will be dedicated to the analysis of this category by thoroughly studying the structuring methods of this specific series. Since there is only one case study

3. The Narrative Structures of Triple and Double Function Plots

of the discovery/confrontation plot, the approach of this category will be generalized, but it will be strengthened by the data and the concrete evidence of the whole theoretical approach of this book.

Discovery/confrontation plot narratives are built in a manner in which the characters and the audience see the Other at the same time, and then the confrontation part starts right away. There is no need for confirmation, since the antagonistic forces are extensive and the main characters have to defend themselves from early on. As is evident, these narratives have a much quicker rhythm and do not usually have extensive durations. In order to have a better understanding of this plot category, we have to analyze the structure of the following case study.

Black Summer—*A Structural Analysis*

Black Summer is an American zombie apocalypse series, created by Karl Schaefer and John Hyams. The first season was released on Netflix on April 11, 2019, and it has been renewed for an eight-episode second season.[21] The story of the series takes place six weeks after the start of a zombie apocalypse, when Rose (Jaime King) is separated from her daughter, Anna (Zoe Marlett). Rose starts a challenging journey with a lot of obstacles, but nothing will stop her until she finds her daughter. As Jaime King comments about the protagonist, "Thrust alongside a small group of American refugees, she must brave a hostile new world and make brutal decisions during the most-deadly summer of a zombie apocalypse."[22]

The series was ordered as a spin-off prequel to *Z Nation* (Syfy, 2014–2018), an American action/horror/comedy post-apocaptic TV series which was also created by Schaefer and Engler. At a Comic-Con panel, Schaefer noted that *Black Summer* was not going to be episodic, but would instead be an eight-hour unified work that it was not intended to be the funny version of *The Walking Dead* that *Z Nation* is, but instead an old-school, scary, zombie narrative.[23]

From this statement by the creator we can extract two important points regarding *Black Summer*. First of all, this series is a fine example of a pure horror narrative with no hybrid elements. Apart from Schaefer, this notion was echoed by producer Jodi Binstock, who stated that the series is "not tongue-in-cheek, it's very very serious: it's as if the zombie apocalypse really happened in 2018 and explores what that would be for all of us."[24] Even Stephen King praised the series for its horror elements,

The Netflix Vision of Horror

stating, "Just when you think there's no more scare left in zombies, this comes along. Existential hell in the suburbs, stripped to the bone."[25] It is also worth mentioning that *Black Summer* belongs to the Horror of Armageddon type, making it one of only three examples in the corpus of this type of horror (along with *Santa Clarita Diet* and *V Wars*, both of which deal with the notion of a human transforming into an Other through transmission).

The second notion that is extracted from Schaefer's statement is that this series was designed and structured as a unified narrative and not in an episodic manner like *Z Nation*, a declaration that confirms the argument of this book. *Black Summer* has eight episodes and a total duration of 257 minutes. It is worth mentioning that the episodes do not have a stable duration, their length ranging from twenty to forty-four minutes. Its narrative follows the three-act structure, but since it belongs to the discovery/confrontation plot category, the percentages of its acts do not behave as in the classical model of narration. In order to thoroughly analyze the narrative of *Black Summer*, we have to see the fifteen beats of the overarching story. Hence, the beats of the series' narrative are the following:

Opening Image (1 min.): The first scene of the series establishes the dystopian and damaged society of the fictional world, while the tone and the rhythm of the narrative are initiated. The opening shots have empty streets with no people, while the viewers hear loud sirens. Then we are introduced to the main character of the narrative, Rose, and her family, which consists of her husband, Patrick (Ty Olsson), and her daughter, Anna. In the Opening Image beat we are familiarized with the apocalyptic world in which the overarching story of the narrative takes place, while we are acquainted with the two main characters who will be the center of the dramatic question: Rose and Anna. The entire narrative of *Black Summer* is based on the strong relationship between a mother and a daughter in a dystopian setting, facts that are encompassed in the first beat of the series.

Theme Stated (11 min.): In the eleventh minute of the narrative, the basic theme of the series is stated in a dialogue scene. As was established in the theoretical analysis of Snyder's approach and demonstrated in the majority of the case studies of the corpus, this technique is very common, many audiovisual works stating their theme in dialogue between the main characters. In *Black Summer*, there is a scene with Rose and Patrick, who are hiding in a house. Patrick is wounded and cannot be accepted in organized accommodation for protection. Patrick urges

3. The Narrative Structures of Triple and Double Function Plots

Rose to leave him behind and go to the stadium to find their daughter by saying, "They don't have a plan for us, Rose. There's no safety net here." The theme of the series is embodied in this specific dialogue scene, which establishes the paranoia of the fictional world and the danger that can be found in the most familiar faces.

Setup (1 min.–18 min.): The first eighteen minutes are dedicated to the construction and introduction of the entire fictional world and of all its components. We are introduced to the dystopian society in which the overarching story takes place, the protagonist of the narrative, Rose, and her daughter, who will initiate the main conflict, which is—most importantly to the premise of the series—centered around the conventions of a zombie apocalypse. This premise is established right after the scene that states the theme of the narrative, when Patrick transforms into a zombie and threatens Rose's life. Rose is in danger and running for her life, but Julius James (Justin Chu Cary) saves her by killing Patrick. Julius is a criminal who took the identity of "Spears," the name of the guard he killed. So Rose teams up with a person but does not know his true identity.

Catalyst (18 min.): After the establishment of all the components of the fictional world and the introduction of the main premise of the story to the audience, the inciting incident takes place and creates the main conflict and the central dramatic question of the narrative. More specifically, in *Black Summer*, we see Julius promise Rose that they will go to the stadium, in which people are accommodated in order to be protected from the zombies, and they will find Anna again. This commitment between two of the main characters of the series initiates the progression of the narrative and creates their central objective, which is for mother and daughter to be reunited again. So, the central dramatic question is whether Rose can find Anna in this dystopian setting, while the main conflict is between the main characters and the Other of the narrative, which are the zombies. The characters have a clear purpose, but the zombies are the main obstacle in the fulfillment of their aim.

Debate (18 min.–41 min.): The rest of the first episode is dedicated to closing the first act. In this part of the narrative, we are introduced to the other main characters of the overarching story, who are in denial about the dangerous situation they have been called to face. Hence, in this beat the audience is introduced to Ryan (Mustafa Alabssi), a deaf survivor who tries to avoid the zombies; Ooh "Sun" Kyungsun (Christine Lee), a Korean woman who is looking for her missing mother; Barbara Watson (Gwynyth Walsh), a woman who has survived without her husband and is not

The Netflix Vision of Horror

sure if he is alive; William Velez (Sal Velez, Jr.), a pole lineman who has a sister and children in Texas; and Lance (Kelsey Flower), a young survivor with no family. In all of the introductory scenes with the aforementioned main characters, the audience continues to live the paranoia of this fictional world, while the characters are in serious danger and unable to comprehend the situation they are called to handle. Finally, in this beat, the audience gets the important information about the true identity of Julius, while the rest of the characters are unaware of this.

Break Into Two (41 min.): At the end of the first episode, we have the first plot point, which changes the course of the narrative and introduces new events that will reassert the main conflict and the dramatic question of the overarching story. In this scene, which takes place at a checkpoint, we see many people being stopped by soldiers, who do not let them pass the gates. After some intense moments, the crowd pushes away the soldiers and passes through the gates. In the crowd are the main characters of the narrative, while on the other side are Barbara, William, and Sun. This action means that our main characters are in the restricted zone and unprotected by any state force, while they struggle to fulfill their initial objective. Finally, it is worth mentioning that although this series has eight episodes, the second act begins at the end of the first episode. This fact in itself shows that the narrative will have a short beginning, but we also have to take into account that the first episode of *Black Summer* is the longest, while the last two episodes have almost half the duration.

B Story (47 min.): At the beginning of the second act, a new secondary storyline begins that helps the proper structuring of this portion of the narrative. This B Story is in accordance with the theme of the narrative, the premise of the overarching story, and the main storyline of the series. In this series, this secondary storyline is about William, Barbara, and Sun, who are driving together in Barbara's car. These three characters are being chased while they are driving their minivan; they believe they are being chased because the other truck wants their fuel. Both vehicles crash into a stopped semitrailer, killing both Barbara and the pick-up truck driver, who later on transform into zombies. The surviving occupants escape their vehicles and flee to an abandoned diner while being chased by the now zombified Barbara and pick-up truck driver. This storyline will be further developed until its course of action coordinates with the main storyline of Rose.

Fun and Games (47 min.–110 min.): The first part of the second act finds our main characters facing obstacles, but the difficulty of the main

3. The Narrative Structures of Triple and Double Function Plots

conflict is at normal levels and the protagonists can handle the situation. At this point in the narrative, the audience watches the main storyline of Rose and Julius heading towards the stadium and the secondary storyline of William and Sun. In the main storyline we see Rose, Spears, Ryan, and Lance find an abandoned school, and they wish to help a child seen running inside the school. Eventually, they realize that a gang of boys who travel through the vents have occupied the school. At the same time, we see the entire beginning of the secondary storyline, which was analyzed in the previous beat, and we see the course of events from the car chase and the death of Barbara, and William and Sun's flight to an abandoned diner.

Midpoint (110 min.): Just before the exact middle of the entire narrative, the Midpoint beat occurs. In this part of the overarching story, suddenly the stakes become higher and the main characters are in real danger, as the threat is upon them. In the midpoint of *Black Summer*, we see the gang of the kids killing Ryan inside the school by shooting him, and then Ryan is turned into a zombie. The kids scatter, while Ryan as a zombie chases Julius and Rose into a dead end. Ultimately, the two main characters are saved, and the undead Ryan is trapped back in the school. In other words, the midpoint is about a main character from the central storyline who becomes a zombie and suddenly represents a threat to the protagonists. The turning of Ryan into a zombie constitutes an important event to the entire narrative, since it shows that no one is safe in this fictional world.

Bad Guys Close In (110 min.–167 min.): The rest of the second act finds all of the main characters in a more difficult position than before, since the antagonistic forces seem to gain ground. Lance is chased by a zombie who forces him to climb on top of a school bus, which gives him a temporary reprieve. The zombie later manages to chase Lance off the bus and into a fire station, where Lance unsuccessfully tries to kill it with a fireman's pickaxe. Afterwards, a man saves Lance's life, but after being bitten during the struggle, Lance thanks the man before killing him while his savior still has his back turned. At the same time, William, Sun, Carmen (Erika Hau), her boyfriend Manny (Edsson Morales), and Phil (Stafford Perry) are trapped inside the diner while undead Barbara and Marvin circle the building. All these characters are trying to find a plan in order to escape, but the tension between the characters is not helping the situation.

All Is Lost (167 min.): In the eleventh beat of the narrative, the events lead the characters to lose all hope and feel that they have little

The Netflix Vision of Horror

chance of defeating the antagonistic forces. At the All Is Lost beat, the characters who are trapped inside the diner fail to implement the plan regarding their escape. More specifically, Phil and William's first plan was to escape using a distraction created by Sun while the remaining four characters attacked the two zombies. This plan backfires and leaves the zombies more distressed than before, forcing everyone back inside. From this point until the end of the second act, the characters do not have any optimism, and the antagonistic forces have the upper hand in this stressful situation.

Dark Night of the Soul (167 min.–186 min.): From the All Is Lost beat until the second plot point, the narrative finds the main characters at their lowest point, with no courage or confidence to go on. Phil grows desperate and summons a meeting with only Carmen and Manny, emerging with a new demand to William: sacrifice Sun to the zombies so the rest can escape. William defends Sun, who convinces the others that Phil has been hiding a bite on his arm, meaning that he will eventually turn into a zombie himself. Everyone turns on Phil and cruelly attacks him. At the same time, Earl (Nyren B. Evelyn)—a mysterious survivor who saved Julius and Rose—Julius, and Rose are walking, seemingly exhausted. Rose is so tired that she hallucinates and sees visions of her daughter. The trio arrives at the diner and sees the two zombies. The main storyline crosses paths with the B Story, while all of the characters seem desperate and hopeless.

Break Into Three (186 min.): At the end of the fifth episode, the second plot point takes place and the narrative enters its third and final act, in which the conflict will be resolved and the dramatic question will be answered. In this scene, the seven main characters join forces and defeat the zombies that have been threatening them for a long time, narratively. As Julius prepares to unload his last two bullets, William drags out a heavily beaten Phil, who is circled by the zombies. Julius shoots and kills one zombie but misses the other one. Earl, Julius, Sun, Carmen, and Manny kill undead Marvin, while William finishes off Phil to prevent reanimation. The group goes inside the diner, and all together search for weapons. They take as many supplies as they can and leave the diner united as a group. The main characters have joined forces against the Other, and all together are marching towards the stadium, in which the main conflict will finally be resolved.

Finale (186 min.–257 min.): The rest of the three episodes function as the end of the third act and, more specifically, to the Finale beat. In this part of the narrative, we see the course of the action that leads

3. The Narrative Structures of Triple and Double Function Plots

to the final resolution and the ultimate answer to the central dramatic question. The group arrives at a trap house, where Manny gets shot and killed by stray bullets. After turning undead, he chases Sun, while Rose and Lance try to escape from a guard. Amidst all the chaos, the group eventually reunites, but just as they are cornered by zombies, the two soldiers from the previous episode kill them and offer to lead them to the stadium. The soldiers discover the true identity of Julius and reveal it to Rose. She eventually kills them and decides to spare Julius. The characters continue their journey, and a lot of them end up zombies or dead. At the end, they arrive at the stadium, and Rose is reunited with her daughter, Anna.

Final Image (257 min.): The last beat of the narrative is the final scene that the audience witnesses. In *Black Summer*, the Final Image beat finds the three remaining characters—Rose, Julius, and Sun—who have managed to survive against the antagonistic forces, arriving at the stadium. Reaching the inside of the empty stadium, Rose is reunited with her daughter. Apart from resolving the main conflict of the entire narrative, this last scene of the series shows the massive change that has occurred to the fictional world and to the protagonist. In the Opening Image we had a family in real danger that was ready to break apart, while the Final Image shows the same family reuniting in a dystopian setting, but away from the real danger. The main characters are safe, the dramatic question has been answered and the narrative is ready to finish.

Black Summer is another example of a series that follows all of the fifteen beats of the classical model of narration described by Snyder. Based on the above analysis, it is clear that the series is structured based on the three-act model but that the duration of each act deviates from the general rule. The first act of the series is 16 percent, the second act is 56 percent, while the third act is 28 percent. It is clear that we do not have a balanced distribution of the narrative, and the action is divided disproportionally into the three acts. The first act is by far the shortest of all of the case studies of this corpus, while the rest of the percentage that was meant to be at the beginning of the narrative is apportioned to the other two acts.

Of course, this is highly connected to the plot type each audiovisual work belongs to. *Black Summer* belongs in the discovery/confrontation plot category, meaning that its narrative incorporates only two of the four essential plot functions. The discovery function is at the first act and more specifically at the Setup beat, in which Rose is attacked by Patrick, who has just been transformed into a zombie. Both the audience

The Netflix Vision of Horror

and the protagonist are becoming familiarized with the Other of the narrative at the same time; therefore there is no need for the onset function, and the series introduces the discovery function as the first integral part of its plot. There is no need for the confirmation function, since all of the characters are already part of this dystopian world and are constantly being threatened by the antagonistic forces of the narrative. Consequently, from the discovery function, the narrative proceeds to the confrontation function. As previously said, this function is mainly incorporated into the third act, since that is the part of the narrative which is reserved for the acceleration of developments and the resolution of the conflict. *Black Summer* is no exception to this rule and, even if there are scenes of opposition during the second act, the main part of this function occurs at the Finale beat.

Black Summer is the last case study, and the results of its analysis are compatible and consistent with the rest of the data of the present and the previous chapter. This series is a rare example of a double-function plot that uses the classical model of narration in its favor by adapting the three acts to the special needs of the narrative. Even though it has only two essential plot functions, nevertheless it is consistent with Snyder's approach and incorporates all of the fifteen beats of the three-act structure into its narrative. Hence, *Black Summer* is another important example of how the new ways of consumption and distribution of the new media have blurred the lines between series and filmic narratives.

* * *

The discovery/confrontation plot category is a unique case in the present study, since the corpus has only one narrative that follows this type. As mentioned before, the double-function plots are rare for long-form narratives, since they are meant for shorter stories. Nevertheless, *Black Summer* is a sufficient example of how an extensive series can incorporate only two essential functions into its narrative and still follow the classical model of narration and use the entire fifteen beats. Since we are talking about one case study, the conclusions regarding this category will be based only on the data from this series. This leaves room for debate, but nonetheless gives a formable guideline that can be used in combination with the rest of the data from the other plot categories of the corpus.

In order to be complete, we must examine the percentage distribution of the action into the fifteen beats of *Black Summer*. In the following table, we can see the specific data that were extracted from the above analysis.

3. The Narrative Structures of Triple and Double Function Plots

Table 14. 15–Beat Sheet

	Black Summer
Opening Image	1%
Theme Stated	4%
Setup	<7%
Catalyst	7%
Debate	7%–16%
Break Into Two	16%
B Story	18%
Fun and Games	18%–43%
Midpoint	43%
Bad Guys Close In	43%–65%
All Is Lost	65%
Dark Night of the Soul	65%–72%
Break Into Three	72%
Finale	72%–100%
Final Image	100%

It is clear that the narrative rushes to introduce the fictional world and tries to move on the confrontation function quickly. The first act is only 16 percent of the entire narrative, meaning it is smaller by 9 percent than the standard three-act model. Each of the five beats of the first act are shorter than expected, and the Catalyst is place right after the end of the Setup beat, which only happens to this one case study in the corpus. Then, the second act and its seven beats put the narrative on the right track, leaving the final act around 28 percent in order to conclude the overarching story of the series. Of course, in order to extract more precise conventions, we have to compare this structure with Snyder's approach and with the prototype model of narration of Netflix Original horror series, the complex discovery plot.

Table 15. Plot Categories Comparison

	Snyder's Approach	Complex Discovery Plot	Discovery/Confrontation Plot
Opening Image	1%	1%	1%
Theme Stated	5%	6%	4%
Setup	<9%	<11%	<7%
Catalyst	11%	12%	7%
Debate	11%–25%	12%–24%	7%–16%
Break Into Two	25%	24%	16%
B Story	27%	27%	18%
Fun and Games	27%–50%	27%–50%	18%–43%
Midpoint	50%	50%	43%
Bad Guys Close In	50%–68%	50%–66%	43%–65%
All Is Lost	68%	66%	65%
Dark Night of the Soul	68%–75%	66%–75%	65%–72%
Break Into Three	75%	75%	72%
Finale	75%–100%	75%–100%	72%–100%
Final Image	100%	100%	100%

The comparison of the three models of narration on the above table can give us a well-defined picture of the way the narratives of the

3. The Narrative Structures of Triple and Double Function Plots

discovery/confrontation plot category work. As mentioned, each beat of the first act of the discovery/confrontation plot is smaller by far than either Snyder's approach or the complex discovery plot. This leads to a standard start of the second act that has approximately the same duration as the other two models, but the key element in the expansion of the middle part of the discovery/confrontation model is the Bad Guys Close In beat. In Snyder's approach it has a duration of 18 percent of the entire narrative, while this percentage is 16 percent in the complex discovery plot. In the discovery/confrontation plot we see that this beat rises to 22 percent, an increase of 6 percent compared to the prototype model of narration for Netflix Original horror series. Having this anomaly just after the middle of the narrative, the series continues with a standard form, while it gives more space to the third act, which is longer by 3 percent than either of the other two models of narration.

As established through examining the other models of narration, these irregularities in the way the series structure their narratives come directly from the essential plot functions they incorporate into their overarching story. The discovery/confrontation plot category has a narration pattern in which the characters learn about the Other and then confront it. It is common sense that since these narratives leave half of the plot functions out of their plots, their structure will have significant discrepancies compared to the prototype model.

In the second chapter in the analysis of the complex discovery plot, it was proven that the onset function is highly connected with the first act, and more specifically with the opening beats of this act. Since the discovery/confrontation plot category does not include this function in its overarching stories, it is logical that this model of narration will have considerably shorter first acts. The narrative does not have to familiarize the audience with the fictional world in thorough detail, but rather starts the action much earlier than the series that have a complex discovery plot. Having the discovery function that is connected with both the first and the second acts, the discovery/confrontation plot prefers to link this function with the first act and then prepare the fictional world for the confrontation that is the vital substance of the overarching story. *Black Summer* has placed the discovery function in the Setup beat, meaning in the first 7 percent of the narrative, and then the course of the action leads to the main characters' conflict with the antagonistic forces.

Thus, the second act is dedicated forming the basis of the confrontation function that will be fully developed and resolved in the third act. In this final portion of the narrative, we see the course of action towards the final resolution and the ultimate answer to the central dramatic question. This is the reason the confrontation function is highly connected to the Finale beat, the longest and most essential part of the third act.

In conclusion, based on the two plot functions these narratives incorporate into their overarching story, the discovery/confrontation plot category has a much shorter first act that establishes the discovery function, an extensive second act that sets the basis of the opposition between the main characters and the antagonistic forces, and a slightly longer third act in which the confrontation function occurs.

A Comparison to the Triple and Double Function Plot Categories

In this chapter, I analyzed the three different plot categories that deviate from the general rule of the prototype structure that was established in the previous chapter regarding the complex discovery plot, which incorporates all four of the essential functions and whose acts have a balanced distribution that is similar to the general model of classical narration. In the conclusion of this chapter, I will compare these three plot categories and extract some final data from this analysis.

In the corpus of this analysis, there were two categories that belong to the triple-function plot family—the discovery plot and the discovery/confirmation/confrontation plot—but only one double-function category, the discovery/confrontation plot. If we compare them, one preliminary observation is that the main utility and action distribution of the triple-function plot categories is very similar to the prototype category of Netflix Original horror series. Since they only omit one plot function in their overarching stories, their narrative structures do not deviate significantly, and they obey most of the conventions of the complex discovery plot. In the discovery plot, the first acts are longer by drawing from the second act, while in the discovery/confirmation/confrontation plot the first acts are slightly smaller due to favoring the third acts. Apart from these slightly adjustments to the proportions of the acts, the narratives of these categories are structured in a manner that conforms to the general rules of the three-act structure.

This is the case with the double-function plot category too, but the modifications to the structuring norms are greater than was observed in the triple-function plots. In the discovery/confrontation plot there is

3. The Narrative Structures of Triple and Double Function Plots

a minor first act that consists of only 16 percent of the whole narrative, making it the shortest beginning of the entire corpus under study. This modification creates longer second and third acts that serve the intensity of the conflict and the path through to its resolution.

The common ground of all the case studies, no matter their plot category, is that they indeed follow the general approach of the three-act structure and the fifteen beats as Snyder described them. The complex discovery plot has minor changes to Snyder's approach, and every narrative of the series of this category is structured as a unified audiovisual work which is reminiscent of a long-form film and not a TV show that is depended on episodic storytelling. Obviously, in the triple- and double-function plots, the fifteen beats are adapted to the needs of each category, and their percentages differ in every type of plot. The next table gathers the structuring patterns of each type and summarizes the results of this chapter to provide a more approachable and thorough comparison.

Table 16. Triple- and Double-function Plot Categories

	Discovery Plot	Discovery/ Confirmation/ Confrontation Plot	Discovery/ Confrontation Plot
Opening Image	1%	1%	1%
Theme Stated	6%	5%	4%
Setup	<10%	<9%	<7%
Catalyst	11%	11%	7%
Debate	11%–34%	11%–21%	7%–16%
Break Into Two	34%	21%	16%
B Story	37%	25%	18%

The Netflix Vision of Horror

	Discovery Plot	Discovery/ Confirmation/ Confrontation Plot	Discovery/ Confrontation Plot
Fun and Games	37%–51%	25%–50%	18%–43%
Midpoint	51%	50%	43%
Bad Guys Close In	51%–66%	50%–60%	43%–65%
All Is Lost	66%	60%	65%
Dark Night of the Soul	66%–75%	60%–71%	65%–72%
Break Into Three	75%	71%	72%
Finale	75%–100%	71%–100%	72%–100%
Final Image	100%	100%	100%

Based on this table, it is clear that the major beat which generates an inconsistency between the beginnings of the triple- and double-function plots is the Debate beat. This portion of the narrative that creates the differentiation in the first acts of each category is dedicated to the main characters' reluctance to take the journey of the narrative that is solely based on the main conflict. In the discovery plot, which has a longer first act, the debate gives more time to the beginning of these narratives, since its duration is 23 percent of the entire narrative. In the discovery/confirmation/confrontation plot this beat is much shorter, since it has a duration of 10 percent, and therefore the first acts of these works are slightly more reduced than expected. On the other hand, in the discovery/confrontation plot we see a much shorter Debate beat of a 9 percent duration that starts even earlier than in the previous categories. Consequently, this is the main reason the double-function plot category has such a minor beginning.

3. The Narrative Structures of Triple and Double Function Plots

Regarding the second acts of these three categories, we witness a heterogeneity that creates a different pattern in each model of narration. The key element to the reduction of the expected duration of the second act in the discovery plot category is the Fun and Games beat. While in both the other categories this beat has a total duration of 25 percent of the entire narrative, in the discovery plot it is only 14 percent. This causes a shorter second act in this category (41 percent), while the other two are much closer to the prototype model—in the discovery/confirmation/confrontation pot we have 50 percent, while in the discovery/confrontation, 56 percent. Conclusively, the increased duration of the second act in the discovery/confrontation plot is located at the Bad Guys Close In beat, which is significantly longer than in the other two categories.

Lastly, the duration of the third act is solely connected to the Finale beat, in which there are minor differences in all of the three categories. In the discovery plot, we have a third act that follows the general rule of 25 percent of the entire narrative, while in the other two categories, we have slightly longer endings, with 28 percent (discovery/confrontation plot) and 29 percent (discovery/confirmation/confrontation plot). Based on these adjustments of various beats, the structural models of narration of each of the categories are the following:

Table 17. Comparison of Act Lengths

	Discovery Plot	Discovery/ Confirmation/ Confrontation Plot	Discovery/ Confrontation Plot
First Act	34%	21%	16%
Second Act	41%	50%	56%
Third Act	25%	29%	28%

These variations are strictly connected with the plot functions each category incorporates into its narrative. The triple-function plots maintain a more balanced distribution of action since they miss only one essential function compared to the complex discovery plot. On the other hand, double-function plots have 50 percent of the vital functions of the prototype category and therefore they have more substantial differences in their models compared to the complex discovery plot.

The only category of the above that maintains the onset function is the discovery plot. This function is highly connected with first acts, and consequently the other two categories that miss the onset have reduced beginnings. The discovery function, which has a dual connection with both the first and the second acts, is part of all three of the categories. Hence, none of these narratives are influenced by this function.

Regarding the confirmation, even if two plot categories miss this function, each of them treats it differently. On one hand, we have the discovery plot, which maintains the implications of the discovery function and structures the beginning of the second act by making it shorter than the general rule. On the other hand, the discovery/confrontation plot category structures the second act based on the upcoming ultimate confrontation by creating minor clashes, and therefore its second acts are significantly longer than the general rule. Nevertheless, in both cases the lack of the confirmation function alters the duration of the second act.

Finally, the confrontation function is essential in all of the narratives and highly connected with the third act, and more specifically the Finale beat. Since we are talking about audiovisual horror works, the confrontation between the main character and the Other of the narrative is fundamental to the overarching story. Each of these series is based on a main conflict, and there has to be a confrontation function in order to have the answer to the central dramatic question. This is why all of the case studies incorporate the confrontation function into their plots, and subsequently why every model of narration in this book maintains a balanced third act that is close to the general rule of the three-act structure.

In conclusion, this chapter proves that even if some of the case studies of the corpus do not follow the prototype model or a construction that is closely similar to the general classical narration, nevertheless they all follow the outline of the three-act structure, which they adjust to their specific needs. Each plot category has its own peculiarities, and the general three-act model is not ideal for every type of narration. Therefore, every audiovisual work alters the norms according to its overarching story. All the series can be categorized according to their plot functions, and consequently every plot category follows a specific model of narration that is a variation of the general three-act structure. In the present chapter, I analyzed the model of narration for the rest of the 39 percent of the corpus under study that do not follow the complex discovery plot, and I concluded that all of the Netflix Original horror shows are operating as long-form films in disguise. No matter the distribution of these works, they ultimately function as extensive and unified audiovisual texts that do not rely on the episodic nature of television.

Conclusion

The horror genre is globally an important and integral part of the audiovisual industry and influences pop culture on many levels. This is why I chose this specific genre in order to study the new mechanisms of series narration on one of the most popular SVOD platforms. Since we are living in the beginning of this new streaming era, in which distribution patterns and consumption habits have radically changed, the present study tried to fill the gap in the academic literature regarding the way these audiovisual works are designed. The main argument of the present book was to prove that Netflix Original horror shows are structured in a manner that is closer to filmic texts than to television shows.

In the minds of audience members, conventional television is connected to their domestic space and works as part of their furniture, while it has been associated with the term "television flow," meaning the continuous transmission of different programs. This medium is linked with a practice of watching diverse shows that do not have a common ground in a constant manner. Of course, nowadays this way of consuming television content seems archaic, and the technological evolution of the medium combined with the presence of the new media has introduced the audience to new ways of distribution and viewing.

SVOD platforms abolished the tradition of conventional television flow and offered their content based on personalization. Now, viewers do not need to have their weekly appointment with their favorite series, and instead SVOD platforms offer them entire seasons at the same time. Netflix is a pioneer of this distribution technique, and its original content is created in order to be consumable via binge-watching. As is logical, this vital transformation of the medium influenced the narratives themselves, since they started to be created as unified narration and not episodic storytelling.

In order for this analysis to be done systematically and methodically, I created a corpus that was based on strict criteria: First, the

Conclusion

analysis was limited to the first seasons of Netflix Original Horror series, since they have a repeatable formula for each season. Second, the analysis was based on the content that is available on the U.S. version of the platform. Third, the series that were eligible for this study were from 2013, the inaugural year of Netflix Original content, until the end of 2019, the year this study began. Fourth, the series had to be original productions by Netflix, and not an acquisition of the platform for international distribution. Fifth, all of the series had to be fictional shows, since reality content has other structuring norms. And last, since Netflix uses the term horror flexibly, all of the series had to acknowledged as part of the genre by either IMDb or Rotten Tomatoes. So, from an initial corpus of twenty-four shows, the final audiovisual corpus consisted of thirteen Netflix Original Horror series. These thirteen series were the foundation of this study, since it was based on hard evidence and data extracted from their narratives.

After identifying the material to be analyzed, the academic research started. In this book, I used two important theoretical tools coming from different fields. The first, coming from screenwriting studies, was the three-act structure and the classical model of narration. Since I wanted to prove that these series behave like long-form films, I used the three-act model in order to observe the norms and constructions of their narratives. Because the generalized three-act model can fall into simplifications that will lead to problematic and false data, I used a more detailed approach to the classical narration, the one of the fifteen beats introduced by Blake Snyder. Based on Snyder's approach, each classical narrative can be divided into fifteen parts that serve as a beat-by-beat analysis of the three-act structure. The first five beats are the first act, the next seven beats are the second act, while the rest of the three beats are the third act.

The second important theoretical tool comes from horror studies and is Noel Carroll's analysis of different categories of plots in this specific genre. Carroll identifies four essential plot functions that can be found in the narratives of the horror genre, no matter the medium. More specifically, the four functions are the onset, discovery, confirmation, and confrontation. Depending on which of these functions each narrative incorporates into its plot, we can divide the series into different plot categories. The most important and widespread category is the one that serves as a prototype narrative because it incorporates all of the four functions, the complex discovery plot. Then, Carroll identifies other categories of horror plot that miss one or even more of the

Conclusion

above four functions. Based on this approach, apart from the prototype category, there are several other categories that can be described as triple-function and double-function plots (depending on the number of the essential functions they use).

In the first chapter I created the corpus under study, I displayed the theoretical tools of this study and I analyzed the material. The first important finding was that these series indeed behave like long-form and unified audiovisual narratives, while staying faithful to their objective of being for binge-watch consumption. Netflix Original horror series are based on overarching stories with a beginning, a middle, and an end, as they do not rely on episodic narration with the emphasis being on the units than the entire structure. Another outcome of the analysis that was conducted in the first chapter was that the majority of the works in the corpus follow the complex discovery plot, since they incorporate all of the four functions into their narratives. The rest of the series can be divided into three plot categories: two triple-function plots and one double-function plot. According to these findings, I tried to thoroughly analyze the mechanisms of narration of each category and form a structuring outline of each model. The next two chapters of this book were dedicated to this task.

The second chapter was based on the analysis of the complex discovery plot, the category that applies to more than 61 percent of the entire corpus. This category contains *Chilling Adventures of Sabrina* (Netflix, 2018–present), *Diablero* (Netflix, 2018–present), *Ghoul* (Netflix, 2018), *Hemlock Grove* (Netflix, 2013–2015), *Marianne* (Netflix, 2019), *Stranger Things* (Netflix, 2016–present), *Typewriter* (Netflix, 2019–present), and *V Wars* (Netflix, 2019–present). From these eight case studies that incorporate all four of the plot functions, the analysis concludes that the complex discovery plot category faithfully follows the three-act structure outline, and all of these series have a similar distribution of their action to the 25 percent–50 percent–25 percent rule of the standard classical model.

Moreover, based on the analysis of the prototype model of Netflix Original horror series, it is clear that the four essential plot functions that are incorporated into the complex discovery plot are linked with precise parts of the overarching narrative of a series. Specifically, the onset function takes place at the beginning of the first act, the discovery function can be either at the end of the first act or at the beginning of the second act, the confirmation function is linked with the second act, while the confrontation function is mainly connected with the Finale

Conclusion

beat at the third act. Therefore, the key to the balanced distribution of the action into acts is the existence of all four of the plot functions, which are highly connected with the structuring methods of each narrative. While the second chapter of the book established this connection between the plot function and the structuring of the narrative, the question that raised was what happens if a series misses one or even two of the essential functions.

The third chapter of the present book tried to answer that question by thoroughly analyzing the rest of the case studies that do not follow the complex discovery plot. The remaining 39 percent of the series of this study are part of triple- or even double-function plot categories, and even if they follow the three-act structure regarding their overarching story, nevertheless they adapt it to their own needs. Particularly, in this chapter I analyzed the discovery plot category, which incorporates the onset, the discovery, and the confrontation functions with the series *Chambers* (Netflix, 2019) and *The Haunting of Hill House* (Netflix, 2018); the discovery/confirmation/confrontation plot category with the series *Santa Clarita Diet* (Netflix, 2017–2019) and *The Order* (Netflix, 2019–present); and the discovery/confrontation plot category with the series *Black Summer* (Netflix, 2019–present), the only double-function plot of the entire study. Based on these series, I defined the characteristics of each category and compared them with the prototype model of the complex discovery plot.

Regarding the discovery plot category, which omits the confirmation function, it follows the same structural conventions as the complex discovery plot, but it adopts a percentage distribution of 34 percent–41 percent–25 percent, more suitable for this category, making the second act shorter than expected. Following the same pattern, the discovery/confirmation/confrontation plot has a 21 percent–50 percent–29 percent action distribution, the more convenient for this category, making the first act shorter than usual. Finally, the only double-function plot category of the corpus, the discovery/confrontation plot, has much shorter beginning since its distribution pattern is 16 percent–56 percent–28 percent. All of the above findings confirm the discoveries and the outcome of the analysis of the previous chapters about the important connection of the plot functions with the structuring model of narration of every series. Each of the above categories adjust the distribution of their action according to the absence of the respective essential functions: the discovery plot omits the confirmation function that is connected with the second act, and therefore its second act is shorter;

Conclusion

the discovery/confirmation/confrontation plot omits the onset function that is usually placed in the beginning of the narrative, so its first act is shorter; and the discovery/confrontation plot omits both the onset and the confirmation functions and consequently creates a more abnormal distribution that does not resemble the standard and balanced three-act structure.

From the above analysis, it is clear that the episodic series is an evolving medium that is highly affected by the technological progress during the digital era. While conventional television had its own rules regarding narrative structuring that was based on the notion of television flow, the new SVOD platforms reinvented the medium and pushed its narratives into new territories. According to the present study, it is clear that the new narratives of the SVOD audiovisual works are closely connected to cinema conventions, embracing the aspects of media convergence. From the data collected during this study, it is clear that the narratives of an essential genre, horror, are creating a pattern that, no matter the plot category that they belong to, follows the classical filmic narrative model and are created as long-form films.

In conclusion, this book formulated a structuring analysis method regarding a specific series genre and proved that no matter what the plot type of a series, the new distribution and consumption methods of the new media and the SVOD platforms can lead to further blurring of the lines between cinema and television. Even if these specific narratives were created as series, their structuring methods are reminiscent of a filmic narrative that is united and concrete with three distinctive parts in its overarching story—a beginning, a middle and an end. No matter the number of the episodes or their duration, each of the Netflix Original horror series function like long-form films that follow the three-act structure with individual modifications as needed per category.

Thus, the present study has consolidated a tangible theoretical tool that forms the basis of an overall approach regarding the narratives of fictional shows exclusively created by Netflix, and this tool can be the basis of additional readings and discoveries regarding different genres and cycles. Finally, based on the present study, series genre can be furthered studied, as new narratives will continue to emerge in the upcoming years. Binge-watching practices are now a part of our everyday life, and fictional shows are highly influenced by the new consumption experience.

Filmography

Alfred Hitchcock Presents (CBS, 1955–1965)
Arrested Development (Fox, Netflix, 2003–present)
Bewitched (ABC, 1964–1972)
Black Summer (Netflix, 2019–present)
Bloodline (Netflix, 2015–2017)
Buffy the Vampire Slayer (WB-UPN, 1997–2003)
Cabin Fever (Roth, 2002)
Casablanca (Curtiz, 1942)
Castlevania (Netflix 2017–2018)
Chambers (Netflix, 2019)
Chilling Adventures of Sabrina (Netflix, 2018–present)
Crazyhead (E4, Netflix, 2016)
Dark Shadows (ABC, 1966–1971)
Daybreak (Netflix, 2019)
Devilman: Crybaby (Netflix, 2018)
Diablero (Netflix, 2018–present)
E.T. the Extra-Terrestrial (Spielberg, 1982)
The Exorcist (Friedkin, 1973)
Ghoul (Netflix, 2018)
Glitch (ABC, Netflix, 2015–2019)
The Goonies (Donner, 1985)
The Handmaid's Tale (Hulu, 2017–present)
Haunted (2018–present)
The Haunting of Hill House (Netflix, 2018)
Hemlock Grove (Netflix, 2013–2015)
Hostel (Roth, 2005)
House of Cards (Netflix, 2013–2018)
Immortals (BluTV, 2018)
Jaws (Spielberg, 1975)
Kabaneri of the Iron Fortress: The Battle of Unato (Araki, 2019)
Kolchak: The Night Stalker (ABC, 1974–1975)
Lilyhammer (NRK, 2012–2014)
Love Death + Robots (Netflix, 2019–present)
The Mandalorian (Disney+, 2019–present)
Marianne (Netflix, 2019)
The Morning Show (Apple TV+, 2019–present)
Orange Is the New Black (Netflix, 2013–2019)
The Order (Netflix, 2019–present)
Prank Encounters (2019–present)
Rosemary's Baby (Polanski, 1968)
Sabrina, the Teenage Witch (ABC, The WB, 1996–2003)
Santa Clarita Diet (Netflix, 2017–2019)
Scream (MTV, 2015–2016)
Slasher (Super Channel, Chiller, Netflix, 2016–present)
Stand by Me (Reiner, 1986)
Stranger Things (Netflix, 2016–present)
Supernatural (WB-CW, 2005–present)
The Thing (Carpenter, 1982)
Thriller (NBC, 1960–1962)
Twilight Zone (CBS, 1959–1964)
Twin Peaks (ABC, 1990–1991)
Typewriter (Netflix, 2019–present)
V for Vendetta (McTeigue, 2006)
V Wars (Netflix, 2019–present)
The Vampire Diaries (CW, 2009–2017)
The Walking Dead (AMC, 2010–present)
The X-Files (FOX, 1993–2002)
Z Nation (Syfy, 2014–2018)

Appendix A: Series Corpus

Table 17. Basic Data on the Series Corpus

Series	Number of Episodes	Total Duration	Hybrid Genre(s)	Country	Year (1st Season)
Black Summer	8	257 minutes	—	USA	2019
Chambers	10	412 minutes	Fantasy Horror	USA	2019
Chilling Adventures of Sabrina	10	560 minutes	Fantasy Horror	USA	2018
Diablero	8	302 minutes	—	Mexico	2018
Ghoul	3	127 minutes	—	India	2018
The Haunting of Hill House	10	555 minutes	—	USA	2018
Hemlock Grove	13	656 minutes	Fantasy Horror	USA	2013
Marianne	8	350 minutes	—	France	2019

Appendix A

Series	Number of Episodes	Total Duration	Hybrid Genre(s)	Country	Year (1st Season)
The Order	10	445 minutes	Fantasy Horror	USA	2019
Santa Clarita Diet	10	262 minutes	Comedy Horror	USA	2017
Stranger Things	8	383 minutes	Fantasy Horror	USA	2016
Typewriter	5	234 minutes	___	India	2019
V Wars	10	395 minutes	___	USA	2019

Appendix B: Three-Act Structures

Table 18. Three-Act Percentage Breakdowns

Series	First Act	Second Act	Third Act
Black Summer	16%	56%	28%
Chambers	32%	42%	26%
Chilling Adventures of Sabrina	21%	55%	24%
Diablero	25%	51%	24%
Ghoul	25%	50%	25%
The Haunting of Hill House	37%	40%	23%
Hemlock Grove	22%	53%	25%
Marianne	28%	47%	25%

Appendix B

Series	First Act	Second Act	Third Act
The Order	22%	50%	28%
Santa Clarita Diet	20%	50%	30%
Stranger Things	26%	50%	24%
Typewriter	21%	55%	24%
V Wars	23%	51%	26%

Appendix C: Types of Plot and Horror

Table 19. Plot and Horror Types

Series	Type of Plot	Type of Horror
Black Summer	Discovery/Confrontation Plot	Horror of Armageddon
Chambers	Discovery Plot	Horror of the Demonic
Chilling Adventures of Sabrina	Complex Discovery Plot	Horror of the Demonic
Diablero	Complex Discovery Plot	Horror of the Demonic
Ghoul	Complex Discovery Plot	Horror of the Demonic
The Haunting of Hill House	Discovery Plot	Horror of the Demonic
Hemlock Grove	Complex Discovery Plot	Horror of the Demonic
Marianne	Complex Discovery Plot	Horror of the Demonic

Appendix C

Series	Type of Plot	Type of Horror
The Order	Discovery/Confirmation/Confrontation Plot	Horror of the Demonic
Santa Clarita Diet	Discovery/Confirmation/Confrontation Plot	Horror of Armageddon
Stranger Things	Complex Discovery Plot	Horror of the Demonic
Typewriter	Complex Discovery Plot	Horror of the Demonic
V Wars	Complex Discovery Plot	Horror of Armageddon

Chapter Notes

Introduction

1. Anne Dunn, "The Genres of Television," 128.
2. Raymond Williams, *Television: Technology and Cultural Form*, 89–90. For more on television flow, see also Gregory A. Waller, "Flow, Genre, and the Television Text," 59–61.
3. Sarah Kozloff, "Narrative Theory and Television," 72.
4. Jeremy G. Butler, *Television: Critical Methods and Applications*, 29.
5. Jason Mittell, *Complex TV*, 16.
6. Djoumi Baker, "Terms of Excess Binge-Viewing as Epic-Viewing in the Netflix Era," 41.
7. Alan Sepinwall, "Why Matt Weiner 'Would Lose.'"
8. For more, see Timothy Havens, "Netflix: Streaming Channel Brands."

Chapter One

1. Internet Live Stats, http://www.internetlivestats.com/internet-users.
2. Anthony N. Smith, *Storytelling Industries*, 52.
3. Erik Pedersen, "SVOD Study: 101M Disney+ Subs."
4. Maíra Bianchini and Maria Carmem Jacob de Souza, "Netflix and Innovation in Arrested Development's Narrative Construction," 102.
5. For more, see Amanda Lotz, *Portals*.
6. Nancy Hass, "And the Award for the Next HBO Goes To."
7. Ramón Lobato, *Netflix Nations*, 11.
8. Kevin McDonald and Daniel Smith-Rowsey, "Introduction," in *The Netflix Effect*, 1.
9. Smith, *Storytelling Industries*, 1.
10. Mareike Jenner, *Netflix and the Re-invention of Television*, 2.
11. Mario Klarer, "Putting Television 'Aside,'" 205.
12. James Poniewozik, "Go Ahead, Binge-Watch That TV Show."
13. Mareike Jenner, "Is This TVIV?," 268.
14. Sidneyeve Matrix, "The Netflix Effect," 120.
15. Jason Gilbert, "Netflix's 'Post-Play' Feature."
16. Casey J. McCormick, "Forward Is the Battle Cry," 101.
17. Klarer, "Putting Television 'Aside,'" 216.
18. Gaby Allrath, Marion Gymnich, and Carola Surkamp, "Introduction: Towards a Narratology of TV Series," 3.
19. Sean O'Sullivan, "Six Elements of Serial Narrative," 50–53.
20. Anne Dunn, "The Genres of Television," 130.
21. Sotiris Petridis, *Tileoptiko Senario: Domes kai Texnikes*, 9.
22. Jeremy G. Butler, *Television: Critical Methods and Applications*, 28.
23. Martie Cook, *Write to TV*, 49.
24. Jim Pagels, "Stop Binge-Watching TV."
25. Veronica Innocenti and Guglielmo Pescatore, "Changing Series," 10.
26. Kathryn VanArendonk, "Theorizing the Television Episode," 66.
27. David Bordwell, *Narration in the Fiction Film*, 156.
28. For more, see Victor Shklovsky, "Art as Technique."
29. Peter Hant, *Das Drehbuch: Praktische Filmdramaturgie*, 75.

Notes—Chapter One

30. For a modern edition, see Aristotle, *Poetics*, translated by Stephen Halliwell (Cambridge: Harvard University Press, 1995).
31. Constance Nash and Virginia Oakey, *The Screenwriter's Handbook*.
32. Syd Field, *Screenplay*.
33. Matthias Brütsch, "The Three-Act Structure," 302.
34. Christopher Vogler, *The Writer's Journey*, [PAGE].
35. Paul Joseph Gulino, *Screenwriting*.
36. Blake Snyder, *Save the Cat! The Last Book on Screenwriting You'll Ever Need*.
37. For example, for three-act structuring and short films see Linda J. Cowgill, *Writing Short Films*.
38. Brütsch, "The Three-Act Structure," 302.
39. Christina Kallas-Kalogeropoulou, *Senario*, 136–138.
40. *Ibid.*, 151–154, 249–250.
41. *Ibid.*, 275–277.
42. Snyder, *Save the Cat*, 67–96.
43. Brütsch, "The Three-Act Structure," 320.
44. Adam Hart, *Monstrous Forms*, 187.
45. Jason Lynch, "Here's the Recipe Netflix Uses."
46. See Ralph Cohen, "History and Genre," 205–206; Hans Robert Jauss, *Towards an Aesthetic of Reception*, 80; and Steve Neale, *Genre*, 19.
47. J.A. Cuddon, "Introduction," in *The Penguin Book of Horror Stories*, 11.
48. Rick Worland, *The Horror Film: An Introduction*, 25.
49. Viktória Prohászková, "The Genre of Horror," 132.
50. Dominic Strinati, *An Introduction to Studying Popular Culture*, 82.
51. Sotiris Petridis, *Anatomy of the Slasher Film*, 1.
52. Brigid Cherry, *Horror*, 37.
53. Roberta Pearson, "Cult Television as Digital Television's Cutting Edge," 106.
54. For more, see the first chapter, "The TV in TV Horror: Production and Broadcast Contexts," of Lorna Jowett and Stacey Abbott, *TV Horror*.
55. Matt Hills, *The Pleasures of Horror*, 112.
56. Stephen King, *Danse Macabre*, 235.
57. Drew Beard, "Introduction: Paranormal TV," 152.
58. Lisa Schmidt, "Television: Horror's 'Original' Home," 161.
59. Stacey Abbott, "Loss Is Part of the Deal," 157.
60. See Andrew Tudor, "Genre."
61. Christine Gledhill, "Rethinking Genre," 221.
62. Jason Mittell, "A Cultural Approach to Television Genre Theory," 3.
63. Jason Mittell, *Genre and Television*, 9.
64. For more on the term "quality TV," see Jane Feuer, "HBO and the Concept of Quality TV," 145–157.
65. Djoumi Baker, "Terms of Excess Binge-Viewing," 40.
66. See Jonathan Gray, *Show Sold Separately*, 23–46.
67. Noel Carroll, *The Philosophy of Horror*, 99.
68. *Ibid.*, 99–100.
69. *Ibid.*, 101–103.
70. Charles Derry, *Dark Dreams 2.0*, 21–106.
71. I coined this term with that usage in my book *Anatomy of the Slasher Film: A Theoretical Analysis*, from which I am borrowing the analysis of the "Other."
72. Kevin Thomas, "The Other," 331.
73. For more information, see Robert R. Williams, *Recognition: Fichte and Hegel on the Other*.
74. See Jean-Paul Sartre, *Being and Nothingness*.
75. See Simone de Beauvoir, *The Second Sex*.
76. See Emmanuel Levinas, *Totality and Infinity*.
77. See Julia Kristeva, *Powers of Horror*.
78. See Jacques Lacan, *Écrits*.
79. Vivian Sobchack, "Bringing It All Back Home," 45.
80. For more information regarding the Other, see Jacques Lacan, *The Seminar of Jacques Lacan*, 235–247.
81. Dylan Evans, *An Introductory Dictionary of Lacanian Psychoanalysis*, 135–136.

Notes—Chapter Two

82. Patrick Jemmer, "The O(the)r (O)the(r)...," 9.
83. Slavoj Žižek, *How to Read Lacan*, 11.
84. See Julia Kristeva, *Powers of Horror*.
85. Robin Wood, *Hollywood: From Vietnam to Reagan... and Beyond*, 65.
86. Cary Morrison, "Creature Conflict," 172.
87. Stephen T. Asma, "Monsters on the Brain," 958.
88. For more information, see Stephen T. Asma, *On Monsters: An Unnatural History of Our Worst Fears*.
89. Carroll, *The Philosophy of Horror*, 108–109.
90. *Ibid.*, 110.
91. *Ibid.*, 110.
92. *Ibid.*, 116.

Chapter Two

1. For more around the story of the series, see Lesley Goldberg, "Kiernan Shipka to Star as Sabrina in Netflix 'Riverdale' Spinoff."
2. Nellie Andreeva, "Sabrina the Teenage Witch Series Picked Up."
3. In Natalie Abrams, "Why the Sabrina the Teenage Witch Series Went to Netflix over the CW."
4. In Samantha Highfill, "Chilling Adventures of Sabrina."
5. Constance Grady, "Netflix's Chilling Adventures of Sabrina Is a Messy, Gorgeous Thrill Ride."
6. Meagan Navarro, "Netflix's "Chilling Adventures of Sabrina" Is Delightful Satanic Witchery."
7. For more on the Christmas special episode, see Rick Porter, "'Chilling Adventures of Sabrina' Gets a Holiday Special on Netflix."
8. Jennifer Maas, "'Chilling Adventures of Sabrina': Here's How They Turned the Holiday Episode Around So Quickly."
9. For more on the adaptation, see Ariel León, "Netflix prepara 'Diablero,' serie de fantasía filmada en México."
10. John Hecht, "Netflix Orders Mexican Horror Series Diablero."
11. Kristen Lopez, "Netflix's Diablero Season 1 Review."
12. Mikayla Daniels, "Diablero Review: Is the Netflix Series the New Supernatural?"
13. Joel Keller, "Stream It or Skip It: 'Diablero' on Netflix."
14. Editorial Desk, "Ghoul Screening."
15. Rahul Desai, "Ghoul Review: The Demons Within."
16. Evan Dickson, "Blumhouse Partnering with Ivanhoe and Phantom."
17. Akhil Arora, "Netflix Adds Three New Originals to India Slate."
18. Akhil Arora, "How Netflix's Ghoul Came to Be."
19. Udita Jhunjhunwala, "'Ghoul' Director Patrick Graham."
20. Rohan Naahar, "Ghoul Review: Netflix's Sacred Games Follow-Up."
21. Nellie Andreeva, "Netflix Nears Order for Eli Roth Horror Drama 'Hemlock Grove.'"
22. Sean Ludwig, "Netflix Says More Members Watched 'Hemlock Grove.'"
23. Brian Stelter, "Netflix Does Well in 2013 Primetime Emmy Nominations."
24. Nellie Andreeva, "Netflix Renews 'Hemlock Grove' for Third and Final Season."
25. Jack Wilhelmi, "Why Hemlock Grove Is Netflix's Most Underrated Horror Series."
26. Alison Willmore, "Netflix's New Series 'Hemlock Grove.'"
27. John Squires, "Netflix's 'Marianne' Will Not Be Returning for a Second Season."
28. Meagan Navarro, "Marianne Is Netflix's Most Terrifying Original Horror Yet."
29. Elena Nicolaou, "Exactly What Makes Marianne the Scariest Show on Netflix."
30. In Kylie Klein-Nixon, "Black Spot, Marianne."
31. For example, *Casablanca* (Curtiz, 1942) is one of the films which show that temporal or chronological shifts are represented in classical film narrative, in which the emphasis is on the maintenance of spatial and temporal coherence. From more, see Russell J.A. Kilbourn, *Cinema, Memory, Modernity*, 15.
32. Caitlin Gallagher, "Is Hawkins a

Notes—Chapter Three

Real Town? 'Stranger Things' Will Make You Nostalgic."

33. Philli Mlynar, "Unpacking the '80s nostalgia of the 'Stranger Things' Soundtrack."

34. Neil Genzlinger, "Review: With 'Stranger Things,' Netflix Delivers an Eerie Nostalgia Fix."

35. Kory Grow, "'Stranger Things': How Two Brothers Created Summer"s Biggest TV Hit."

36. Joseph M. Sirianni, "Nostalgic Things: Stranger Things," 190.

37. See Hanh Nguyen, "Stranger Things: Barb Gets a Lot More Than Justice in Season 2."

38. See Laura Bradley, "How Stranger Things Season 2 Brought Justice for Barb."

39. Patrick Frater, "Netflix Sets 'Typewriter' as Ghostly Goa-Set Indian Original Series."

40. Joseph Knoop, "Netflix's Typewriter."

41. Aditya Shrikrishna, "Netflix's 'Typewriter' Review: The Kids Are All Not Right."

42. In Yadunandan Singh, "Ian Somerhalder Believes 'V-Wars' Predicted the Coronavirus."

43. For more, see Daniel Furn, "When Is V Wars Season 2 Released on Netflix?"

44. Isaac Feldberg, "The Return of Ian Somerhalder, Thanks to V-Wars."

Chapter Three

1. Noel Carroll, *The Philosophy of Horror*, 108.

2. Carita Rizzo, "Series Mania Marks 10th Anniversary."

3. Dave Nemetz, "Chambers Cancelled at Netflix."

4. The convention that sex equals danger or even death is highly connected with the horror genre in both film and television. Barbara Creed states that horror's obsession with blood, particularly the bleeding body of woman, suggests that castration anxiety is a central concern of the genre, while the woman's body is slashed and mutilated to signify not only her own castrated state but also the possibility of castration for the male (for more, see Barbara Creed, "Horror and the Monstrous-Feminine," 74, and Barbara Creed, "Film and Psychoanalysis," 83). Stereotyped gender representation was connected with the genre for many decades, but according to Kevin J. Wetmore, after the events of 9/11 gender politics were reshaped by empowering women, which allowed gender to be ignored as a concern (see Kevin J. Wetmore, *Post-9/11 Horror in American Cinema*, 195). For more on this matter, see J. Carol Clover, *Men, Women and Chain Saws*, and Richard Nowell, *Blood Money*.

5. Lucy Mangan, "Chambers Review—Not Even Uma Thurman Can Save This."

6. Ariana Romero, "How the Chambers Finale Changes Everything."

7. Melanie Robson, "Five Shots, Twice Disappeared," 2.

8. See David Trottier, *The Screenwriter's Bible*.

9. In my article "TV Mini-Series or Long-Form Film? Narrative Analysis of The Haunting of Hill House," I conducted a preliminary narrative analysis of this series based on theoretical tools from screenwriting studies.

10. Carroll, *The Philosophy of Horror*, 110.

11. Nellie Andreeva, "Drew Barrymore Comedy 'Santa Clarita Diet.'"

12. Nellie Andreeva, "'Santa Clarita Diet' Canceled by Netflix After 3 Seasons."

13. In Ariana Bacle, "Santa Clarita Diet Creator Calls New Zombie Comedy a Romantic Piece."

14. *Ibid*.

15. Linda Williams, "When the Woman Looks," 64.

16. Denise Petski, "The Order Horror Drama Series Renewed for Season 2 by Netflix."

17. Marty Brown, "The Order."

18. Michael Ahr, "The Order Review (Spoiler-Free)."

19. Samantha Nelson, "Netflix's Dark Fantasy The Order Is an Absurdist Match."

20. Carroll, *The Philosophy of Horror*, 111.

21. Nellie Andreeva, "'Black Summer'

Notes—Chapter Three

Starring Jaime King Renewed for Season 2 by Netflix."

22. Lesley Goldberg, "'Z Nation' Spinoff Starring Jaime King a Go at Netflix."

23. In Christian Long, "Black Summer: Z Nation Spin-Off Starring Jaime King Headed to Netflix."

24. In James Collins, "Inside Making Z Nation."

25. Dustin Rowles, "Netflix's Phenomenal 'Black Summer' Finds an Unexpected Champion."

Bibliography

Abbott, Stacey. "Loss Is Part of the Deal: Love, Fear and Mourning in TV Horror." In *Emotions in Contemporary TV Series*, edited by Alberto N. García. London: Palgrave Macmillan, 2016.
Abrams, Natalie. "Why the Sabrina the Teenage Witch Series Went to Netflix Over the CW." *Entertainment Weekly*, January 7, 2018. Accessed January 25, 2020.
Ahr, Michael. "The Order Review (Spoiler-Free)." *Den of Geek*, March 8, 2019. Accessed January 28, 2020.
Allrath, Gaby, Marion Gymnich, and Carola Surkamp. "Introduction: Towards a Narratology of TV Series." In *Narrative Strategies in Television Series*, edited by Gaby Allrath and Marion Gymnich. London: Palgrave Macmillan, 2005.
Andreeva, Nellie. "'Black Summer' Starring Jaime King Renewed for Season 2 by Netflix." *Deadline Hollywood*, November 20, 2019. Accessed November 30, 2019.
Andreeva, Nellie. "Drew Barrymore Comedy 'Santa Clarita Diet' Renewed for Season 2 by Netflix." *Deadline Hollywood*, March 29, 2017. Accessed March 20, 2020.
Andreeva, Nellie. "Netflix Nears Order for Eli Roth Horror Drama 'Hemlock Grove' from Eli Roth and Gaumont International Television." *Deadline Hollywood*, December 12, 2011. Accessed March 18, 2020.
Andreeva, Nellie. "Netflix Renews 'Hemlock Grove' for Third and Final Season." *Deadline Hollywood*, September 2, 2014. Accessed March 18, 2020.
Andreeva, Nellie. "Sabrina the Teenage Witch Series Picked Up by Netflix with 2-Season Order." *Deadline Hollywood*, December 1, 2017. Accessed February 20, 2020.
Andreeva, Nellie. "'Santa Clarita Diet' Canceled by Netflix After 3 Seasons." *Deadline Hollywood*, April 26, 2019. Accessed March 20, 2020.
Aristotle. *Poetics*. Translated by Stephen Halliwell. Cambridge, MA: Harvard University Press, 1995.
Arora, Akhil. "How Netflix's Ghoul Came to Be: 14 Hours a Day for Over a Month in a 'Leaky, Damp, and Horrible Smelling' Place." *NDTV*, August 21, 2018. Accessed February 20, 2020.
Arora, Akhil. "Netflix Adds Three New Originals to India Slate." *Gadgets*, February 23, 2018. Accessed February 20, 2020.
Asma, Stephen T. "Monsters on the Brain: An Evolutionary Epistemology of Horror." *Social Research* 82, no. 4 (2014): 941–968.
Asma, Stephen T. *On Monsters: An Unnatural History of Our Worst Fears*. New York: Oxford University Press, 2009.
Bacle, Ariana. "Santa Clarita Diet Creator Calls New Zombie Comedy a Romantic Piece." *Entertainment Weekly*, February 3, 2017. Accessed March 26, 2020.
Baker, Djoumi. "Terms of Excess Binge-Viewing as Epic-Viewing in the Netflix Era." In *The Age of Netflix: Critical Essays on Streaming Media, Digital Delivery and Instant Access*, edited by Cory Barker and Myc Wiatrowski. Jefferson, NC: McFarland, 2017.
Beard, Drew. "Introduction: Paranormal TV." *Horror Studies* 4, no. 2 (2013): 151–158.
Beauvoir, Simone de. *The Second Sex*, translated by H.M. Parshley. New York: Vintage, 1989.

Bibliography

Bianchini, Maíra, and Maria Carmem Jacob de Souza. "Netflix and Innovation in Arrested Development's Narrative Construction." In *The Age of Netflix: Critical Essays on Streaming Media, Digital Delivery and Instant Access*, edited by Cory Barker and Myc Wiatrowski. Jefferson, NC: McFarland, 2017.
Bordwell, David. *Narration in the Fiction Film*. New York: Routledge, 2013.
Bradley, Laura. "How Stranger Things Season 2 Brought Justice for Barb." *Vanity Fair*, October 27, 2017. Accessed January 31, 2020.
Brown, Marty. "The Order." *Common Sense Media*, March 13, 2019. Accessed January 28, 2020.
Brütsch, Matthias. "The Three-Act Structure: Myth or Magical Formula?" *Journal of Screenwriting* 6, no. 3 (2015): 301–326.
Butler, Jeremy G. *Television: Critical Methods and Applications*. Belmont, CA: Wadsworth, 1994.
Carroll, Noel. *The Philosophy of Horror, or Paradoxes of the Heart*. New York: Routledge, 1990.
Cherry, Brigid. *Horror*. New York: Routledge, 2009.
Clover, J. Carol. *Men, Women and Chain Saws. Gender in the Modern Horror Film*. Princeton, NJ: Princeton University Press, 1992.
Cohen, Ralph. "History and Genre." *New Literary History* 17, no. 2 (Winter 1986): 205–206.
Collins, James. "Inside Making Z Nation with Producer and Director Jodi Binstock." Mandy.com, November 23, 2018. Accessed November 30, 2019.
Cook, Martie. *Write to TV: Out of Your Head and Onto the Screen*. Oxford: Elsevier, 2007.
Cowgill, Linda J. *Writing Short Films: Structure and Content for Screenwriters*. Hollywood: Lone Eagle, 1997.
Creed, Barbara. "Film and Psychoanalysis." In *The Oxford Guide to Film Studies*, edited by John Hill and Pamela Church Gibson. Oxford: Oxford University Press, 1998.
Creed, Barbara. "Horror and the Monstrous-Feminine: An Imaginary Abjection." In *Horror, The Film Reader*, edited by Mark Jancovich. New York: Routledge, 2002.
Cuddon, J.A. "Introduction." In *The Penguin Book of Horror Stories*, edited by J.A. Cuddon. New York: Penguin, 1984.
Daniels, Mikayla. "Diablero Review: Is the Netflix Series the New Supernatural?" *Netflix Life*, February 5, 2019. Accessed January 20, 2020.
Derry, Charles. *Dark Dreams 2.0: A Psychological History of the Modern Horror Film from the 1950s to the 21st Century*. Jefferson, NC: McFarland, 2009.
Desai, Rahul. "Ghoul Review: The Demons Within." *Film Companion*, August 22, 2018. Accessed November 24, 2019.
Dickson, Evan. "Blumhouse Partnering with Ivanhoe and Phantom to Make Horror Films in India." *Collider*, September 3, 2014. Retrieved November 24, 2019.
Dunn, Anne. "The Genres of Television." In *Narrative and Media*, edited by Helen Fulton, Rosemary Huisman, Julian Murphet, and Anne Dunn. Cambridge, MA: Cambridge University Press, 2005.
Editorial Desk. "Ghoul Screening: Anurag Kashyap, Jim Sarbh and Sanya Malhotra Walk the Black carpet." *The Indian Express*, August 22, 2018. Accessed November 24, 2019.
Evans, Dylan. *An Introductory Dictionary of Lacanian Psychoanalysis*. New York: Routledge, 1996.
Feldberg, Isaac. "The Return of Ian Somerhalder, Thanks to V-Wars." *Boston Globe*, December 5, 2019. Accessed January 9, 2020.
Feuer, Jane. "HBO and the Concept of Quality TV." In *Quality TV: Contemporary American Television and Beyond*, edited by Janet McCabe and Kim Akass, 145–157. New York: I.B. Tauris, 2007.
Field, Syd. *Screenplay: The Foundations of Screenwriting*. New York: Dell, 1979.
Frater, Patrick. "Netflix Sets 'Typewriter' as Ghostly Goa-Set Indian Original Series." *Variety*, November 8, 2018. Accessed March 10, 2020.

Bibliography

Furn, Daniel. "When Is V Wars Season 2 Released on Netflix? What's Going to Happen?" *Radio Times*, March 11, 2020. Accessed March 12, 2020.

Gallagher, Caitlin. "Is Hawkins a Real Town? 'Stranger Things' Will Make You Nostalgic for These Other '80s Classics." *Bustle*, July 15, 2016. Accessed January 2, 2020.

Genzlinger, Neil. "Review: With 'Stranger Things,' Netflix Delivers an Eerie Nostalgia Fix." *New York Times*, July 14, 2016. Accessed January 13, 2020.

Gilbert, Jason. "Netflix's 'Post-Play' Feature Will Suck You into More TV Show Marathons." *Huffington Post*, August 16, 2012. Accessed February 5, 2020.

Gledhill, Christine. "Rethinking Genre." In *Reinventing Film Studies*, edited by Christine Gledhill and Linda Williams. London: Arnold, 2000.

Goldberg, Lesley. "Kiernan Shipka to Star as Sabrina in Netflix 'Riverdale' Spinoff." *Hollywood Reporter*, January 5, 2018. Accessed March 1, 2020.

Goldberg, Lesley. "'Z Nation' Spinoff Starring Jaime King a Go at Netflix." *Hollywood Reporter*, July 19, 2018. Accessed November 30, 2019.

Grady, Constance. "Netflix's Chilling Adventures of Sabrina Is a Messy, Gorgeous Thrill Ride." *Vox*, October 26, 2018. Accessed November 27, 2019.

Gray, Jonathan. *Show Sold Separately: Promos, Spoilers, and Other Media Paratexts*. New York: New York University Press, 2009.

Grow, Kory. "'Stranger Things': How Two Brothers Created Summer's Biggest TV Hit." *Rolling Stone*, August 3, 2016. Accessed January 13, 2020.

Gulino, Paul Joseph. *Screenwriting: The Sequence Approach*. New York: Continuum, 2004.

Hant, Peter. *Das Drehbuch: Praktische Filmdramaturgie [The Screenplay: Practical Dramaturgy of the Film]*. Waldeck: Felicitas Hübner, 1992.

Hart, Adam. *Monstrous Forms: Moving Image Horror Across Media*. New York: Oxford University Press, 2019.

Hass, Nancy. "And the Award for the Next HBO Goes To." *GQ*, January 29, 2013. Accessed January 23, 2020.

Havens, Timothy. "Netflix: Streaming Channel Brands as Global Meaning Systems." In *From Networks to Netflix: A Guide to Changing Channels*, edited by Derek Johnson. New York: Routledge, 2018.

Hecht, John. "Netflix Orders Mexican Horror Series Diablero." *The Hollywood Reporter*, August 2, 2017. Accessed January 20, 2020.

Highfill, Samantha. "Chilling Adventures of Sabrina Cast Previews a Darker Show Than You Might Expect." *Entertainment Weekly*, September 13, 2018. Retrieved February 20, 2020.

Hills, Matt. *The Pleasures of Horror*. New York: Bloomsbury Academic, 2005.

Innocenti, Veronica, and Guglielmo Pescatore. "Changing Series: Narrative Models and the Role of the Viewer in Contemporary Television Seriality." *Between* 4, no. 8 (2015): 1–15.

Jauss, Hans Robert. *Towards an Aesthetic of Reception*. Brighton: Harvester, 1982.

Jemmer, Patrick. "The O(the)r (O)the(r)..." In *Engage Newcastle Volume 1—Café Philosophique: A Season of "The Other"*, edited by Patrick Jemmer. Newcastle: Newcastle Philosophy Society, 2010.

Jenner, Mareike. "Is This TVIV? On Netflix, TVIII and Binge-Watching." *New Media and Society* 18, no. 2 (2016): 257–273.

Jenner, Mareike. *Netflix and the Re-invention of Television*. London: Palgrave Macmillan, 2018.

Jhunjhunwala, Udita. "'Ghoul' Director Patrick Graham: 'I wanted to bring a new, old legend to the forefront.'" Scroll.in. August 22, 2018. Accessed January 20, 2020.

Jowett, Lorna, and Stacey Abbott. *TV Horror: Investigating the Darker Side of the Small Screen (Investigating Cult TV)*. New York: I.B. Tauris, 2013.

Kallas-Kalogeropoulou, Christina. *Senario: H texni tis Epinoisis kai tis Afigisis ston Kinimatografo [Screenplay: The Art of Invention and Narration in Cinema]*. Athens: Nefeli, 2006.

Bibliography

Keller, Joel. "Stream It or Skip It: 'Diablero' on Netflix, Where a Demon Hunter and a Priest Try to Find a Little Girl." *Decider,* December 21, 2018. Accessed January 20, 2020.

Kilbourn, Russell J.A. *Cinema, Memory, Modernity: The Representation of Memory from the Art Film to Transnational Cinema.* New York: Routledge, 2010.

King, Stephen. *Danse Macabre.* New York: Gallery, 1981.

Klarer, Mario. "Putting Television 'Aside': Novel Narration in House of Cards." *New Review of Film and Television Studies* 12, no. 2 (2014): 203–220.

Klein-Nixon, Kylie. "Black Spot, Marianne: Why Netflix's French Female-Led Horrors Rule." *Stuff,* December 1, 2019. Accessed March 2, 2020.

Knoop, Joseph. "Netflix's Typewriter: Here's Why Everyone's Talking About This New Horror Series." *IGN Southeast Asia,* July 30, 2019. Accessed January 30, 2020.

Kozloff, Sarah. "Narrative Theory and Television." In *Channels of Discourse, Reassembled: Television and Contemporary Criticism,* edited by Robert Clyde Allen. New York: Routledge, 1992.

Kristeva, Julia. *Powers of Horror: An Essay on Abjection,* translated by Leon S. Roudiez. New York: Columbia University Press, 1982.

Kristeva, Julia. *Strangers to Ourselves.* New York: Columbia University Press, 1991.

Lacan, Jacques. *Écrits: The First Complete Edition in English,* translated by Bruce Fink. New York: W.W. Norton, 2006.

Lacan, Jacques. *The Seminar of Jacques Lacan, Book II. The Ego in Freud's Theory and in the Technique of Psychoanalysis, 1954–1955,* translated by Sylvana Tomaselli. New York: W.W. Norton, 1991.

León, Ariel. "Netflix prepara "Diablero," serie de fantasía filmada en México." *El Universal,* August 2, 2017 (in Spanish). Accessed January 30, 2020.

Levinas, Emmanuel. *Totality and Infinity: An Essay on Exteriority,* translated by Alfonso Lingis. Netherlands: Kluwer Academic, 1991.

Lobato, Ramón. *Netflix Nations: The Geography of Digital Distribution.* New York: New York University Press, 2019.

Long, Christian. "Black Summer: Z Nation Spin-Off Starring Jaime King Headed to Netflix." *Syfy,* July 19, 2018. Accessed November 30, 2019.

Lopez, Kristen. "Netflix's Diablero Season 1 Review." *IGN,* December 27, 2018. Accessed January 20, 2020.

Lotz, Amanda. Portals: A Treatise on Internet-Distributed Television. Ann Arbor: University of Michigan Press, 2017.

Ludwig, Sean. "Netflix Says More Members Watched 'Hemlock Grove' on First Weekend Than 'House of Cards.'" *Venture Beat,* April 22, 2013. Accessed March 18, 2020.

Lynch, Jason. "Here's the Recipe Netflix Uses to Make Bingeworthy TV." *QUARTZ,* March 20, 2015. Accessed November 7, 2019.

Maas, Jennifer. "'Chilling Adventures of Sabrina': Here's How They Turned the Holiday Episode Around So Quickly." *The Wrap,* December 9, 2018. Accessed March 1, 2020.

Mangan, Lucy. "Chambers Review—Not Even Uma Thurman Can Save This Supernatural Slog." *The Guardian,* April 26, 2019. Accessed December 18, 2019.

Matrix, Sidneyeve. "The Netflix Effect: Teens, Binge Watching, and On-Demand Digital Media Trends." *Jeunesse: Young People, Texts, Cultures* 6, no. 1 (2014): 119–138.

McCormick, Casey J. "Forward Is the Battle Cry: Binge-Viewing Netflix's House of Cards." In *The Netflix Effect: Technology and Entertainment in the 21st Century,* edited by Kevin McDonald and Daniel Smith-Rowsey. New York: Bloomsbury Academic, 2016.

McDonald, Kevin, and Smith-Rowsey, Daniel. "Introduction." In *The Netflix Effect: Technology and Entertainment in the 21st Century,* edited by Kevin McDonald and Daniel Smith-Rowsey. New York: Bloomsbury Academic, 2016.

Mittell, Jason. *Complex TV: The Poetics of Contemporary Television Storytelling.* New York: New York University Press, 2015.

Bibliography

Mittell, Jason. "A Cultural Approach to Television Genre Theory." *Cinema Journal* 40, no. 3 (Spring 2001): 3–24.
Mittell, Jason. *Genre and Television: From Cop Shows to Cartoons in American Culture.* New York: Routledge, 2004.
Mlynar, Phillip. "Unpacking the '80s Nostalgia of the 'Stranger Things' Soundtrack *Mashable,* July 25, 2016. Accessed January 23, 2020.
Morrison, Cary. "Creature Conflict: Man, Monster and the Metaphor of Intractable Social Conflict." In *Monsters and the Monstrous. Myths and Metaphors of Enduring Evil,* edited by Paul L. Yoder and Peter Mario Kreuter. Oxford: Inter-Disciplinary, 2004.
Nash, Constance, and Virginia Oakey. *The Screenwriter's Handbook: What to Write, How to Write It, Where to Sell It.* New York: Barnes and Noble, 1978.
Naahar, Rohan. "Ghoul Review: Netflix's Sacred Games Follow-Up Is Even Braver, Scary in Unexpected Ways." *Hindustan Times,* August 31, 2018. Accessed March 20, 2020.
Navarro, Meagan. "Marianne Is Netflix's Most Terrifying Original Horror Yet." *Bloody Disgusting,* September 18, 2019. Accessed March 2, 2020.
Navarro, Meagan. "Netflix's "Chilling Adventures of Sabrina" Is Delightful Satanic Witchery Full of Halloween Magic." *Bloody Disgusting,* October 15, 2018. Accessed January 27, 2020.
Neale, Steve. *Genre.* London: BFI, 1980.
Nelson, Samantha. "Netflix's Dark Fantasy The Order Is an Absurdist Match for What We Do in the Shadows." *The Verge,* March 4, 2019. Accessed January 28, 2020.
Nemetz, Dave. "Chambers Cancelled at Netflix." *TV Line,* June 18, 2019. Accessed December 18, 2019.
Nguyen, Hanh. "Stranger Things: Barb Gets a Lot More Than Justice in Season 2." *IndieWire,* October 28, 2017. Accessed January 31, 2020.
Nicolaou, Elena. "Exactly What Makes Marianne the Scariest Show on Netflix." *Refinery29,* September 19, 2019. Accessed March 2, 2020.
Nowell, Richard. *Blood Money: A History of the First Teen Slasher Film Cycle.* New York: Continuum, 2011.
O'Sullivan, Sean. "Six Elements of Serial Narrative." *Narrative* 27, no. 1 (2019): 49–64.
Pagels, Jim. "Stop Binge-Watching TV." *Slate,* July 9, 2012. Accessed November 23, 2019.
Pearson Roberta. "Cult Television as Digital Television's Cutting Edge." In *Television as Digital Media (Console-ing Passions),* edited by James Bennett and Niki Strange. Durham, NC: Duke University Press, 2011.
Pedersen, Erik. "SVOD Study: 101M Disney+ Subs Among Five Platforms Combining for 529M by 2025." *Deadline,* November 11, 2019. Accessed February 3, 2020.
Petridis, Sotiris. *Anatomy of the Slasher Film: A Theoretical Analysis.* Jefferson, NC: McFarland, 2019.
Petridis, Sotiris. *Tileoptiko Senario: Domes kai Texnikes Suggrafis Makras Optikoakoustikis Afigisis* [*Television Screenplay: Structures and Techniques of Writing Long Audiovisual Narrative*]. Athens: Writers Guild of Greece, 2018.
Petridis, Sotiris. "TV Mini-Series or Long-Form Film? Narrative Analysis of The Haunting of Hill House." *Journal of Screenwriting* 11, no. 2 (2020): 207–220.
Petski, Denise. "The Order Horror Drama Series Renewed for Season 2 by Netflix." *Deadline Hollywood,* March 28, 2019. Accessed January 28, 2020.
Poniewozik, James. "Go Ahead, Binge-Watch That TV Show." *Time,* July 10, 2012. Accessed November 20, 2019.
Porter, Rick. "'Chilling Adventures of Sabrina' Gets a Holiday Special on Netflix." *Hollywood Reporter,* November 12, 2018. Accessed November 12, 2019.
Prohászková, Viktória. "The Genre of Horror." *American International Journal of Contemporary Research* 2, no. 4 (April 2012): 132–142.

Bibliography

Rizzo, Carita. "Series Mania Marks 10th Anniversary with Star-Studded Return to Lille." *Variety*, March 22, 2019. Accessed December 11, 2019.

Robson, Melanie. "Five Shots, Twice Disappeared: Staging Memory Through the Long Take in The Haunting of Hill House (2018)." *Mise-en-scène: The Journal of Film and Visual Narration* 4, no. 1 (2019): 1–17.

Romero, Ariana. "How 'The Chambers' Finale Changes Everything We Know About Sasha and Becky." *Refinery29*, April 29, 2019. Accessed December 18, 2019.

Rowles, "Dustin. Netflix's Phenomenal 'Black Summer' Finds an Unexpected Champion." *UPROXX*, May 11, 2019. Accessed November 30, 2019.

Sartre, Jean-Paul. *Being and Nothingness: An Essay on Phenomenological Ontology*. Translated by Hazel E. Barnes. New York: Routledge, 2003.

Schmidt, Lisa. "Television: Horror's 'Original' Home." *Horror Studies* 4, no. 2 (2013): 159–171.

Sepinwall, Alan. "Why Matt Weiner 'Would Lose' If He Wanted to Make a Weekly Netflix Show." *Uproxx*, January 26, 2016. Accessed January 30, 2020.

Shklovsky, Victor. "Art as Technique." In *Russian Formalist Criticism: Four Essays*, 2nd edition, edited by Lee T. Lemon and Marion J. Reis. Lincoln: University of Nebraska Press, 2012.

Shrikrishna, Aditya. "Netflix's 'Typewriter' Review: The Kids Are All Not Right." *New Indian Express*, August 1, 2019. Accessed January 30, 2020.

Singh, Yadunandan. "Ian Somerhalder Believes 'V-Wars' Predicted the Coronavirus." *Play Crazy Game*, March 11, 2020. Accessed March 12, 2020.

Sirianni, Joseph M. "Nostalgic Things: Stranger Things and the Pervasiveness of Nostalgic Television." In *Netflix Nostalgia: Streaming the Past on Demand*, edited by Kathryn Pallister. Lanham, MD: Lexington, 2019.

Smith, Anthony N. *Storytelling Industries: Narrative Production in the 21st Century*. London: Palgrave Macmillan, 2018.

Snyder, Blake. *Save the Cat! The Last Book on Screenwriting You'll Ever Need*. Studio City, CA: Michael Wiese, 2005.

Sobchack, Vivian. "Bringing It All Back Home: Family Economy and Generic Exchange." In *The Dread of Difference: Gender and the Horror Film*, edited by Barry Keith Grant. Austin: University of Texas Press, 1996.

Squires, John. "Netflix's 'Marianne' Will Not Be Returning for a Second Season." *Bloody Disgusting*, March 2, 2020. Accessed March 2, 2020.

Stelter, Brian. "Netflix Does Well in 2013 Primetime Emmy Nominations." *New York Times*, July 18, 2013. Accessed March 18, 2020.

Strinati, Dominic. *An Introduction to Studying Popular Culture*. New York: Routledge, 2000.

Thomas, Kevin. "The Other." *Peace Review* 14, no. 3 (2002): 331–336.

Trottier, David. *The Screenwriter's Bible: A Complete Guide to Writing, Formatting, and Selling Your Script*. 3rd edition. West Hollywood, CA: Silman-James, 1998.

Tudor, Andrew. "Genre." In *Film Genre Reader IV*, edited by Barry Keith Grant. Austin: University of Texas Press, 2012.

VanArendonk, Kathryn. "Theorizing the Television Episode." *Narrative* 27, no. 1 (2019): 65–82.

Vogler, Christopher. *The Writer's Journey: Mythic Structure for Writers*. Studio City, CA: Michael Wiese, 1998.

Waller, Gregory A. "Flow, Genre, and the Television Text." In *In the Eye of the Beholder: Critical Perspectives in Popular Film and Television*, edited by Gary R. Edgerton, Michael T. Marsden, and Jack Nachbar. Bowling Green, OH: Bowling Green State University Press, 1997.

Wetmore, Kevin J. *Post-9/11 Horror in American Cinema*. New York: Continuum, 2012.

Wilhelmi, Jack. "Why Hemlock Grove Is Netflix's Most Underrated Horror Series." *Screen Rant*, February 14, 2020. Accessed March 18, 2020.

Bibliography

Williams, Linda. "When the Woman Looks." In *Horror: The Film Reader,* edited by Mark Jancovich. New York: Routledge, 2002.
Williams, Raymond. *Television: Technology and Cultural Form.* Glasgow: Fontana/Collins, 1974.
Williams, Robert R. *Recognition: Fichte and Hegel on the Other.* New York: State University of New York Press, 1992.
Willmore, Alison. "Netflix's New Series 'Hemlock Grove' Is a Ramshackle, Sometimes Interesting Mess of Supernatural Themes and Teen Angst." *IndieWire,* April 19, 2013. Accessed January 31, 2020.
Wood, Robin. *Hollywood: From Vietnam to Reagan ... and Beyond.* New York: Columbia University Press, 2003.
Worland, Rick. *The Horror Film: An Introduction.* Malden, MA: Blackwell, 2007.
Žižek, Slavoj. *How to Read Lacan.* New York: W.W. Norton, 2006.

Index

Abbott, Stacey 20, 21, 172, 177, 179
ABC 20, 21, 22, 41, 42, 163
Abrams, Natalie 173, 177
Al Jazeera 8
Alfred Hitchcock Presents 21, 163
Allrath, Gaby 171, 177
Amazon Prime Video 7
AMC 21, 163
Andreeva, Nellie 173, 174, 177
Apple TV+ 3, 4, 7, 163
Aristotle 13, 172, 177
Arora, Akhil 173, 177
Arrested Development 60, 163, 171, 178
Asma, Stephen T. 27, 173, 177
audiovisual industry 2, 157

Bacle, Ariana 174, 177
Baker, Djoumi 171, 172, 177
Beard, Drew 21, 172, 177
Beauvoir, Simone de 26, 172, 177
Bewitched 42, 163
binge-watch(ing) 2, 7, 10, 12, 18, 22, 23, 25, 29, 31, 38, 157, 159, 161, 171, 179, 181
Black Summer 5, 23, 29, 30, 36, 101, 140, 141, 142, 143, 144, 145, 147, 148, 149, 151, 160, 163, 165, 167, 169, 174, 175, 177, 180, 182
Bloodline 19, 163
Bordwell, David 13, 171, 178
Bradley, Laura 174, 178
brands 3, 83, 171, 179
Brütsch, Matthias 13, 18, 172, 178
Buffy the Vampire Slayer 21, 163
Butler, Jeremy G. 2, 12, 171, 178

Cabin Fever 60, 163
Carroll, Noel 25, 26, 28, 29, 84, 101, 102, 120, 140, 158, 172, 173, 174, 178
Casablanca 163, 173
Castlevania 23, 163
CBS 21, 163
CGTN 8
Chambers 5, 23, 24, 29, 30, 36, 101, 102, 103, 105, 106, 108, 109, 115, 117, 119, 160, 163, 165, 167, 169, 174, 180, 181, 182

Cherry, Brigid 20, 172, 178
Chilling Adventures of Sabrina 5, 23, 24, 29, 31, 36, 41, 47, 94, 95, 96, 97, 98, 99, 159, 163, 165, 167, 169, 173, 179, 180, 181
cliffhanger(s) 2, 12, 47, 78, 91
Clover, J. Carol 174, 178
CNN 8
Cohen, Ralph 34, 109, 172, 178
Collins, James 175, 178, 183
Cook, Martie 171, 178
Cowgill, Linda J. 172, 178
Crazyhead 23, 163
Creed, Barbara 174, 178
Cuddon, J.A. 19, 172, 178
CW 21, 41, 48, 163, 173, 177

Dark Shadows 21, 163
Daybreak 23, 163
Derry, Charles 26, 172, 178
Devilman: Crybaby 23, 163
Diablero 5, 23, 29, 36, 41, 47, 48, 49, 50, 52, 53, 94, 95, 96, 97, 98, 159, 163, 165, 167, 169, 173, 178, 179, 180
Disney+ 4, 7, 163, 171, 181
DVD 8, 10

E.T. the Extra-Terrestrial 72, 163
Evans, Dylan 172, 178
The Exorcist 42, 163

Feuer, Jane 172, 178
Field, Syd 13, 172, 178
five-act structure 12
flow 1, 2, 3, 157, 161, 171, 182
formulaic 1
four-act structure 12
FOX 21, 60, 163,

Ghoul 5, 23, 25, 29, 32, 36, 41, 53, 54, 56, 57, 58, 59, 79, 94, 95, 96, 97, 98, 159, 163, 165, 167, 169, 173, 177, 178, 179, 181
Gledhill, Christine 22, 172, 179
Glitch 22, 163
The Goonies 72, 163
Gulino, Paul Joseph 14, 172, 179

185

Index

The Handmaid's Tale 53, 163
Hant, Peter 171, 179
Hart, Adam 18, 172, 179
Haunted 23, 163
The Haunting of Hill House 5, 24, 29, 34, 36, 101, 109, 110, 111, 115, 116, 117, 119, 160, 163, 165, 167, 169, 174, 181, 182
Havens, Timothy 3, 171, 179
HBO Max 7
Hemlock Grove 3, 5, 9, 24, 25, 29, 32, 36, 41, 59, 60, 61, 62, 64, 65, 94, 95, 96, 97, 98, 159, 163, 165, 167, 169, 173, 177, 180, 182, 183
Hills, Matt 20, 172, 179
Hostel 60, 163
House of Cards 9, 10, 11, 60, 163, 180

Immortals 23, 163
Innocenti, Veronica 12, 171, 179

Jauss, Hans Robert 172, 179
Jaws 72, 163
Jenner, Mareike 171, 179

Kabaneri of the Iron Fortress: The Battle of Unato 23, 163
Kallas-Kalogeropoulou, Christina 172, 179
Klarer, Mario 11, 171, 180
Kolchak: The Night Stalker 21, 163
Kristeva, Julia 26, 27, 172, 173, 180

Lacan, Jacques 26, 27, 172, 173, 178, 180, 183
Lilyhammer 10, 163
Love Death + Robots 23, 163

The Mandalorian 4, 163
Marianne 5, 24, 29, 33, 36, 41, 66, 67, 68, 69, 70, 71, 93, 94, 95, 96, 97, 98, 159, 163, 165, 167, 169, 173, 180, 181, 182
Mittell, Jason 2, 24, 171, 172, 181
The Morning Show 4, 163
MTV 8, 9, 163

NBC 21, 163
NRK 10, 163

Orange Is the New Black 9, 163
The Order 5, 24, 29, 34, 36, 101, 128, 129, 130, 131, 132, 133, 134, 135, 136, 139, 160, 163, 166, 168, 170, 174, 180, 181
Other 26, 27, 28, 38, 40, 65, 91, 97, 98, 99, 102, 104, 114, 116, 121, 128, 134, 139, 141, 142, 143, 146, 148, 151, 156, 172, 179, 182, 183

Pagels, Jim 12, 171, 181
Pescatore, Guglielmo 12, 171, 179
Prank Encounters 23, 163

Rosemary's Baby 42, 163

Sabrina, the Teenage Witch 41, 163
Santa Clarita Diet 5, 24, 29, 33, 36, 101, 121, 122, 123, 127, 128, 135, 136, 139, 142, 160, 163, 166, 168, 170, 174, 177
Sartre, Jean-Paul 26, 172, 182
Scream 9, 163
Sirianni, Joseph M. 73, 174, 182
Slasher 22, 163, 172, 181
Snyder, Blake 14, 15, 17, 18, 38, 39, 42, 47, 48, 54, 58, 60, 66, 73, 79, 84, 85, 91, 92, 93, 94, 96, 103, 108, 110, 116, 117, 118, 122, 129, 134, 135, 136, 137, 138, 142, 147, 148, 149, 150, 151, 153, 158, 172, 182
Stand by Me 72, 163
Stranger Things 5, 24, 29, 33, 36, 41, 72, 73, 78, 93, 94, 95, 96, 97, 98, 99, 159, 163, 166, 168, 170, 174, 178, 179, 181, 182
Supernatural (TV Series) 21, 48, 163, 173, 178

The Thing 72, 163
Thriller 21, 163
Twilight Zone 21, 163
Twin Peaks 20, 163
Typewriter 5, 24, 29, 35, 36, 41, 78, 79, 80, 81, 83, 84, 94, 95, 96, 97, 98, 99, 159, 163, 166, 168, 170, 174, 178, 180, 182

V for Vendetta 53, 163
V Wars 5, 24, 29, 35, 36, 41, 84, 85, 87, 88, 90, 91, 94, 95, 96, 97, 98, 142, 159, 163, 166, 168, 170, 174, 178, 182
The Vampire Diaries 21, 163

The Walking Dead 21, 141, 163
Wetmore, Kevin J. 174, 182
Williams, Linda 128, 174, 179, 183
Williams, Raymond 1, 171, 183
Wood, Robin 27, 173, 183
Worland, Rick 19, 172, 183

The X-Files 21, 163

Z Nation 141, 142, 163, 175, 178, 179, 180
Žižek, Slavoj 27, 173, 183

www.ingramcontent.com/pod-product-compliance
Lightning Source LLC
Chambersburg PA
CBHW020837020526
44114CB00040B/1243